DIGITAL GIRLHOODS

KATHERINE A. PHELPS

DIGITAL GIRLHOODS

TEMPLE UNIVERSITY PRESS
Philadelphia • *Rome* • *Tokyo*

TEMPLE UNIVERSITY PRESS
Philadelphia, Pennsylvania 19122
tupress.temple.edu

Library of Congress Cataloging-in-Publication Data

Names: Phelps, Katherine A., 1987– author.
Title: Digital girlhoods / Katherine A. Phelps.
Description: Philadelphia : Temple University Press, 2025. | Includes
   bibliographical references and index. | Summary: "Explores the nuanced
   and complex relationships that American tween girls have with social
   media and the meanings they give to it, from its pitfalls to its
   potential, and its powerful possibilities for tween girls in creating
   more equitable futures"— Provided by publisher.
Identifiers: LCCN 2024030591 (print) | LCCN 2024030592 (ebook) | ISBN
   9781439925805 (cloth) | ISBN 9781439925812 (paperback) | ISBN
   9781439925829 (pdf)
Subjects: LCSH: Preteen girls—United States. | Social media and
   preteens—United States. | Identity (Psychology) in adolescence.
Classification: LCC HQ711.15 (print) | LCC HQ711.15 (ebook)
LC record available at https://lccn.loc.gov/2024030591
LC ebook record available at https://lccn.loc.gov/2024030592

9 8 7 6 5 4 3 2 1

For the tween girls

Contents

Acknowledgments

This book did not come to fruition without the guidance, support, and love of many. It is a true privilege to acknowledge those folks and the members of my community who have helped me along the path of this project.

This work began in 2013 as a question that lingered and grew into a multi-method study titled "Digital Vanguards: Tween Girls' Online Performances and the Construction of Modern American Girlhoods." And now it has come to its current form, my first book. I feel as I imagine many do when they come to the end of a writing process . . . It will never land as "complete" because, as with any piece of scholarship, we social scientists contribute to ongoing discussions in small, mighty, and always unfinished ways. I am excited by the thought of the conversations and questions this book might kindle, especially as girls and girlhoods have garnered more attention in recent years. We have so much to learn from them.

I would like to begin by thanking my editor Shaun Vigil, who saw value in the project and has been a steadfast voice and sure hand in guiding me through the process. From our first meeting, you made me feel confident that I could do this. You made it feel like less of a mountain. Thank you to everyone I have worked with at Temple University Press, including Will Forrest and Gary Kramer; thank you for your patience and for answering my many questions. Sincere thanks to the anonymous readers of the manuscript, whose thoughtful recommendations made the work stronger.

Thank you to the scholars who drove this work and framed this project. Though far too numerous to list here, their names and contributions are woven throughout the text, and I am glad to lend my voice to the chorus.

My tremendous gratitude to my doctoral dissertation committee: Dr. Andrea Leverentz, Dr. Leslie Wang, and Dr. Chris Bobel. Thank you for your time, energy, and investment in me as a scholar. I feel especially proud to share this accomplishment with Chris, who also published her first book with Temple University Press. I am certainly in good company.

I also must thank Matthew Gregory, for whom I was a teaching assistant when I started my doctoral program at the University of Massachusetts-Boston back in 2013. You showed me how cool sociology is. You showed me what it means to engage a lecture hall full of students. You shared your expertise, your wisdom, your wit, and whiskey. I imagine that if we had not had those conversations out behind Wheatley Hall looking over the harbor, this book would not have come into existence. You realized there was a thread I needed to follow, and you encouraged me to follow it.

To my Ph.D. cohort, what fun we had on Wheatley fourth and in that far-too-small office. What a genuinely kind, hilarious, hardworking crew of humans. It was a sincere privilege to be in your presence during those years of Very Long Days as we trudged our way toward becoming academics. What an absolute blast in the beauty and the mess of it.

Thank you to the Gender and Women's Studies Department at the University of Wisconsin–Madison. My gratitude to Judy Houck for supporting me in this pursuit and for checking in on me during the process. Thank you to Lachrista Greco for moments of respite and laughter. Thank you to Leigh Senderowicz and Sara Chadwick for your kindness and support. To Nina Valeo Cooke, thank you for being such an advocate for me and for your warmth. Jamie Gratrix, thank you for the coffee dates, for your sincere enthusiasm about this book, and for being a breathing space and style inspiration who brought joy on difficult days.

My dear Susan Nelson, though you are no longer just down the hall, you are always near, and that makes me so glad. You are a true balm; I could wander campus with you forever, and we could stop and eat pastries whenever we please and sit and listen to the water. Being in your presence is among my most favorite and simplest joys.

Autumn Miller and Ying Dai, it has been such a pleasure to work with you, learn from you, and watch you grow as scholars. Thank you so much for being champions of this project and for your belief in me.

To Dr. Julianne Siegfriedt and Dr. Whitney Gecker, I am endlessly grateful for our little coven. May our many adventures in academia continue, and may we always take the time to come together for true respite. Thank you for bringing me perspective and peace. I love you both to the moon and stars.

To my Boston family, our connection forged in the classrooms at Simmons, my original responsible birds, Molly, Sarah, and Brenna, you have all been such important touchstones for this project, but more importantly, you have been there through it all. Here is to many more moments of getting to celebrate one another, from the momentous occasions to the mundanity.

To the one and only Sandy Locke, you have been a champion of my choices and heartbeat of my life for the last near twenty years. You are one of the smartest and bravest people I know. What an amazing privilege to grow with you. Now that we have four children between us, three of them daughters, I seek your grit and wisdom daily as we navigate the wild ride that is Parenthood. I am glad we are on it together.

Angela Bonilla, you inspire me always and in all ways. Ian Hall and Sarah Bottjen, you are warmth embodied—thank you for loving our family as we get to love yours. Devyn Brown, you are sunbeams and the sweetness of morning walks. To Mar, gorgeous friend, thank you for bringing your brilliant art to my being and bearing witness to how it blooms. Alex Bildsoe, Bailey Preston, and Mary Neigel, I am thankful the beat goes on in our little foursome. To the Ruth Badder Disc Burns, for being the ultimate (ha!) respite during summer months, and to Madeline Hayes in particular for reminding me what I am capable of.

To my dear friend Mike Kelly: you are one of my favorite humans on the planet. Thank you for understanding this accomplishment and showing me that my work is worthy of celebrating.

To Dr. Frankie Frank, you inspire me. You challenge me. You help me to soar. Thank you for lending your heart and labor to this book. You have added at least a decade to my life from the laughs alone. You have somehow made me appreciate cats, which was no easy feat. You have my heart forever, and there is so much more to come for us.

My students, past and present, have been the energy and sustenance, graciously giving of themselves in our classroom. You are the reason I get excited to come to campus every day and the reason I want to keep asking questions and doing this work. You brilliant, gentle, hilarious humans—thank you.

A brief but spectacular thank you to Chris Pureka for being a central companion in my headphones for many years of my life now. Your music means so much to me.

To my wonderful in-laws, Lynne, Wayne, and Ben, I treasure you. Thank you for all you do. I hit the absolute jackpot when I became a member of the Clark family.

To my siblings, Addie and Ty, what a phenomenal gift to not only love your siblings, but to like them. Any time I get to spend with both of you is the best of times. Thank you for the space you gave me to talk about the book, to share in the journey during the highlights and hard moments. You are both endlessly inspiring to me, and the courage you demonstrate daily in your pursuits—education, the arts, advocacy—is a towering motivation. Having you, Ty, as my big brother, and you, Addie, as my twin, is wondrous comfort.

Helene and Ellsworth, words fail, really. Thank you for being my parents, for being Mom and Dad. Thank you for loving me so well. I would not be who I am without you. I hope you can both feel daily how much you mean to me; the level of gratitude for all you have given me defies language. You have made it possible.

My children Kraemer and Vivian, you teach me something new every day. You remind me to slow down, be present to what is in front of me, take deep breaths, step away. In the years since getting my doctorate and writing this book, I have gotten to watch you grow, learn, and explore. You are both the kindest, coolest, funniest, most creative, dynamic, heart-bursting little humans, and I am so proud to know you. I love being your mom.

Joe Clark: as I write this, you are standing in the kitchen, making dinner, laughing at something on your computer, and my whole being is filled to the brim with peace and love. Jobs, kids, house—through all the must-dos and want-to-dos, you are the constant joy of my days. Two pillars. Bow and stern. A fruitful garden. A full heart. I sure am glad we chose Wisconsin and that we chose each other. Thank you for literally everything you do and for knowing that I could do this and get it done. I love you. Let's go on a bike ride and a paddle together.

And finally, endless regard for the tween girls who shared their time, experiences, and voices for this project. Thank you, thank you, thank you.

DIGITAL GIRLHOODS

1

AMERICAN TWEEN GIRLS SIGNING ON

"Navigating the complexity of modern life as a girl is a
full-time job."

—CASSELL AND CRAMER 2008:68

In April 2016, a Fox news story out of Tampa, Florida, warned parent viewers about the dangers of sexual predators using social media and other
Internet sites to target children. Along with the anchor commentary, the
news network showed a public service announcement (PSA) video produced
as a collaboration between the U.S. Department of Justice and the National
Center for Missing and Exploited Children. In the video, a young White[1] girl
(portrayed by an older female actor) sits in a pink-walled bedroom in front
of her computer. She is characterized as being about thirteen or fourteen
years old. Her curly blond hair is tied back with a headband, and her cheeks
are flushed. She slowly removes her pink tank top—undressing for someone
through the web camera who she *thinks* she knows but who is, in actuality,
a stranger.

The two-minute video then shows an older White male on his computer
watching the girl undress on the screen. Falsely posing as a younger male peer,
the man solicits the girl for further explicit content. When the girl refuses,
the man, continuing to pose as a known peer, threatens to circulate the video
of her undressing to all her friends. As the video ends, a text card flashes on
the screen, reading, "Anything private you share online could be used against
you. If someone demands sexual images from you, stop immediately and report it." The Fox news story positioned the PSA video as something "parents
need to see," a reminder that "the web can be a dangerous place, and that teens
are easy targets, preyed upon time after time" (Tampa Fox 13 2016). This news
story is far from the only example showcasing the potential threat of sexual

predators online; what seems to occur time after time is the framing of young girls as primary targets for male sexual predators online. By the time they enter adolescence, girls have been warned repeatedly about the dangers of sharing images and videos in public digital spaces, and especially sharing content that shows their bodies.

There is a societal fear *for* girls in public spaces and for what may happen *to* girls in public spaces. But there is also a fear *of* girls (Doyle 2019). This old story is packaged in a new way for the digital age. Moral panics about youth (Banet-Weiser 2014; Cohen 1972; Driscoll and Gregg 2008; McRobbie and Thornton 1995; Thiel-Stern 2014) driven by adult fears of young people having sex, girls being targeted by men and boys for sex, girls being seen as objects for sex, girls desiring sex, girls engaging in risky (i.e., sexual) behavior, and girls damaging their reputations based on any of these behaviors are not new. But because the Internet has grown well beyond a mere cultural touchstone in the last two decades, and we are now seeing near ubiquitous use of social media platforms among American youth (Nesi, Mann, and Robb 2023; Pearson 2023; Vogels, Gelles-Watnick, and Massarat 2022), moral panic surrounding girls' bodies and sexualities has seen a marked revival in the contemporary digital age.

Media plays a particularly powerful role in constructing moral panic around American girls and their bodies (Driscoll and Gregg 2008; McRobbie and Thornton 1995; Thiel-Stern 2014). As demonstrated by the story at the start of this chapter, narrative emphasis from news media in recent years has often been placed on the dangers wrought by the Internet: cyberbullying, mental health crises, sexualization, low self-esteem, negative body image, and online predators. As the old story goes, much of what defines contemporary moral panics is a nostalgic sensation and longing for some distant golden age marked by social stability and strong moral discipline (Cohen 1972; McRobbie and Thornton 1995). The alarmist, adult-centered response to girls being online—and more specifically, girls making their bodies visible and available online—would seem to suggest that social media is lacking stability and discipline. As McRobbie and Thornton (1995) explore in their revamped conceptualizations of Cohen's (1972) theory of moral panics, concern for and about youth manifests via the perceived threat of young people having too much free time and the question of "Where are their parents?" This concern not only incites broad social anxieties but also discerns a culturally manufactured need for heightened surveillance of young people. Driscoll and Gregg examine this reaction in their work on moral panics, youth, and YouTube when they write,

> Part of what we want to unravel here is the simultaneous obsession with and presumption of youth perpetuated by public and popular

representations of "global" online participation. These characterizations imply that online behavior takes place in an "Other" (unknown)
space, dangerously adrift from established forms of social interaction
(and hence surveillance, regulation, and discipline) and that "Youth"
is their most reliable and helpful label. At the time of writing, You-
Tube acts as the archetype of this phenomenon. Its status as a point
of origin for a "moral panic" is evident in the sheer number of fronts
for anxiety it harbors (2008:73).

My work, in part, considers YouTube as a site of production for contemporary tween girl digital cultures specifically through analysis of a tween girl–
driven YouTube trend called "Am I Pretty or Ugly?" As demonstrated in more
depth in the coming pages, the news media, mass media, and adult-centered
response to the Pretty or Ugly YouTube trend exposed anxieties that have
come to the fore once again regarding girls' bodies, made plain through alarm
over girls' social media participation. Shayla Thiel-Stern writes in her work
on moral panics and girls in public space:

> Gendered moral panics are recycled, redistributed, and reconstituted
> in a nearly constant historical cycle. Moreover, panics related to teen
> girls might be seen as so insignificant as to hardly count as arousing
> social anxiety. Nonetheless, the same concerns about the appropriate
> performance of femininity and girlhood and the same cultural wor-
> ries about teen girls' behaviors (and the potential consequences of those
> behaviors) continue to be the same, even over more than a century
> (2014:16).

The most recent cultural shift resulting in a notable uptick of protectionist discourses around girls is the irrefutable popularity and significant use
of social media among American tween girls today. This moral panic about
girls online is hypergendered and informed by entrenched, overarching narratives of girlhood in the United States that tend to paint girls (especially tween
and teen girls) in simplistic ways: as salacious, sexual provocateurs who are
distractions or temptations for boys and men; as badly behaved, aggressive,
or even criminal; or as innocent, passive victims preyed on by boys and men.
These narratives are jejune, well-trodden as the Madonna-Whore myth, and
exacerbated by social and cultural shifts in phenomena such as popular culture, technology, fashion, and mass media (Banet-Weiser 2014; Best and Bogle
2014; Thiel-Stern 2014). American tween girls know they are being represented in popular and public media in ways that reproduce stereotypes, reify harmful tropes, and do not represent the authentic, dynamic mosaics of their lived
experiences (Bulger et al. 2021). As Cassell and Cramer (2008) suggest in the

epigraph, girls must traverse shifty terrain, managing the bristling expectations and fraught assumptions that imbue girlhood with social, cultural, and political meaning.

I did not grow up with social media in the same way as the current generation.[2] I dabbled on Myspace (released in 2003) during my senior year of high school, selecting my "Top 8" friends and curating my layout. I chatted and gossiped on AOL Instant Messenger (AIM) with peers, carefully crafting my "away" message if another family member needed the computer or, in the days of dial up, the landline phone. Thinking of it in these nostalgic terms only affirms my feeling of incredulity in seeing what social media has become over the last two decades (Anderson et al. 2022; Bennett 2023). I was just entering college as an undergraduate student when Facebook took off, and at that point, it was only accessible to college students, not the social networking behemoth we know today. Notably, however, Facebook use by young people has dropped off massively in the last handful of years, with TikTok, Instagram, and Snapchat now among the most favored platforms—though still not as popular as YouTube, which has a 95 percent user rate among thirteen- to seventeen-year-olds.[3]

I did not spend my tween years posting selfies and sharing "stories." I spent those years building worlds for my Barbie dolls, playing board games and soccer, going to parties in friends' basements, and tying up the landline phone for hours (much to my parents' chagrin). Tween girls today are much the same. They are still playing with Barbie and going to see the much talked about 2023 movie by the same name. They are still playing board games and soccer. They are still goofing off outside, having parties, and sharing secrets. But there is one blatant difference between how tween girls are developing today versus in my own millennial generation: their social worlds are unequivocally marked by an increasingly blurry line between physical and digital worlds (Buckingham 2013a; boyd 2014; Nesi, Mann, and Robb 2023; Palfrey and Gasser 2016). Tween girls in America today are growing up on social media.

Key Terms

To clarify some terms, who or what is a girl? Using Jessalynn Keller's framing, I situate girlhood subjectivities as "discursively produced through historical, cultural, and social contexts, rather than a static and biological or age-based category that is universally valid" (2016:3). Theorist Catherine Driscoll similarly defines girl as "an assemblage of social and cultural issues and questions rather than a field of physical facts" (2002:14). A girl is not necessarily defined by a certain age, race, or even sex category assigned at birth. Popular media dubbed 2023 "The Year of the Girl" (*Dazed, The Cut, Elle, NPR*), with intense social and political interest around girl culture, most notably how adult women have been reclaiming and celebrating elements of girlhood and femininity, especially those aesthetically in line with popular films like *Barbie*, the cultural phenomenon of Taylor Swift's The Eras Tour, and social media trends such as "Girl Dinner." In this way, *girl* can be understood as a sensibility: a set of ideas, concerns, desires, and affects relative to a particular time, place, and social, cultural, and political context.

In this research, I understand American girlhood as defined by and made legible to the broader American public via cultural anxieties and related expectations and stereotypes surrounding female children's and adolescent's bodies and sexualities. These definitions are necessarily raced, classed, abled, and gendered. Girlhoods are broadly understood in the United States in relation to a restrictive, culturally inscribed gender binary that codes certain behaviors, activities, language, and expressions as belonging to girls (feminine) and others as belonging to boys (masculine). I frame girlhoods as associated with gendered behaviors of how girls may yield to and accommodate social and cultural expectations about their bodies and sexualities, resist and subvert those expectations, or do both at the same time (Butler 1990; Schilt and Westbrook 2009; West and Zimmerman 1987).

Girlhoods are ever shifting, transforming, and being altered according to specific times, places, and circumstances. When one takes an intersectional approach (Crenshaw 1989; Smith, Frazier, and Smith 1977), exploring a prism of girlhoods mediated by nationality, race, ethnicity, age, ability, size, region, sexuality, and beyond, it becomes clear how stereotypes about girls—as well as biases—converge to create our relationships with girls themselves at individual, interpersonal, and institutional levels. Tween girls' identities as girls do not exist in a vacuum or as individuals. We must think about their identities in relation to the historical moment, the institutions of which they are part, the communities they touch, and the communities they build. Only by seeing all these elements operating together as a whole, as an interlocking system that shapes the social and political conditions of their lives, does it become possible to consider solutions that actually grant girls the power to be and do anything—a power that has thus far been experienced mainly in theory.

Consideration of the politics of place are essential for imagining and contextualizing processes of girlhoods. Rentschler and Mitchell (2016) argue that focus on place renders meanings of girlhoods via their interaction with sociopolitical, historical, and media discourses. Vanner (2019) assures us that focus on location "enables a political analysis of the ways in which girlhood is uniquely gendered, sexed, raced, and classed in different spaces" (120). In this work, I think about girlhoods within the context of the digital age in contemporary America. The labels *America* and *American* are not necessarily suggestive of research subjects' only or primary national identity or sense of belonging in any straightforward way. Rather, I use *America(n)* in this context in recognition of how girlhood cultural scripts are produced and disseminated across media landscapes within a specific geographic, spatial, and national cultural context. The production of digital girlhoods by tween girls themselves troubles limiting and oppressive representations, cultivating new imaginings and nuanced possibilities of girlhood embodiments across and within various subjectivities and identities.

Girlhood is often framed as a monolithic, idealized category in which the diverse experiences of girls are flattened to fit a societal norm. Who is the ideal girl in the American imagination? Who is the innocent girl in need of protection? She tends to be White, of middle- to upper-class circumstance, visibly able-bodied, educated, heterosexual, born in the United States, and growing up in the mythic nuclear family model (Coontz 1993). This is the American girl the media tells tween girls they should aspire to embody, the girl the media presents as the most vulnerable target for sexual predators. My research recognizes the reality of many and varied girlhoods and the nuances therein, subject to shift and change depending on how dimensions of difference intersect. In relation to how *girl* is categorized on social media, "nowadays, the category of girl in the contemporary mediascape extends to include the tween-age girl who is between 9 and 14 as well as older women in their 30s and 40s who are often referred to as girls" (Hill 2017:121). This expansion is reified by the recent, remarkable surge of intrigue around all things girl, from teenage girls' mental health and well-being (CDC 2023) to girls' place in popular culture, to ubiquitous pink, hyperfeminine fashion trends and "hot girl walks" (Miller 2023).

This research also considers the province of youth, particularly in digital space. Driscoll and Gregg's definition of youth culture aligns well with my purview of tween girlhoods online:

> Across the rhetorical tropes that dominate Western media—youth-as-trouble, youth-as-fun, youth-as-future and youth-as-confusing tribe—youth emerges as a liminal troubling category perfect for engagement with the uncertainties of the future, and youth culture as a category that slips between what look, by opposition, like more stable and coherent categories (see Valentine, Skelton and Chambers 1998; Driscoll 2002). Youth culture is most usefully defined as a field of artifacts, identities, and practices which are circulated by youth as about and for youth (2008:78).

American youth are now living fluidly between offline and online spaces and engaging in self- and social development in ways specific to their generation (boyd 2014; Buckingham, Bragg, and Kehily 2014; Farman 2012; Palfrey and

Gasser 2016). The transition from adolescence to adulthood is facilitated by online participation, and specifically social media participation. Prior to the rise of the Internet and the near ubiquitous use of social media platforms as part of daily life, youth employed immediate peer groups, interactions in social spaces, relationships with friends and family, and media such as television and film to gauge where they fell in the scheme of what is "normal" in terms of body and behavior and build identities based on what is reflected back at them by these various agents.

While this process is still occurring, the Internet has also become a crucial agent of identity development (Farrell 2022; Kennedy 2020; Malvini Redden and Way 2017; Yau and Reich 2019). The social conditions of young people's lives are reflected through social media participation and creation, and social interactions, relationships, and self-expression occur online with as much regularity and normalcy (if not more) as in any offline space. This has especially become the case for young people who came into tween- and teenhood during the COVID-19 pandemic, when virtually all peer interaction moved into the digital realm (Bulger et al. 2021), revealing important new information about how American youth navigate self- and social development through social media participation. We have yet to fully understand the impacts of the pandemic on young people in this context.

Along with girls, girlhoods, and youth, I situate *tween* in certain terms in this work. *Tween* as an idea and classification emerges with and through the production of popular media. In addition to its characterization as a consumer demographic and highly gendered, markedly feminine preadolescent-to-adolescent life stage, *tween* is also a discursive, constructed category that is not static, sometimes contradictory, and often filled with cultural anxieties and tensions (García-Gómez 2018; Kennedy 2018). Tween girls are constructed as "fun" (Coulter 2021) and packaged and sold as such. In the landscape of marketing and consumerism, tween girls are represented as carefree, empowered, confident—and notably hyperfeminine. They are still children but burgeoning, on the cusp of becoming women. As author Jessica Bennett notes from a parent interview in her piece "Being 13" (2023), tweens can be understood as "half adult, half child . . . [eating] a Lunchable while at a fancy hair appointment."

Tween girls are hearts, stars, rainbows, flowers, and bubble gum. They are princess crowns, disco balls, lip gloss, glitter, peace signs, and smiley faces. They are pop culture, postfeminist girl power, and "riot grrrl" punk sensibility rolled into one, made palatable through neoliberal, capitalist co-optation. Mattie Kahn, author of *Young and Restless: The Girls Who Sparked America's Revolutions* (2023a), writes in an op-ed piece for *InStyle* that "girls as spenders are cheered; girls as citizens are sidelined" (2023b). Tween girls are constructed as powerful individuals in processes of consumption but bereft of recognizable collective social power, except in the purview of popular culture (e.g., celebrities and tween icons such as Taylor Swift can have major influence over tweens within shared fandom, but this influence rarely translates to how tweens might wield tangible social or political power to affect policy or material conditions). *Tween* is a category that precedes adolescence but is entirely bound up with it. Melanie Kennedy's 2018 monograph *Tweenhood: Femininity and Celebrity in Tween Popular Culture* considers how tween girlhoods are produced and constitutively expressed through both capitalism and feminism as a "transitional stage" in which tween girls work on and develop the self through consumption of celebrity. Kennedy frames tweenhood as "a construct of the postfeminist cultural context" (2018:3); a tween girl is sold empowerment in a system that keeps her disempowered.

Tween girls exist in a liminal space between childhood and adulthood, which influences their consumptive patterns and behaviors. Tween girls play around with makeup. They follow beauty tutorials. They are interested in knowing, following, and, in some cases, setting trends. They are fascinated by—at times, obsessed with—celebrities. Investment in popular culture, beauty and body work, and fashion drive tween girl consumer behavior. Tween girls are consistently engaging with media "beyond their years," which informs their existence in a liminal space (García-Gómez 2018; Renold and Ringrose 2011). They are girls who are not yet grown up but exhibit markers of adulthood via interest in certain kinds of content, types of dress, patterns of language, and modes of behavior. They are in the process of becoming. They are also heavily laden with culturally constructed and projected conditions of female adolescence, including low self-esteem, negative body image, sexual uncertainty, fraught homosocial relationships, and a rejection of parental guidance in favor of peer approval (Crann 2017).

The Matter of Tween Girls Online

I chose to examine the tween girl category in this research because it is the demographic whose members are creating and posting "Am I Pretty or Ugly?" YouTube videos; they are also making their foray into the world of social media and "digitally networked publics" (boyd 2010; De Leyn et al. 2021). Because federal law dictates that a person must be thirteen years old to have a social media profile across various platforms (Children's Online Privacy Protection Rule, or COPPA), girls younger than thirteen become an all at once hypervisible and invisible demographic in digital space. I am interested in the dynamic exchange and dissonance of how tween girls are represented in public and popular media and culture, how they are targeted in the consumer marketplace (especially in relation to being in crisis and sold empowerment and self-esteem in contemporary confidence culture) (Orgad and Gill 2022), and how they are representing themselves on social media and demonstrating a much more complex landscape of American girlhoods today. Tween girl selves are constituted and can be understood in a context of social media participation, digital space use, and content creation. When a tween girl posts a video on YouTube asking the world, "Am I pretty or ugly?" she is also asking, "Who am I?"

Over the last decade in the United States, social media participation has become the new normal for American youth. In her work on digitally networked publics and teenagers, danah boyd addresses how adults tend to view youth participation on social media in stark terms, as utopian or dystopian. But, as boyd suggests, what teenagers are doing on social media is more complicated; it "mirrors, magnifies, and makes more visible the good, bad, and ugly of everyday life" (2014:24). Though there has been a significant increase in academic inquiry on the matter of social media impacts on young people across a considerable variety of geopolitical and cultural contexts, we remain overall uncertain of the potential impacts and mediations that social media participation has on tween girls' lives, for better or worse (Anderson et al. 2022; Valkenburg, Meier, and Beyens 2022; Valkenburg et al. 2022).

Public opinion and academic scholarship are frequently divided on the matter. Some suggest that social media, and the Internet more broadly, is a safe and useful space for girls to express themselves in myriad ways and engage in topics that matter to their gendered selves, such as body image, sexuality, menstruation, friendship, intimate relationships, and social justice and activism (Anderson et al. 2022; Bulger et al. 2021; Burnette, Kwitowski, and Mazzeo 2017; Davis 2010; De Leyn et al. 2021; Ging and O'Higgins Norman 2016; Hammond, Cooper, and Jordan 2018; Kanai 2019b; Kearney 2011; Mendes, Ringrose, and Keller 2019; Kennedy 2020; Markey and Daniels 2022; Mazzarella 2010; Shields Dobson 2011; Stern 1999; Takayoshi 1999; Wade 2024). Others contend that the content girls are creating and posting on social media (e.g., selfies, TikToks, snaps, and stories) is indicative of an ongoing "crisis of girlhood" (Choukas-Bradley et al. 2022; Cohen, Newton-John, and Slater 2018; Nurka 2014; Sales 2016; Chen, Luo, and Chen 2020) characterized by phenomena such as sexual objectification, sexism, body dissatisfaction, and other gendered social ills. People in the latter camp argue that social media is a vehicle that furthers gendered oppression, increases sexualization and objectification of girls, fosters patterns of unhealthy comparison, and promotes low self-esteem.

It would be quite easy to fall into one of these camps. I argue instead that the realities of how social media impacts American tween girls—and, more importantly, the realities of their relationships with social media—are more nuanced and multivalent. Tween girls' social media use encompasses all the above: good and bad, risk and reward, pitfalls and potentials. And tween girls' other identities, including race, sexuality, queerness, size, and ability, to name a few, certainly hold weight in how tween girls relate to and participate on social media and how adults and institutions respond to that participation. As girlhood studies scholar Marnina Gonick suggests, social and cultural anxieties about girlhood "[do] not . . . get conferred equally or in the same way on all girls" (2003:4, see also Rentschler and Mitchell 2014).

While in some ways social media can and does reproduce, reify, or even magnify problematic social ills, such as the ongoing objectification and sexualization of girls, these ills do not find their origin in social media. Objectification and sexualization have long been recognizable in narratives of American girlhoods (Egan 2013; Thiel-Stern 2014). We certainly should not be dismissive of potential harms of social media, but to consider them as existing in a vacuum or as the only side to the story obfuscates another truth: that social media is also a place where tween girls can make themselves central to conversations happening about their lives and create content that speaks to who they are. Much of the moral panic surrounding tween girls today is not about social media in and of itself, but more so, as the story goes, about the novelty of social media, the "new-ness" of the technology and what we are learning about it, and the sense on the part of many tween girl caretakers that social media feels unfamiliar, unregulated, and, therefore, unsafe. The moral panic manifests as a fear of the unknown, which unsurprisingly translates to increased anxiety about tween girls' visibility online and participation in public digital spaces—and, more specifically, about what it means to make their bodies visible in those spaces. Kennedy and Coulter reflect on this question in the introduction to a special issue of the *Girlhood Studies* journal titled "Locating Tween Girls."

> The cultural visibility of tweenhood, and the subject of the tween—one bound up with deep-rooted assumptions about race, beauty, and consumer culture—is a site onto and through which contemporary social anxieties and debates about vulnerable group members' uses and navigations of new media (newer at least than the platforms and technologies girls' studies scholars such as Harris were writing about over a decade ago) get projected (2018:2).

Tween girl participation on social media is complicated and worth our collective attention. Rather than immediately resorting to alarmism and a despair mindset that casts tween girls as either in trouble or causing trouble (Harris 2004a), I suggest that tween girls' content creation and social media participation are consequential invitations to listen, ask questions, and ultimately understand more about what matters to them today across and within their identities and interests. Tween girls are more media literate than in the past because social media is intrinsically bound up with their development and the sensibilities of their cultural conditions. Even if a tween girl is not actively participating on social media platforms, this fact can tell us much about how she is experiencing her social world (Bennett 2023). What do tween girlhoods look like and feel like in America today? And why and how does social media matter to tween girls?

While I offer a critique of the current heightened desire to control and restrict girls online, I do not want to be glib and suggest that tween girls' social media use is somehow simple, straightforward, and devoid of risk. Social media platforms are owned by private corporations. Participation is mediated, and content creation is subject to scrutiny and surveillance (Farrell 2022; Wade 2019a). Algorithms suggest and promote specific content that drives consumer behaviors. Girls' social media practices are not immune to existing structural inequities and power dynamics, and there is risk involved in participation. But tween girls know this. Their social media participation and engagement is a direct reflection of their social lives as a whole: nuanced and complicated, sometimes overwrought or overwhelming, sometimes practical, often playful, and at times plainly beneficial to tween girls themselves. What I hope to emphasize is that the impulse to protect girls by pulling them off social media, keeping them away from platforms, and policing and restricting their bodies and sexualities in these digital spaces substantiates damaging and persisting dominant narratives of girlhood and hegemonic gender norms that continually devalue girls, dismiss them, and tell them that they do not belong, that their value is wrapped up in aesthetic capital (Anderson et al. 2010), and that their worth (and liability) is situated squarely in the framing of their bodies as culturally fraught spaces, the sites of so many enduring social anxieties.

Tween girls have been taking up digital space and forging their own paths in the digital arena since the dawn of public Internet use and the rise of content creation (Kearney 2006; Kearney 2011; Keller 2019; Keller and Ryan 2018; Takayoshi 1999). They are the vanguards of the personal profile, cultivating networked publics (boyd 2010) and communities and creating content that speaks directly to their positionalities as tween girls in America (Keller 2019; Kennedy 2020; Shields Dobson 2015; Thiel-Stern 2014). Rather than use the term *user-generated content*, defined as online users generating content to disseminate information about products and brands, I use the broader term *content creation*, which includes contribution of content/information by digital media users for an audience. Pew Research defines *content creation* as "the creation of the material people contribute to the online world" (Lenhart, Fallows, and Horrigan 2004). I do not include sexting or texting in this definition because these kinds of digital communication may not take place on social media applications and are most often shared specifically and interpersonally between individual cellular phone numbers (Barrense-Dias et al. 2017; García-Gómez 2018; Gordon-Messer et al. 2013; Hasinoff 2015; Klettke, Hallford, and Mellor 2014). That said, if an image is shared via Snapchat or other social media application, it falls under the category of content creation. I consider any digital content created for an audience on a social media platform (whether for a group of friends on Snapchat or as a publicly available video on YouTube) as content creation.

The content tween girls create online is an assemblage of cultural artifacts I refer to as *digital girlhoods*. Digital girlhoods are all at once the tangible cultural material that tween girls create and produce on and across social media platforms (selfies, images, reels, stories, videos, vlogs, etc.) and the processes of becoming and enacting tweenhood and girlhood online that constitute and illuminate the liminal space between childhood wonder and adult interests in explicitly gendered ways. Digital girlhoods are both the creation by tween girls of sites of inquiry to understand more about contemporary tween girl digital cultures and the phenomenon of how tween girlhoods as a category of being and embodiment are constituted and made legible via social media participation today. American tween girls give meaning to contemporary American tween girlhoods as they create within and navigate digital space through the ongoing cultural and social production of digital girlhoods.

Digital girlhoods give us tremendous insight into how tween girls in the United States navigate, embody, and resist contemporary paradigms of "doing girlhood" (Currie, Kelly, and Pomerantz 2009) and the stringent expectations associated with ideal girlhood, which continue to privilege Whiteness, thinness, cis-hetness, and able-bodiedness. But beyond rendering a deeper, richer understanding of persistent and dominant cultural models of American girlhoods, digital girlhoods keenly demonstrate how tween girls use social media as a tool for visibility, self-representation, image control, social capital, community building, and connection. Tween girls' participation on social media has the potential to foster meaningful change for girls as members of an oppressed demographic, create counternarratives, and contribute to social, cultural, economic, and political strides toward gender equity (Mendes, Ringrose, and Keller 2019; Preston-Sidler 2015; Wade 2019a).

There is tremendous potential in situating social media as a tool tween girls are leveraging for visibility and political participation in social and cultural discourses about their own lives. But social media is still messy. The often contradictory narratives that tween girls present on these platforms (when it comes to gender and sexuality in particular) shed light on the completely contradictory and conflicting social conditions that currently structure tween girls' lives (Attwood, Hakim, and Winch 2017; García-Gómez 2018; Vares, Jackson, and Gill 2011; Renold and Ringrose 2011). Social conditions are further complicated depending on the identities of the tween girl in question. Popular culture and mass media tell girls to be confident, but not too confident. Be vulnerable, but do not show too much of yourself online. Be authentic, but only in appropriately self-effacing ways. Be pretty, but not vain. Be thin, but not too thin, but certainly not fat. Be smart, but not too smart. Be active, but do not bypass the boys. Be a leader, but in a suitably feminine way. Be sexy, but not slutty.

This endless list of paradoxes, set against a backdrop of constructed ideal femininity (White, thin, pretty, able-bodied, educated, middle to upper class, etc.), is reinforced and policed by institutions, adults, and girls themselves, both individually and interpersonally. Contrasting expectations are bound up with decades-old notions of postfeminism and newer, shinier, polished iterations of feminist ideology that are notably neoliberal, individualistic, and built on the premise of constant consumption to achieve empowerment (Banet-Weiser 2018; Orgad and Gill 2022; Zeisler 2016). Tween girls are, after all, a market demographic (Banet-Weiser 2014; Kennedy and Coulter 2018; Kennedy 2018). Within contemporary confidence culture, American girls are supposed to be sure of themselves, but with all these competing, contradictory expectations, they are surely confused. What is a girl to do?

Tween girls embody and negotiate these many contradictions via social media participation because it is their modus operandi of communication today. If we want to understand more about girlhoods in contemporary America, we need look no further than TikTok, Instagram, Snapchat, or YouTube. How are tween girls living and experiencing girlhood in the digital age? I ask this question not only because of the lightning speed at which things seem to move and change these days (especially when it comes to which social media platforms are most popular and what starts trending or goes viral) but also because in the midst of all this change, some things remain notably unwavering—or at least, resurface again and again. These things include the ever-familiar, adult-driven moral panic, fear, and anxiety that define and shape dominant, restrictive ideas about what it means to be a successful tween girl in the United States. I deem these attitudes responsible, in no small part, for the ongoing oppression, suppression, and restriction of girls across identities and circumstances from full opportunity in social, cultural, and political life.

I argue that TikTok as a specific platform, for example, is not the thing that matters. Indeed, the TikTok platform is quite like other social media applications that have come before and will come after (e.g., Vine, Musical.ly). We cannot reasonably separate the astronomic rise of TikTok's popularity from the context of the global COVID-19 pandemic and the collective shift into lockdown (De Leyn et al. 2021; Kennedy 2020)—the reality that so many American youth were at home, with cell phones and laptops as the primary conduits for connection to peers, social groups, popular culture, and political events (Bennett 2023; Bulger et al. 2021). What matters is TikTok as the unmistakable realm of youth culture and production (Jennings 2019). Part of what makes TikTok what it is in the current moment is the sheer volume of content being created and shared, and tween girls are highly visible and prolific content creators on the app.

The essence and ethos of TikTok is what resonates, and that essence and ethos will proliferate onto the next social media platform that gains traction. The social media app BeReal was, for a moment, a GenZ obsession, and it has now declined in popularity. Though it launched in 2020, the app did not see significant usership until 2022, further reifying the mysterious ways in which platforms start to trend among users and lose their shine seemingly overnight. BeReal asks users to "be real" and "show your friends who you really are, for once" (Rush 2022), removing the opportunity to add filters, edit photos, and meticulously curate content and putting a fresh spin on authenticity and vulnerability (something I speak to in more depth in later chapters). The tween girls I interviewed for this research articulated various reasons for using different social media applications (e.g., Snapchat for communicating with small groups of friends vs. Instagram and TikTok for scrolling through content vs. YouTube for posting public videos), but they made a larger point that it is not the app that matters, but rather what social media can be used for more generally in self and social development and what it means to them. They brought up themes of visibility, self-esteem, desirability, relationships, celebrity, popularity, privacy, and safety.

Taking a step back and considering how social media has evolved as a whole, from Myspace to YouTube to Tumblr to Facebook to Instagram to TikTok, we see that these platforms are spaces where content is created and shared, and that content reflects what tween girls care about and what they may be going through. Many interests and issues relevant to tween girls remain the same as in decades past. Certainly, social ills such as body dissatisfaction among young girls and the desire to fit in are not new (Brown and Gilligan 1992; Brumberg 1997; Orenstein 1994). But being able to share the minutiae of a day, giving the world a glimpse into your bedroom, your intimate spaces, your private life, speaking publicly to issues that impact you, and making your body visible on a public forum *is* new. Though we are only just beginning to grasp the impacts of social media participation on young people and tween and teenage girls in particular (De Leyn et al. 2021; Jarman et al. 2021; Nesi 2020; Maes and Vandenbosch 2022; Markey and Daniels 2022; Steinsbekk et al. 2021), research and resulting scholarship is finding that the gendered impacts of social media use are not clean, easy to categorize, or rendered essential across girlhood identities. When we put tween girl voices front and center, we learn that social media is both positive and negative (maybe even neutral), rewarding and frustrating, good and bad. There exists an exciting opportunity to continue to learn more about what these platforms mean to some of their most prolific users, so long as we are willing to ask questions and let tween girls speak for themselves.

Am I Pretty or Ugly?

How does social media, now a primary mode of social development, communication, and expression for tween girls, interact with historical and contemporary expectations of what tween girls are, how they are supposed to look and behave? How are the answers to these questions complicated by race, ethnicity, social class, gender identity, sexuality, and ability? I sought to understand more by talking with tween girls themselves, as well as investigating a tween girl–driven YouTube trend as a primary example of contemporary digital girlhoods.

Between October 2016 and March 2017, I interviewed twenty-six tween girls from a variety of racial and socioeconomic backgrounds. All were between the ages of ten and thirteen and living in Wisconsin. I asked them about their experiences on social media, how they use it in their daily lives, and what it means to them. Through these interviews, I learned that social media is not just important to them; it is a tool and vehicle they use to gain some semblance of control over how others see them and how they see themselves. It is a meaningful avenue for garnering visibility, social capital, and self-esteem. Though not without drawbacks, including its "drama-filled" moments (to use their terminology) and the reasons they are told to be wary, especially regarding public versus private content, social media is held up as a crucial mechanism for community building, maintaining connections with friends and peers, and developing and engaging interests. Much has changed in the last handful of years surrounding social media in the context of the COVID-19 pandemic, but recent scholarship reifies and affirms these findings (Anderson et al. 2022; Keller 2016; Bulger et al. 2021; Nesi, Mann, and Robb 2023; Wade 2019a). Tween girls are savvy, strategic, and thoughtful in how they use social media and create digital girlhoods.

In addition to conducting interviews, I analyzed 260 YouTube videos from the prominent YouTube trend "Am I Pretty or Ugly?" The Pretty or Ugly YouTube trend began in 2011 with a handful of tween girls posting individual, publicly available videos on YouTube asking, "Am I pretty or ugly?" (or some variation thereof) and requesting that viewers leave comments about their appearances. The videos became so rampant on YouTube that they were recognized by the site as trending, and unsurprisingly, news media stories and other videos on YouTube started popping up in response to the trend. To date, it is estimated that more than one million Pretty or Ugly videos have been posted to YouTube by the tween girl demographic (Banet-Weiser 2014; Gallo

2013; Perle 2013; Rossie 2015), and in recent years, similar kinds of videos in which posters ask viewers to assess their appearance have trended on TikTok.

I became aware of the Pretty or Ugly YouTube trend in the fall of 2013 when I came across a news story published on the *Slate* magazine website titled "Young Girls Ask, 'Am I Pretty or Ugly?' on YouTube" (Waldman 2013). My initial reaction to learning about the trend was predictably aligned with much of the public and news media reaction to it at the time, boiling down to feelings of "this is so sad" and "we can't believe girls are asking this question." Reporters and media commentators were disturbed by the existence of the trend and suspicious of girls' motives for posting this kind of video. But mostly, they focused on how sad and troubling they believed it to be. One source lamented,

> Most [of the videos] come with a feigned nonchalance. . . . [What's] particularly disconcerting about these inquiries by young girls, who barely know who they are as individuals, is that the focus on looks at such a young age comes from insecurity and needing to be validated, even by those they don't know (Maldonado 2013:para. 9).

Meanwhile, other sources sang a different tune, criticizing the Pretty or Ugly videos for what they saw as their attention-seeking nature. In the same 2013 *Slate* article, author Katy Waldman writes of one of the girls in a Pretty or Ugly video: "She smiles coyly, feigns insecurity. . . . [Maybe] she craves validation; maybe she is secretly consumed by doubt. Either way, she looks like she is having an awesome time." So in one sense and reading of the trend, girls are feigning nonchalance. In another, they are feigning insecurity. Could it be that both are happening at the same time? Or is it possible that the girls making these videos are, in fact, not feigning anything?

The more I investigated the trend and the backlash on the part of many adult authority figures, the more I wondered about the seeming shock and awe at tween girls asking this pretty or ugly question when it is a question American society has collectively characterized as a natural part of growing up as a girl for more than a century (Brumberg 1997; Orenstein 1994). The obvious difference from decades past is that the tween girls taking part in this trend are not just asking their family, friends, or immediate peer groups to assess their appearances; they are asking the world on a highly popular public digital platform where anyone with access to YouTube could see and comment on the videos. And while this trend peaked on YouTube nearly a decade ago and may no longer seem relevant, there is no denying the enduring importance of being pretty in embodying "successful" girlhood (Adams and Bettis 2003; Harris 2004b; Currie, Kelly, and Pomerantz 2009; Sands

2012), demonstrative of how this question of continues to pop up regardless of the social media platform du jour.

"Where are the parents?" was yet another sentiment made popular in news media response to the trend. Commentators leveled blame against parents for not keeping a closer eye on their daughters, who they felt, by nature of their age and gender, had no business making public YouTube videos for any potential Internet predator, pedophile, or troll to see. Still other sources framed the matter as girls "setting themselves up" for cyberbullying (Kennedy 2013). Among the parental, popular, and news media response to the trend, the common denominator appears to be a protective attitude toward girls, a suggestion that the girls making these videos do not fully comprehend the risks associated with posting them and the potential repercussions. Many vilified tween girls for being attention seeking—but why is this trait necessarily bad, especially when girlhood concerns and interests are so often dismissed and disparaged? Little has been done to examine the social conditions surrounding the Pretty or Ugly trend, and critical inquiry into why tween girls might use the specific platform of YouTube to ask this age-old question is notably absent.

Public perceptions and media representations of girls (in both news media and popular culture) have greatly contributed to contrasting dominant narratives about girls that position them as either innocent and in need of protection or as dangerous, promiscuous, and rebellious. Abiding paradigms of "girls in trouble" versus "girls as trouble," "can-do girls" versus "at-risk girls" (Harris 2004a), reinforce harmful girlhood stereotypes related to race and class and continually position girls as an oppressed, marginalized, and vulnerable population. In recent years, news stories about girls sharing private information via the Internet have spread far and wide and have resulted in increased policing of girls' behavior, especially in reference to acting or appearing sexy online.

In certain states, young people can be prosecuted for sharing sexy images or videos (Best and Bogle 2014; Hasinoff 2015). What began as discrete news media moments and individual reporting on incidents of sharing sexual content is now legible as a far-reaching cultural phenomenon and source of moral panic, manifesting as a fear of what could happen to girls' bodies—and of what girls' bodies are capable of. Sady Doyle writes in her book *Dead Blondes and Bad Mothers* that there is a "madness that ensues when a society locates the threat to its own existence in the body of the young girl" (2019:6). An entire social values system—one that simultaneously obsesses over and fears sex, purports to believe in self-love while constantly pushing for self-improvement, and emphasizes personal fulfillment measured by a heteronormative notion of happy family life concurrent with an entrenched ethos of individualism, competition, and capitalist enterprise—is being cast onto the bodies of today's American girls.

Competing Cultural Models: Innocent Girls Who Need Protection and "Girl Power!"

A clear avenue that helps situate these dueling dualisms is Andrew Cherlin's theory of competing cultural models, which he defines as ways of viewing and understanding social life. In his 2010 book *The Marriage Go Round*, Cherlin thinks about marriage and divorce in the United States as competing cultural models. On the one hand, people in the United States love marriage. The wedding services industry in the United States earned yearly revenue somewhere north of $57 billion in 2021 and upward of $70 billion in 2023 (McCain 2023). American society considers marriage the ideal end point for every monogamous, romantic relationship. Yet divorce has become a very common occurrence in this country in the last half century. Divorce, though not regularly viewed as a desirable event or outcome and not always welcomed, is accepted, an unmistakably established norm. Cherlin argues that much of this contradiction has to do with competing models of what Americans are effectively conditioned into desiring—a happy, fulfilling marriage and home life, as well as individualism in identity, achievement, and success in the workplace. I use Cherlin's framework of competing cultural models to shed light on the contested nature of girlhood in America today, shaped by two competing cultural models that provide girls with conflicting guidelines on identity, appearance, and behavior: innocent girls who need protection versus "Girl Power!"

With each new development in media, technology, and fashion (or other cultural shift) comes another turn of the moral panic cycle perpetuated by girls participating in the public sphere. In the innocent girls who need protection cultural model, girls have historically been represented and thought of as "in crisis" (Banet-Weiser 2015; Harris 2004a; Mazzarella and Pecora 2007; Rentschler and Mitchell 2014). Constructions of girls as in crisis have been heavily marked by race and class connotations, situating girls as either in trouble or as trouble, "can-do" or "at risk" (Abrams 2003; Downe 2005; Harris 2004a). The social thrust of protectionist discourse around girls is White centered; girls of color, especially Black, Brown, and Indigenous girls in lower-economic circumstances, are framed in crisis in a different way from White girls and girls in middle- and upper-economic circumstances, often toward criminalization, adultification, or narratives of delinquency (Carter Andrews et al. 2019; Morris 2015; Wade 2019a). Girls with disabilities have been rendered essentially invisible in broader cultural discourse around girls in crisis because disability so often obfuscates gender, race, and sexual subjectivities, even as experiences of disability are themselves vast and impossible to essentialize (Hill 2017; Wendell 1997). Expectations of ideal girlhood are not experienced the same way across identities. Sarah Banet-Weiser writes,

> It is the Can-Do girl who has been scripted as a national "problem"; her body has been the site of public national investment, cultivated and imagined as a future citizen, an investment circulated in an economy of visibility. In contrast, the At-Risk girl is always already at risk because of her raced and classed body (2018:82).

Through a more specific lens of tweenhood, De Leyn et al. write that "in the Global North, childhood is oftentimes nostalgically imagined as a state of innocence, naivety, and protection (Sabry and Mansour 2019). Adolescence on the other hand is considered a phase of expanding autonomy but also of reckless risk-taking (Durham 2017)" (2021:3). As an added layer to the discursive girlhood studies framing of the can-do girl and the at-risk girl, the *tween girl* exists somewhere between these imaginings of innocence and needing protection versus expanding autonomy and recklessness by virtue of liminality and slippage in the tween category.

Considering how girls' bodies are restricted in the name of protection, we can point to several examples, such as the ongoing promotion of virginity prominent across many social arenas, especially in Christian denominations and within public education. Girls routinely have earlier curfews than cis male siblings or peers and are more often monitored by parents outside of the home. Sex education in public schools (if it exists at all) rarely discusses girls' sexualities with any nuance, let alone entertaining the possibility of girls identifying with nonhetero desires. Curriculum most often focuses on menstruation, anatomy, and reproductive cycles (and frankly, the information is severely lacking in depth and detail). While this knowledge is important, it does little to question how sex education, even if advertised as comprehensive, fails to promote transparent and direct conversations about desire, queer experiences, pleasure, and the cultivation of sexual subjectivities. Boys are framed as active sexual agents, and girls are passive receivers or victims (Fields 2008; Fine and McClelland 2007; Orenstein 2016; Tolman 2005). This curriculum reproduces a restrictive and simplistic gender binary.

It seems American society would collectively prefer not to acknowledge girls as sexual subjects capable of desiring and asserting that desire, yet girlhood itself is sexualized throughout American public and popular media. If attention is paid to girls' sexualities in the sex ed curriculum, they are often represented in terms of romanticism, emotional connection, and emotional intimacy rather than corporeal drive and desire for physical pleasure. When we consider this reality through a lens of disability justice, girls with disabilities, whether cognitive or physical, are more likely to be viewed as entirely nonsexual or lacking sexual subjectivity and agency. The framework of girlhood innocence becomes even more firmly entrenched, and efforts toward protection are escalated (Fine 1988; Hill 2017; Steele and Goldblatt 2020; Stienstra 2015; Tepper 2000). The invisibility of girls with disabilities across social institutions, including media, renders their self-representation in new media landscapes even more important in intersectional analyses of tween girls' embodied experiences (Hill 2017; Reinke and Todd 2016).

School dress codes unjustly target girls and punish them for wearing "sexual" clothing (leggings that fit the form, for example), yet girls are effectively encouraged to wear such clothing through media messaging, marketing from mass retailers, and its availability in the places where they consume (or where parents consume for them). Peggy Orenstein, author of *Girls and Sex* (2016), argues that, though perhaps well intentioned, parents and educators alienate girls from their own bodies by exacerbating their vulnerability and positioning sex as something to fear, all under the banner of protection. Sarah Banet-Weiser suggests,

> The recent spate of books and other cultural products warning about the sexualization of girls confirms the raced and classed nature of the moral panic; as R. Danielle Egan (2013) argues about the regulation imposed on the sexual practices of middle class girls, "the white bourgeois body has been conceptualized as pure, hygienic, and emblematic of restraint and rationality; and the middle- and upper-class child the embodiment of innocence, purity, and the bright future of the class, race, and nation" (2014:88).

The projection of adult anxieties, fears, and moral panic onto girls' bodies ultimately places an onus on girls to protect themselves from boys and men, dress modestly, behave appropriately, and take full responsibility for their bodies as distractions to boys and men at best—and targets for sexual violence at worst.

The second cultural model is "Girl Power!" The term "Girl Power!" was born out of the third wave feminist movement of the late 1980s and early 1990s and coined by members of the feminist punk band Bikini Kill, who also wrote and published the Riot Grrrl manifesto in 1991. Originally, the "Girl Power!" sentiment encapsulated an underground, do-it-yourself, antiestablishment feminist ethic focused on intersectionality and inclusion, as well as individualism, choice, and agency—notably set apart from the collectivist politics and dubious, homogenizing "sisterhood is global" rhetoric of the feminist second wave. "Girl Power!" was a movement established by girls for girls, and it centered reclaiming, owning, and celebrating the identity of *girl*, emphasizing neofemininities, confidence, independence, subcultural performance, and choice (Riordan 2001).

Over time, the girl power idea has become intensely bound up with consumer culture, a cornerstone of postfeminist ideology and, more recently, a recognizable thread in the resurgence of popular feminism (Banet-Weiser 2018; Zeisler 2016). Postfeminism posits and parades the myth of achieved gender equality: the belief that we are beyond feminism, that we no longer need it. Postfeminist sensibility (Adamson 2017; Gill 2007; McRobbie 2008) can be understood acutely through the feminist politics of late 1990s and early 2000s media such as *Ally McBeal* and *Sex and the City*, which champion a particular brand of female empowerment marked by Whiteness, wealth, individualism, neoliberalism, and adaptation to masculine-coded spaces while performing conventional femininity via beauty and body work (Tasker and Negra 2007). Postfeminism is especially and particularly concerned with the body as project (Gill 2007).

More recently, feminist scholarship on "confidence culture" (Orgad and Gill 2022) and "empowerment" (Banet-Weiser 2018) has complicated the postfeminist sensibility through recognition of an unmistakable rise in feminist branding, "femvertising," and popular feminisms available for purchase. Orgad and Gill (2022) identify the paradox of the confidence revolution that has emerged alongside increasingly stringent expectations and standards of body and beauty, professional success, and familial success. This "have it all" narrative comes from postfeminism and is played out in how "Girl Power!" is packaged and sold. "Girl Power!" glosses over the specificity of oppressions faced by tween girls at various intersections of identity. It is very White, cishet, ableist, and thin oriented. These competing cultural models of innocent girls who need protection and "Girl Power!" demonstrate how contradictory social and cultural conditions create the paradox and dilemma of "ideal girlhood" (Renold and Ringrose 2013). Though rooted in postfeminist notions that feminism has done its job and that gendered empowerment can be achieved and maintained through the performance of ideal femininity, the more recent twist on popular feminism promotes authenticity, vulnerability, and the promise of empowerment and confidence through continual, individual work on the self. Popular feminism suggests that if tween girls are indeed in crisis, they can readily buy their way out and achieve confidence through consumption, so long as they also be themselves.

Thus, rather than destabilizing entrenched gender norms that continue to oppress girls with marginalized identities that mark them as "trouble" or "at risk" by virtue of raced and classed embodiments—or disrupting a logic of White, middle-class girls as at once in need of protection and confident, bold, empowered, and future subjects—"Girl Power!" and its promise delivered by purchase functions as a distraction from enduring gender inequities. "Girl Power!" has been turned into a capitalist project, and the body along with it. From British pop band sensation the Spice Girls of the early aughts to astronaut Barbie ("If you can dream it, you can be it!") to *Frozen*'s Elsa (2013) to T-shirts you can buy with just one click ("I'm a Girl . . . What's your Superpower?"), tween girls are certainly a primary market for self-empowerment via consumption (Banet-Weiser 2014; Kennedy and Coulter 2018; Kennedy 2018).

The coexistence and discordance of these competing cultural models illuminate how American culture simultaneously values girls' opportunities for achievement and ability to assert themselves, speak their minds, and exhibit success in historically male/masculine dominated arenas such as sports, science, and technology, while continuing to value them for their beauty, presumed innocence, gentleness, femininity, and purity. And again, it depends greatly on which girls we are talking about, as competing cultural models play out differently and inform adult responses to girlhood narratives based on race, class, ability, gender, and sexual expression.

Surveillance and policing of tween girls online has increased in recent years alongside the proliferation of resources that seek to equip girls with tools to not only smartly and safely navigate digital spaces but also take full advantage of the rewards, pleasures, and opportunities those spaces have to offer. It matters that we are seeing more recognition of tween girls as agential subjects on social media. The stories news media feature, however, are often (and predictably) the most extreme and sensational, as they capitalize on public anxieties and panics about tween girls and sex, cyberbullying, suicide, and other social ills associated with digital youth culture, making it seem as though young people cannot be trusted to *not* engage in risky online behaviors (Attia 2023). But the tween girls I interviewed shared that they frequently talk to their parents and peers about safe social media use and value privacy and protection online, keenly balancing the benefits of making certain content public in these contemporary economies of visibility (Banet-Weiser 2014; Shields Dobson 2015).

It is the feeling of social media as a less restricted place that allows for both the alarmist responses on the part of adults and the possibilities of freedom and authenticity of expression exercised by young people online. There is ambiguity and ambivalence in how tween girls feel about social media and express themselves on these platforms. Often, tween girls conform to conventional ideas of femininity or resist and subvert these conventions. Conformity and resistance frequently happen at the same time, in the same performance, and sometimes in the same breath. These moments of seeming contradiction are embodied manifestations and reflections of the contradictory and paradoxical nature of achieving ideal girlhood today. Just as in their physical worlds, tween girls on social media must reckon with the constrained agency and normative Whiteness, cisgendered-ness, ableism, and classism of the "innocent girls who need protection" model and the discordant messaging in popular and consumer culture that they can be anything and do anything according to the "Girl Power!" model. Tween girls are certainly not wholly empowered, nor are they passive victims. It is precisely in the in between that tween girls live their lives and grapple with themselves in processes of becoming agential subjects on social media.

Methods and Ethics

This research presents novel understandings of how tween girls negotiate the competing cultural models of innocent girls who need protection and "Girl Power!" via participation on social media platforms and how they give meaning to their experiences as tween girls and social media users in a digitally driven society. As danah boyd writes, "social media platforms have been taken up around the globe at an unprecedented speed, revealing the extraordinary nature of the social media phenomenon. For this reason alone, it is imperative to analyze the phenomenon of social media" (2014:2).

This is a multimethod study. The first method is a textual analysis of YouTube videos from the Pretty or Ugly YouTube trend that began in 2011, peaked in 2013 (my best guess), and continues today at a low rumble with new videos being created and uploaded, the trend itself replicated to varying degrees on other platforms such as TikTok. The second method is in-depth interviews with tween girls between the ages of ten and thirteen living in Wisconsin. This research takes a cultural studies approach and captures interplay between a tangible example of how tween girls perform their bodies online and make themselves visible on social media (on YouTube specifically) and how tween girls themselves articulate and characterize the why and how behind their social media participation and content creation (Sloan and Quan-Haase 2016).

Textual analysis (Smith 2017) of Pretty or Ugly YouTube videos reveals interesting patterns of language and body performance that demonstrate notable variations in how tween girls present themselves within the context of this trend. I analyzed 260 Pretty or Ugly videos posted publicly and available for anyone on YouTube to view. My sample predominantly featured White tween girls between the conjectural ages of ten and fourteen years old. All the tween girl subjects in the videos had access and ability to post to YouTube channels, whether their own channels (technically illegal for those under thirteen years old) or the channels of family members or friends. Videos in the trend vary according to how a girl presents herself and where the video is shot (most often in a bedroom, sometimes a bathroom, rarely a kitchen or other living area in a home, and quite rarely outside or in a public space). The videos range in length from ten seconds to several minutes long but often follow a similar formula or script. A tween girl records herself with a laptop, tablet, or mobile phone, and the video usually goes something like this:

> Hi! Um, I was, um I just wanted to make a video to see, because my friends keep calling me, like, ugly, and then some people call me pretty or whatever. So, I just wanted to get people's response from YouTube. Um, am I ugly or pretty? Tell me the truth. Leave comments below so I can like, read them. So, thank you! Bye!

This video script comes from Kerrigan,[4] a young White girl approximately eleven or twelve years old who wears a red Hollister sweatshirt and plays with her blond hair while she speaks, swiveling around on a desk chair in the room where she records the video. Kerrigan's video demonstrates the overall ethos of the Pretty or Ugly trend and a specific formula recognizable across a significant number of the videos. A tween girl making one of these videos often references friends or peers at school or some other faction of her social life commenting on her appearance. She frames her question as a desire to learn the truth and implores YouTube viewers to be honest with her and comment on whether she is pretty or ugly. She often projects a sense of objectivity onto the YouTube audience, recognized as a network of strangers, people she does not know but a community she can tap into nonetheless. This objectivity seems to be what she wants and her ostensible reason for making the video public on a wide-reaching platform like YouTube: she is getting mixed messages from friends and other people she knows in physical space such as at school, and she can perhaps garner a more objective assessment of her appearance from people she does not know in digital space.

I analyzed 260 of these videos, but there are upward of an estimated one million available to view (Gallo 2013; Perle 2013; Rossie 2015). A Pretty or Ugly video might only have a handful of views, or it may have gone viral and garnered millions of views; videos with more clicks and views helped catalyze the Pretty or Ugly video trope as a trend. Public response to the trend, as well as my own assessment of it, substantiates that it is most certainly a trend among tween girls, driven by this demographic. Tween girls contributed to the growing nature of the trend by watching other girls post videos and then posting their own. Many girls posting Pretty or Ugly videos explicitly identify seeing other girls posting the videos as motivation for making and posting one.

YouTube video results are not generated randomly in searches (Burgess and Green 2018). Specific search terms are required to view desired content. Because of the large volume of videos in the trend, I created a fairly diverse sample through the application of four different configurations of a set of search terms: 1) "Am I pretty or ugly?" 2) "Am I ugly or pretty?" 3) "Am I pretty?" 4) "Am I ugly?" I reviewed video results to determine relevance to the trend and ensured that each video in my sample met the following criteria: it must be generated by one of the four specified search terms; the title of the video must include the words *pretty, ugly,* or some combination thereof; the subject(s) of the video must identify as *girl* or have an assumed sex category of *girl*;[5] and the subject(s) of the video must have an estimated age of fourteen or younger.

The ethical considerations of this research are not straightforward, and I made several context-specific decisions. Though I cannot know for certain the intent of video subjects in terms of wanting to reach a broad audience or wanting only friends and family to watch, as every video I analyzed was public and available to view without a specific login, password, or requirement to follow or subscribe to the YouTube channel in question and because the girls in the videos are crowdsourcing for honesty about their appearances, my ethical standpoint follows that the girls in the videos understood to a reasonable degree that their videos could be watched by any number of people. I did not seek out any information about video subject identity beyond what was posted by the creator (title of video, username, YouTube channel name, date of posting), and I chose to use pseudonyms for analysis of the videos because even though the videos are posted publicly, the video subjects are minors (Graham et al. 2013; Greig, Taylor, and MacKay 2013; Sui, Sui, and Rhodes 2022), and I wanted to establish some degree of anonymity.

I generated a sample of 260 Pretty or Ugly YouTube videos by selecting sixty-five videos from the results of each of the four search terms listed. I cleared my Internet history between each search term and vetted each video for relevance and to ensure there were no repeats in the sample. I did not select videos based on number of views or comments. Though I thought about analyzing comments on the videos in addition to the videos themselves, as doing so might indicate popularity of certain videos in the trend and provide compelling data on notions of "micro-celebrity" (Abidin 2018; Banet-Weiser 2017; Jerslev 2016; Marwick 2013b), it was outside the scope of this research. It is a fruitful vein of analysis that warrants further examination and has already been addressed by at least one scholar (Rossie 2015). I was focused on investigating how tween girls perform their bodies publicly and present themselves on social media in asking this question on YouTube specifically and analyzing what social and cultural meanings of contemporary American girlhoods emerge from individual videos as well as the existence of the Pretty or Ugly YouTube trend as a whole.

I coded the video transcripts and wrote observational notes and memos after viewing each video. These notes included information such as the girl's perceived gender identity and expression, racial identity, age, dress, demeanor, body language, and the environment in which the video was filmed (bedroom, bathroom, shared space in a home, etc.). I also looked at body language and considered how much of a girl's body was visible in a video (e.g., close-up, face only, full body, etc.).

The demographic breakdown of the 260 Pretty or Ugly videos in my sample included a total of 269 video subjects, as seven of the videos in my sample featured more than one girl. Six of the videos featured two girls, and one featured four girls. In terms of perceived racial categories, 214 of the videos featured girls who were assumed White, twenty-four featured girls assumed Black, twenty-one featured girls assumed Latina, three featured girls assumed Asian, one featured a girl who was mixed race (she identifies herself in this way in the video), and the six remaining videos were classified as other or undetermined, as I was not able to reasonably perceive racial category for those video subjects, whether their faces and bodies were somewhat obscured or covered or they were not close enough to the web camera. There is a great deal of Whiteness centered within the trend I explore in more detail in subsequent chapters.

In the second part of my study, I conducted in-depth interviews with twenty-six ten- to thirteen-year-old girls over a six-month period between the end of 2016 and the beginning of 2017. Even though we have seen increased attention in research and scholarship toward female adolescents and social media in recent years, there is still a dearth of research that actively centers the voices and experiences of tween girls growing up with social media (Bulger et al. 2021; De Leyn et al. 2021; García-Gómez 2018). I wanted to know more about the experiences, practices, and content creations of tween girls on social media in relation to the competing cultural models American tween girls exist within. Pairing interviews with tween girls with the textual analysis of the tween girl–driven Pretty or Ugly YouTube trend allowed me to develop a richer understanding of contemporary American girlhoods in the digital age. The YouTube trend is a tangible, public example of digital girlhoods, and the specific tensions this trend calls forth are a compelling demonstration of how tween girls negotiate, conform to, and resist the cultural models of innocent girls who need protection and "Girl Power!" The interviews with the twenty-six tween girls provide rich insight into the trend, as I showed interviewees a sample of Pretty or Ugly videos and asked for their reactions. The interviews also allowed me to see more gradation and distinction between how adult authority figures and public media perceive tween girls in terms of their social media behavior and what tween girls are actually doing on social media. Not unlike how girls are represented in popular media and culture through overly simplistic tropes and stereotypes, the realities of tween girls' lives on social media are much more complicated.

The logic of my study design seeks to understand how tween girls as social actors give meaning to their social worlds in a specific cultural and temporal context (Warren and Karner 2010). Understanding tween girls to be the main target demographic for "Girl Power!" and the self-esteem market (Banet-Weiser 2014), as well as a demographic that adults seek to protect (and police and control), I question how and why tween girls use social media, how they navigate the social conditions of competing cultural models of girlhoods, and what the implications of their social media use are. Tween girls use social media in part to reconcile and make sense of what is happening to them in physical spaces—school, home, with friends, peers, and in other social activities.

I got institutional approval from the University of Massachusetts Boston review board to conduct interviews with ten- to fourteen-year-old girls and recruited study participants through purposive sampling from three sites in Wisconsin: Girls Inc. of Greater Madison, the Boys and Girls Club of Dane County, and the Boys and Girls Club of West Central Wisconsin. These sites serve girls in the tween age category, primarily through after-school programming. Participants were all female adolescents within a specific age range who identify as girls, but they were diverse in terms of race, ethnicity, and socioeconomic circumstance. My interview participants did not have visible disabilities, and I did not ask about disability identity directly, so I cannot speak to the presence of disabilities among interviewees.

Through recruitment materials, I obtained consent from guardians for each girl to participate in a one-on-one interview at the established after-school site. Other eligibility requirements included having regular access (defined as at least one hour each day) to the Internet through use of an Internet-capable device and being self-reportedly active on at least two of the following social media sites: Facebook, Instagram, Musical.ly, Snapchat, Twitter, or YouTube. (Musical.ly was at the height of its popularity during 2016 and 2017 and notably merged with and ultimately became TikTok in 2018. TikTok did not enjoy immense popularity until two years later, with the onset of the COVID-19 global pandemic.)

Interview subjects were recruited by adult liaisons at each site. Program managers assisted in getting word out about the project and distributing study materials to parents and guardians of girls in the programs. Interested parents and guardians were able to reach out to me and ask questions about the study. They provided consent forms granting permission for the girls to participate in the interviews. Girls whose guardians gave their consent were then asked again whether they wanted to participate to ensure that they understood what participation entailed. I scheduled interviews with girls who agreed to participate during after-school hours, and all interviews took place at the respective after-school program sites, settings familiar and comfortable for the girls.

At the outset of each interview, participants signed the assent form, as well as a consent form for audio recording the interviews for analysis. Girls were read the parameters of the study in terms they could understand and given the opportunity to ask questions about the process. Additionally, I made it clear to each participant that they could refuse to answer any questions they did not want to answer, stop the interview, or withdraw from the process altogether at any time. All identifying information was kept strictly confidential throughout the data collection and analysis processes, and each participant was given a pseudonym at the outset of the study. Data was stored in accordance with university policy. Audio recordings of the interviews were deleted on completion of the analysis. A small gift card incentive was given to each girl at the conclusion of her interview. Interview subject demographics are broken down in Table 1.1.

TABLE 1.1: INTERVIEW SUBJECT DEMOGRAPHICS		
Pseudonym	Age	Race
Ariel	10	White
Samantha	10	White
Sinead	10	Black
Scout	10	White
Sierra	10	Black
Genie	10	White
Tessy	10	White
Jazz	10	Black
Taylor	10	White
Marcie	10	White
Pepper	10	White
Fiona	10	White
Constance	10	Latina
Maya	11	Latina
Michelle	11	Black
Dominique	11	Black
Ricki	11	Black
Tania	11	Latina
Breanna	11	White
Jessie	12	Black
Starr	12	Black
Kendra	13	Black
Noelle	13	Black
Dani	13	Black
Chrissy	13	Black
Brooklyn	13	Black

Of the twenty-six tween girls I interviewed, thirteen were Black, ten were White, and three were Latina. Thirteen of the girls were ten years old, six were eleven years old, two were twelve years old, and five were thirteen years old. I had an overrepresentation of younger girls and did not have any fourteen-year-olds in the sample. Twenty-one of the twenty-six girls were living in a more urban area, while the remaining five were in a more rural or smaller town setting. The interviews lasted anywhere between twelve and ninety minutes, around thirty-five minutes on average, with some participants wanting to share more than others. There was no obvious pattern or predictor of interview length in terms of who spoke more or less; the longest interviews were split across interview sites, age, and racial categories. I took field notes during and immediately following each interview to capture specific information about girls' appearances, dress, demeanors, and body language. Each interview was audio recorded and transcribed using a transcription service. I coded field notes as well as interview transcripts for analysis.

The interviews were semistructured and followed an interview guide centered around five themes with suggested questions: 1) basics of online participation, 2) social media behavior and content, 3) digital behavior and gender, 4) the Pretty or Ugly YouTube trend, and 5) perspectives on the importance of social media. During a portion of each interview, I showed each participant a sample of three videos from the Pretty or Ugly trend and asked for her reactions to the videos. All interviewees watched the same three videos, which were randomly selected from my sample of videos for the textual analysis. This catalyzed conversations about social media and gender. In response to the videos, tween girls reflected on how, from their perspectives, girls and boys use social media differently and are judged differently in how they use it.

The interview data revealed a great deal about the experiences of tween girls on social media in the contemporary United States and captured distinct characteristics within tween girls' individual social media use. The girls I interviewed certainly articulated shared themes and experiences, but they also demonstrated significant differences in personal interests, how they use social media, how they experience judgment online, the kinds of choices they make in terms of what and where they post, the degree to which they post and why, how they navigate notions of privacy and safety, and their feelings about their social media participation overall.

I hope to represent these nuances as fully and accurately as possible while recognizing how my role as an adult, White, cis woman researcher informed how girls answered my questions and told me about their experiences and feelings. This research presents the shared meanings created between myself and the tween girls I spoke with (Guba and Lincoln 1994). My focus was to

ensure the girls felt safe and comfortable during the interview process, min-
imizing potential harm while creating space for girls to bring up any topics
they wanted to address in an organic way (Farrell 2022; Willig 2013). Because the girls did not know me outside of the context of the interview, and
given my position as an adult authority figure, I cannot entirely rule out the
possibility of social desirability bias, or them answering questions based on
what they thought I wanted to hear. But I also wanted to be cautious of how
routinely girls are dismissed in their concerns, to follow their lead and be
open to whatever they were telling me as their truths. Regarding my ana-
lytical and ethical position, I kept the interview questions quite open ended
and followed the girls' lead in our conversations, demonstrating a commit-
ment to their perspectives and experiences and centering their voices in the
research.

Tween girls, and girls more generally, are a persistently understudied population. Most of the tween girls I interviewed had never given an interview
before—and never specifically about social media. I wanted to be sensitive
to this reality, giving the girls plenty of space to ask questions and talk about
themes and ideas that came up for them. In analysis, I employed qualitative interpretation frameworks used by girlhood studies scholars (Mitchell
and Reid-Walsh 2008; Singh 2021) and the work of Sorsoli and Tolman, who
write that

> [People] pass regularly from one "state of mind" to another many times
> in a day, often without realizing it, and particularly in response to dif-
> ficult relational experiences. Multiple, even contradictory, perspec-
> tives on any given experience (which can be "voiced" in concert in
> narratives) are not only acceptable but are to be anticipated (2008:497).

Tween girls vocalized quite a bit of ambivalence about social media being
good or bad; they often felt it was both, appreciating certain elements of social media while bemoaning others. Indeed, they had, as Sorsoli and Tolman
suggest, "multiple and contradictory perspectives." These complex and contradictory perspectives speak to the nature of social media as a whole—as
a reflection of social interactions and societal norms and mores, a complicated tapestry that influences tween girls' daily lives, choices, and behaviors
and continually blurs the boundaries between the physical and the digital.
This research presents nuanced accounts of how tween girls "do girlhood"
on social media, how they create digital girlhoods, and how they characterize their experiences online, considering what all this means in a contemporary moment defined by competing cultural models of girlhood and
increased normalization of social media use in the day-to-day lives of American tween girls.

Mapping Digital Girlhoods

Chapter Two further situates and historicizes the contemporary social and cultural conditions of American girlhoods by more thoroughly exploring the origins of the competing cultural models of innocent girls who need protection and "Girl Power!" Looking at how women's and girl's bodies have been and continue to be controlled and restricted over time, I illuminate how overt and covert manifestations of competing cultural models are tangibly felt and embodied by tween girls in the digital cultural landscape. Reflecting on enduring phenomena, theories, and framings such as the Madonna-Whore myth, biopower, docile bodies, stringent gendered aesthetic ideals, and well-worn controlling images of the at-risk girl and the can-do girl in popular media (Hill Collins 1990; hooks 1992), I explore how the tension between protectionist discourses and postfeminist-turned-popular-feminist neoliberal "Girl Power!" results in today's tween girls having to navigate a perpetual push-pull between empowerment and disempowerment.

Mapping this tension onto girls' social media use, Chapter Three explores how the "Girl Power!" cultural model, which emphasizes individualism, empowerment, and confidence via consumption, has fostered the expectation that tween girls make themselves visible online. However, tween girls are notably policed (often by other girls) when modes of visibility resist or subvert conventional and/or acceptable performances of femininity (Attwood, Hakim, and Winch 2017). Tween girls both conform to and resist the conventions and gendered politics of these economies of visibility (Banet-Weiser 2015) in various ways. Visibility on social media has become a normal part of girls' daily routines but also a significant and widely recognized (and sought after) form of social capital among their peers. They exercise control over their self-representations on social media and strategically use social media to engage their interests and build social capital. Tween girls keenly balance the desire to be seen with the pressure of presenting themselves in culturally specific and socially acceptable ways.

Chapter Four digs deeper into the politics of tween girls' visibility on social media through the specific lens of the Pretty or Ugly YouTube trend and the reactions I got from the tween girls I interviewed when I showed them videos from the trend. The Pretty or Ugly trend, as an example of contemporary digital girlhoods, demonstrates clear tensions between empowerment and disempowerment, public and private, confidence and insecurity, and authenticity and affect. The responses my interviewees had to the videos reveal important questions about a digital authenticity values system—what constitutes being real or fake on social media—as well as the idea that being bullied in physical space, such as at school, is a logical or practical motivation behind why a tween girl might post a Pretty or Ugly video on YouTube. Tween girls responded to the Pretty or Ugly videos in complex and often contradictory ways, showcasing how the competing cultural models of girlhood and paradoxes tween girls exist within influence how they relate to one another in their social worlds.

Continuing in this vein of how tween girls relate to each other, Chapter Five takes an in-depth look at a spectrum of tween girl social behavior—ranging from girls bullying girls to relational "drama" between and among girls to intragroup affirmation, homosocial support, and friendship—and investigates how this spectrum plays out on social media. Toxic girl culture is wrought by competing cultural models of innocent girls who need protection and "Girl Power!" This behavioral spectrum is reflected in the meanings tween girls give to social media. Tween girls are conditioned into certain relational behaviors, primarily reflected in media representation of girls as mean, catty, or relationally aggressive (Mikel Brown 2003; Chesney-Lind, Morash, and Irwin 2007; Crann 2017; Currie, Kelly, and Pomerantz 2007; Mcqueeney and Girgenti-Malone 2018; Simmons 2002). There is much social and cultural emphasis on competition among girls, as well as normalization of self-deprecative talk to relate with one another. Tween girls characterize social media as a site where bullying between and among girls can and does occur, but they also view social media, especially apps such as Snapchat, as a crucial vehicle for maintaining continual connection with friends, particularly in terms of seeking and offering support and affirmation. They indicate meaningful connections with friends as a primary motivation for using social media.

Tween girls mainly interact on social media with people and peer networks they already know in physical space (Bulger et al. 2021; De Leyn et al. 2021). This reality goes against some adult-centered fears and perceptions of tween girls engaging in the risky behavior of interacting with strangers and potential predators online. Chapter Six investigates how tween girls are often represented in news and popular media in a simplistic way—either as passive victims of online predation or as reckless and irresponsible in their social media use. Contrary to this popular belief, my research shows that tween girls are keeping much of their content private, interacting primarily with people they know in physical space, following parental guidelines, seeking out "appropriate content" on social media, and internalizing what their parents teach them about approaching social media with a measured amount of fear and caution.

We should not be roundly alarmed or totally emboldened by what tween girls are doing online. The reality is that tween girls are still figuring themselves out. As the creators and negotiators of digital girlhoods, they are using social media as an important tool in processes of self- and social development: to exercise control over how they are seen and how they see themselves, create content they care about, manage relationships, and connect with their communities. In centering tween girls' voices in their experiences with social media and demonstrating how they leverage these platforms (YouTube, Instagram, Snapchat, etc.) to build confidence, gain social capital, create visibility, and foster and manage homosocial relationships, this research offers a fresh approach to American tween girl digital cultures and argues that social media is not the cause of the gendered social ills (low self-esteem, bullying behavior, negative body image, etc.) it is often made out to be. Rather, social media is a consequential tool that tween girls are using in strategic and compelling ways to participate in cultural conversations that so often happen *about* them but generally fail to happen *with* them.

2

CREATING THE SOCIAL CONDITIONS OF
AMERICAN GIRLHOODS

"During [girlhood], we learn to adopt a story about
ourselves—what our value is, what beauty is, what is
harmful and what is normal—and to privilege the feelings,
comfort, perceptions, and power of others over our own.
This training of our minds can lead to the exile of many
parts of the self, to hatred for and the abuse of our own
bodies, the policing of other girls, and a lifetime of
allegiance to values that do not prioritize our safety,
happiness, freedom, or pleasure."
—FEBOS 2021:XIII

"As a term, 'girl' is polarizing: feared for how tightly it
connects youth and desire, reviled for its infantilizing,
passivity-inducing properties. On the face of it, girlishness
is simply dismissed as being frivolous, immature, unmascu-
line, disempowering, reductive. At worst, the girl is an
apolitical neutralizer of direct action. At best, she is simply
enjoying herself with the junk society has given her. In
either state—harmless or neutralizing, hedonic or willfully
ignorant—the girl becomes an attractor of hatred, envy, and
fear. As opposed to mainstream narratives of female
empowerment and their sliding scale of access to power and
resources, the girl is a far more politically ambivalent state."
—QUICHO 2023:PARA. 4

Clinical psychologist and author Mary Pipher theorizes the subject position and construction of the girl as one of crisis and peril and argues that at adolescence, girl selves are lost in social turmoil, going
so far as to refer to the United States as a "girl-destroying place" (1994:44).
Social psychologists have echoed this concern, labeling it the "girl-crisis movement" (Farady 2010). As the opening quotes epitomize, to be a girl is to be
in dilemma, in crisis, in a state of ambivalence. In her widely acclaimed book

Girlhood (2021), author Melissa Febos traces this excision of the self in favor of privileging the needs of others, a gendered phenomenon that often carries over into adulthood. Alex Quicho, a speculative futures scholar, writes frequently about the "girlification" of the Internet and demonstrates in the excerpt at the start of this chapter how girls are all at once loved, loathed, desired, and feared—a perpetually equivocal subject position.

This chapter explores how the contemporary social, cultural, and political conditions of American girlhoods came to be, operating at a nexus of multiple schools of thought, social theories, realities, and imaginings that shape tween girls' lives and constitute the enduring and conflicting cultural models tween girls exist within and are called on to navigate. Throughout the analysis, I take a social constructionist approach to understand the sociopolitical and sociocultural landscape in which American tween girls dwell—not looking for any singular truth but recognizing that *American tween girl* as a category is socially, culturally, and politically determined, indefinite, and subject to shift and change according to time, place, and circumstance. Social constructionism, body politics, Western philosophies, Protestant theology, postfeminism, neoliberalism, digital sociology, contemporary feminisms, and girlhood studies all come together in elucidating how and why social media matters in American tween girls' experiences of living in physical and digital worlds.

The Body

What are the contemporary social conditions of tween girlhoods in the United States today, and how did they come to be? These questions begin with the body. The body has long been theorized as a critical entity and a useful tool in the negotiation of public life and within identity discourses (Bobel and Kwan 2019; Bordo 1993; Douglas 1970; Foucault 1976; Giovanelli and Ostertag 2009). The body can be understood as 1) a sociocultural and historical phenomenon and conduit of social/cultural meaning and value, and 2) an active participant in the social world and agent that may create change (Reischer and Koo 2004). Tween girls doing digital performances of their bodies through selfies, videos, or other content creation on social media become meaningful cultural texts that reveal much about contemporary American girlhoods.

French social theorist Michel Foucault defines biopower as "an explosion of numerous and diverse techniques for achieving the subjugation of bodies and the control of populations" (1976:140). Mechanisms of control by state institutions manage and regulate entire populations of bodies to produce docile bodies, which may be "subjected, used, transformed, and improved" (1976:136). For Foucault, the modern power of social institutions is enacted to produce and normalize bodies toward serving hegemonic ideologies of dominance and deviance. Via the theory of the panopticon, bodies self-regulate through self-surveillance.

Additionally, the proliferation of neoliberalism beyond the economic realm and across a wide swath of social and cultural mechanisms bolsters contemporary expectations of how bodies are supposed to produce, reproduce, self-regulate, discipline, and perform (Adamson 2017; Rose 1999; Rottenberg 2018). The discipline of the body by the self that inhabits the body maintains power relations and protects the status quo. Power, according to Foucault, is not a top-down effect but rather a noncentralized force, neither intrinsically acquired or kept but negotiated in dynamic relationships of push and pull, power and resistance. Foucault's theories of biopower and docile bodies remain salient in historicizing and theorizing the social, cultural, and political functions and constraints of female/feminine/femme bodies.

In the latter half of the twentieth century, Western feminist theorists such as Sandra Lee Bartky (1988) and Susan Bordo (1993) took up Foucault's notions of docile bodies and the self-governing subject, filtering them through a lens of gendered oppression. Female and feminine bodies are regulated in ways distinct from male and masculine bodies and arguably to a more extreme degree, contributing to greater sustained and systemic gender-based oppressions (Diamond and Quinby 1988; King 2004; Reischer and Koo 2004; Weitz 2010). Throughout the twentieth century, the female/feminine body was theorized primarily by way of the reproductive framework, the corporeal project of achieving and maintaining a stringent standard of beauty, and the Madonna-Whore myth. Cultural constructions of beauty and ideal femininity remain principal sites of understanding how gender is performed or achieved, extending to sociopolitical ideas surrounding female/feminine sexual subjectivities. These constructions reproduce corporeal hierarchies that become more complex when taking an intersectional approach, considering race, size, ability, age, and other facets of identity.

Gender is read by others as a successful achievement when the body in question is performing prescribed ideas of masculinity or femininity in a context of cis-het normativity (Bartky 1988; Butler 1990; Westbrook and Schilt 2014; West and Zimmerman 1987). To be effectively read as a woman or girl, the self is responsible for disciplining the body via White-centered Western colonialist constructions of body and beauty work that include (but are not limited to) using cosmetics or makeup, wearing acceptably feminine-coded clothing, removing virtually all body hair, wearing head hair long and straight or wavy rather than short, curly, or kinky, using small gestures and appropriate vocal timbre, and intensely regulating body size toward a thin imperative.

The Power of the Feminine

But where there is power, there is resistance. Female and feminine bodies across intersecting identities are remarkable sites of cultural meaning making, sites where exchanges of power, resistance, violence, and change are made legible over time. Within the canon of body politics, which demonstrates the myriad ways bodies facilitate and mediate lived experiences and navigate a dynamic push-pull between social control and personal agency and autonomy, feminist theory and scholarship has established the inherent power of female and feminine bodies (Bordo 1993; Bobel and Kwan 2011; Doyle 2019; Erdman Farrell 2011; Griffith 2004; Weitz and Kwan 2013).

Author Sady Doyle writes that "men define humanity, and women, insofar as they are not men, are not human. Thus, women must necessarily be put under male control—and to the extent that we resist this control, we are monstrous" (2019:xiii). The feminine has been conceptualized *against* the masculine; that which is not masculine or is a lack of masculine (see Beauvoir 1949 and Irigaray 1985) exists as a threat to cis-hetero, patriarchal social order because it is earthbound, closer to nature, uncontainable, difficult to control in its excess and spectacle, and a provocation to sexual temptation and all other manner of sin.

The Madonna-Whore myth warrants ongoing critique for its exacting depictions of female and feminine sexualities and of women as either pure/chaste/good or promiscuous/loose/bad. There are endless representations and renditions of the power and threat of the female and feminine, as both object and subject. Societally speaking, we create the desirable feminine object and fear the desirous feminine subject but discipline and regulate both. Female and feminine identifying and presenting people have historically been punished for displaying deviance from socially prescribed norms.

Pandora opens the box. Eve eats the apple and unleashes sin on the world. Lesbians during the feminist second wave were deemed by figureheads of the movement such as Betty Friedan as the "lavender menace," considered "toxic" to the mainstream, assimilationist, liberal feminist agenda. Transgender women have been pathologized, policed, and targeted, often experiencing heightened surveillance, violence, and hostility within feminist spaces, so much so that contemporary lexicon includes the acronym TERF (trans-exclusionary radical feminist). Tropes of femininity out of control include the heavily (and falsely) racialized figure of the welfare queen who lives in excess and cheats the state for personal gain (Demby 2013); Glenn Close as the terrifyingly incorrigible Alexandra Forrest in *Fatal Attraction* (1987); Hillary Rodham Clinton, wearing a pantsuit and using powerful political rhetoric, called a criminal, vilified, and openly despised; Kathy Bates's naked, aging, fat body in *About Schmidt* (2003); the problematic spectacle and entertainment of Black men playing fat, Black, and often hypersexualized women in movies and on television—Big Shirley on *Martin* (1992), Eddie Murphy as Rasputia in *Norbit* (2007), and Tyler Perry as Mabel "Madea" Simmons (multiple films); the manipulative bitch; the psycho lesbian; the femme fatale. These tropes of femininity out of control are reproduced time and again, reinforcing the Madonna-Whore myth and demonstrating the downfall of the woman (or girl) who steps out of line. To counter the threat of the excess, powerful female and feminine bodies are disciplined in multiple ways.

Within a neoliberal, postfeminist, consumer feminist landscape, women and girls are themselves complicit in engaging with an oppressive capitalist system of female subordination that sells and promises individually realized empowerment and confidence via consumption but ultimately reinforces perpetual self-regulation, discipline, and bodily improvement. The body remains the project, the most important project, for achieving successful femininity, even with the contemporary resurgence of popular feminism (Banet-Weiser 2018; Orgad and Gill 2022; Rottenberg 2018).

In 2020, a video of celebrity actress turned activist-politician Cynthia Nixon reciting Camille Rainville's poem "Be a Lady They Said" went viral. The poem, originally written and posted on Rainville's personal blog in 2017, chronicles an exhausting thicket of contradictory directives set forth for one to follow to be a lady. An excerpt from the poem reads as follows:

> Be a lady they said. . . . [Tuck] your tummy. Thin your thighs. Tone your calves. Perk up your boobs. Look natural. Be yourself. Be genuine. Be confident. You're trying too hard. You look overdone. Men don't like girls who try too hard.

Standards of feminine beauty in the United States are context driven and pliant (Howard 2018; Stearns 2002; Walker 2007). The relationship between consumer and consumable is dynamic, and the current ethos of celebrating internal and real beauty and promoting body acceptance and self-love is, on the surface, most welcome. The 2023 *Barbie* movie, directed by Greta Gerwig, brings the paradoxes of contemporary American womanhood to the big screen, inciting a great deal of public cultural conversation about (a particular brand of) feminism, gently taking stringent gendered scripts to task, and mocking the patriarchy and toxic masculinity. Yet *Barbie* could hardly be expected to disrupt structures such as White supremacy, imperialism, and capitalism, the continued existence of which are bound up together and contingent on the ongoing oppression of women and girls; the film was, after all, sponsored by Mattel.

On closer inspection, the present-day championing of body positivity and self-love within mainstream "femvertising" (Abitbol and Sternadori 2016; Becker-Herby 2016; Varghese and Kumar 2022) insidiously distracts from larger structural inequities, precludes radical transformation, and serves only to bolster an amoral, capitalist bottom line that cannot create any tangible disruption to oppressive systems as they stand. Even as we see increased representation of different identities in popular media (e.g., a fat Barbie, a trans femme Barbie, a Black Barbie who is also president) and emphasis on body inclusivity and broader acceptance, body positivity remains a capitalistic device divested from radical and revolutionary roots of self-care championed by Black queer feminist thinkers and organizers. As author, fat liberationist, and abolitionist Da'Shaun L. Harrison writes of Black liberation and anti-Black violence in particular, "What is the utility of 'body positivity' if it only seeks to provide one with a false sense of confidence rather than to liberate all from that which cages the body?" (2021:2).

The Racialized Feminine, the "Othered" Body

Black female and feminine bodies have historically been characterized by excess and represented as hypersexual and "out of control" (Hill Collins 1990; hooks 1992; Weitz 2010). The Mammy figure (the dark-skinned, fat, Black, feminine caretaker), on the other hand, manifests excess through care for White children—an unending flow of love and labor that serves the interest of White families, controlled via invisibility of her own family life and interests. The Mammy is nonthreatening, nonsexual, and poses no danger or imposition to the White woman as a potential object of sexual desire for the White man (Bogle 2001). The enduring design of White supremacy seeks to shrink and eradicate feminine Blackness out of fear of Black liberation and abundance. Anti-Black racism and colorism (privileging lighter-skinned members of a particular racial or ethnic group) also bolster misogynoir (Bailey 2021), a particular animus toward Black women and girls.

Whiteness has been and remains the feminine ideal of beauty, even as phenomena such as "Blackfishing" (Balanda 2020; Cherid 2021) become more common among young, White, cisgender female influencers on social media. White women and girls engage in the politics of featurism, co-opting elements of Black and Brown beauty and embodiment and benefiting from those elements (whether in terms of social capital or material capital), yet the enduring privilege of Whiteness shields them from racialized oppression. Skin lightening markets worldwide are only growing (BusinessWire 2022). Featurism becomes more prominent as increased emphasis is placed on having curves in the right places. Lip injections, brow threading, and waist training are all highly popular modes of beauty work (London 2021). Somewhere around 2014, the Brazilian butt lift (BBL) rapidly became a sought-after cosmetic surgery, especially among wealthy White women (Jennings 2021), and as rumors circulated that Kim Kardashian had had butt fillers removed, conversations abounded on social media surrounding the downfall of the BBL moment and a new era of slimmed-down backsides (Rodriguez-Garcia 2023). The target moves once again.

Per the theory of the beauty myth (Wolf 2002), as gender relations change over time and (certain) women and girls gain greater access to power and resources, ideals of feminine aesthetics become increasingly narrow. The already elusive ideal of femininity becomes more elusive (Bordo 1993). Even with a hiked, prevailing emphasis on loving your body, a notably swollen wave of body-positive social media content, and woke brand femvertising, the social and aesthetic capital that come with embodied privilege surrounding proximity to Whiteness, thinness, youth, able-bodiedness, and cis-hetness remain striking. The body of a female pop star may fit the bill of the ideal feminine if she is thin and toned, but the line between toned and muscular is tenuous indeed, and it can be exceptionally easy to cross constructed borders into deviant embodiment. Heightened public discourse and pop culture attention on the appeal of curvy or "slim thicc" women complicate notions of the ideal feminine, and White women are disproportionately rewarded for embodying historically and traditionally Black and Brown corporeal characteristics (hooks 1992; Mosley and Biernat 2021). We need look no further than the Kardashian empire and how it has collectively capitalized on everything from detoxes, diets, and cosmetic surgeries to culturally appropriated hairstyles, lip plumper, waist trainers, shapewear, and the rise and fall of the Brazilian butt lift.

The thin imperative for female and feminine bodies is inextricably bound up with White supremacy (Strings 2019). The well-established moral code of bodies in the West—the code of which bodies are deemed good and worthy and which are deemed bad and in need of correction—is the result of historical differentiation between Whiteness and Blackness (Harrison 2021; Strings 2019); the conflation of thinness with goodness; the emphasis on youth as worthy of celebration and admiration; the separation, isolation, and invisibility of people with disabilities; the proliferation of mass media channels; the rise of the global marketplace, novel modes of consumption, and late capitalist neoliberalism; and the onset of new digital technologies. The hierarchy of bodies that privileges Whiteness, thinness, ability, youth, cis-het normativity, and wealth is legitimated in confluence with increased economic, social, and political opportunities for women, as well as an emphasis on consumerism and the onset of neoliberal economic principles during the Reagan and Clinton eras of the 1980s and 1990s (Eisenstein 2010; Erdman Farrell

2011; Rottenberg 2018). It is no accident that the commercial diet industry in the United States absolutely exploded while the women's liberation movement was gaining substantial ground in the 1970s, seeing success in policy changes and widespread recognition of feminist organizing around a White, liberal feminist agenda fixed on institutional assimilation and gender equality.

Achieving standards of feminine beauty is a direct conduit to female and feminine power within a White supremacist, capitalist, imperialist patriarchy (hooks 1981; hooks 1984)—arguably the most direct. The empowered woman of the 1980s and 1990s was playing by the rules of a man's world, and postfeminist sensibility became prominent alongside the underground, counterculture sensibility and intersectional emphasis of the feminist third wave (Crenshaw 1989; Walker 1992). In rendering the body an individual neoliberal project that promises personal empowerment via consumption toward self-improvement and confidence (Orgad and Gill 2022), women are effectively curbed from external pursuits of power, structural transformation, and collective liberation as they focus inward on corporeal concerns and fundamentally participate in their own oppression from the inside out.

Already privileged female and feminine bodies (White, cis, thin, able-bodied) that quite literally demonstrate personal responsibility, regulation, and self-surveillance achieve more social capital, which translates into increased success in various social institutions and processes such as college admissions, workplace advancement, far-reaching representation in all forms of media, and heightened respect in the political realm. Meanwhile, female and feminine bodies set apart from the White, cis, thin, young, able-bodied ideal are subject to increased scrutiny, policing, discipline, exploitation, and violence. And all the antithetical, impossible expectations associated with the ongoing gendered, raced, and classed neoliberal body project certainly extend to tween girls as well.

Tween Girlhoods and the Body Project

Tween girls across identity categories have historically experienced psychosocial conditioning leading to lower self-worth, low self-efficacy, and body dissatisfaction. This conditioning begins early in life and often carries into adulthood. Negative body image, increased risk of disordered eating practices, and focus on appearance enjoy decades-old recognition as being normal parts of growing up as a girl in the United States (Brown and Gilligan 1992; Brumberg 1997; Hesse-Biber 2006; Orenstein 2016; Pipher 1994). The culturally constructed crisis of negative body image among female adolescents is both born out of the limited social and political power of girls in the United States and reified by it. Disordered eating practices and other elements of self-harm such as cutting are all too common in the body narratives of tween girls (Adler and Adler 2011; Bordo 1993; Hesse-Biber 2006; Leaf and Schrock 2011).

Negative body image and body dissatisfaction carry over into the matter of sexuality, with the simultaneous virginal/hypersexual, Madonna-Whore myth of American girlhood and womanhood rendering the navigation of authentic sexual subjectivities exceedingly complex for tween girls. As Jackson and Vares write,

> In late capitalist societies femininity has become an even more "impossible space" for girls and young women to occupy under contradictory postfeminist conditions where apparent sexual freedoms, amongst others, are clawed back by abiding middle-class respectable femininity and the regulatory discourse of the slut (2015:83).

The hypersexualization of young women in popular media fundamentally contributes to the continued, shared cultural imaginary of female adolescent body dissatisfaction as a foregone conclusion in tween girls' body narratives (Egan 2013). This hypersexualization of girls' bodies also substantiates public anxiety surrounding female adolescent sexualities and contributes to the cyclical nature of gendered moral panics and the reproduction of gendered social control (Buckingham et al. 2010; Renold and Ringrose 2013; Thiel-Stern 2014).

The adultification of Black girls (especially those in lower socioeconomic circumstances) within White supremacist systems has functioned to make Black girlhoods invisible or, at the very least, obscured in broader social and scholarly imaginings (Morris 2015; Stokes 2007; Toliver 2018; Wade 2019a). Representations across media landscapes reify racialized, controlling images of Black girls as being too much or causing trouble, marring the intersections and intricacies of growing up as both Black and girl (Nunn 2018; Rosario, Minor, and Rogers 2021). As Black girlhood studies scholar Dominique Hill writes, "Blackgirls' bodies do not operate as their own and are tattooed by historical tropes and cultural expectations" (2019:278). Too often, Black womanhood and Black girlhood are conflated or mapped onto each other in linear or monolithic ways, belying a reality of varied Black girlhoods, embodiments, and ways of being. Ashleigh Greene Wade writes in her work on Black girlhoods and digital media production that "marking Black Girlhood Studies theory as its own epistemological framework avoids conflating girlhood and womanhood and superimposing Black women's experiences onto those of Black girls" (2019a:14).

Regarding girlhood embodiments and disability, Deborah Stienstra (2015) implores us to consider girls with disabilities as integral to ongoing knowledge building within girlhood studies. Disability studies and girlhood studies scholar Sarah Hill clarifies this point, emphasizing that "disability is often framed as a problem or lack, and that experiences of disability for girls appear to trump or silence other experiences, such as those of sex and gender, and the intersections that exist between these" (2017:114). Furthermore, as Susan Wendell suggests,

> The biological and the social are interactive in creating disability. . . . Societies that are physically constructed and socially organized with the unacknowledged assumption that everyone is healthy, non-disabled, young but adult, shaped according to cultural ideals, and, often, male, create a great deal of disability through sheer neglect of what most people need in order to participate fully in them (1997:106).

Girls have been theorized as disabled by virtue of their existence in patriarchal societies (Young 2005). The subtleties of embodied and lived experiences across identities for girls with disabilities remain woefully underexplored, especially as disability itself can be understood as socially constructed, vast, and context specific. In the United States, girls with disabilities continue to lack significant, meaningful representation in public and popular media, frequently marked as nonsexual or without sexual agency and subjectivity, and presumed to be perpetually child-like in character and interests.

We still have very little empirical scholarship on the experiences of trans, gender queer, and nonbinary girls. Indeed, nonbinary gender identity and expression are often coded as masculine, and nonbinary femme people are often attributed cisgender identities even as they do not identify in this way. Existing literature on experiences of trans youth tends to put youth together into one category, without due attention to specificities of gender identity and expression (Cavalcante 2016; Craig et al. 2015; Horak 2014; Jenzen 2017; Laukkanen 2007; Raun 2016). Additionally, recent attacks on transgender youth across the United States, especially surrounding gender-affirming care, support, and resources as well as participation in social arenas such as school sports and athletics, have not only served to perpetuate violence and harm against trans girls but also bolstered the image of the White, cisgender girl being robbed, her opportunities for empowerment and success contingent on the exclusion of trans girls and cis BIPOC girls. Media studies scholar Jennifer McClearen (2023) is contributing important and novel framings to this area of inquiry.

Only in recent years have we seen more visible, concentrated emphasis on producing media content for tween girls across intersecting identities that employs popular discursive strategies such as body positivity, self-love, personal empowerment, and confidence (Banet-Weiser 2018; Orgad and Gill 2022), but this content is notably raced and classed. Much popular visual media is still underrepresenting or misrepresenting and stereotyping people in minority groups, especially in relation to race, ethnicity, nationality, gender identity, sexuality, size, and disability (Rogers et al. 2021)—more reason why tween girls' self-representations on social media can disrupt enduring and harmful tropes that offer little to no nuance or specificity across and within girlhood identities (Bailey 2021; Hill 2017; Wade 2019a).

Even with increased public attention to girls and somewhat more complex representations of girlhoods in contemporary American media, a tween girl's body, and what she does with it (or what may be done to it), still too often defines who and what a girl is and, moreover, what society expects her to be. Much of the knowledge required to become a successful feminine subject (dress, beauty work, body size regulation, consumption, etc.) is learned, negotiated, and implemented during adolescence, coming into tween girlhood as a social and cultural status, consumer group, and liminal space between childhood and adulthood (Banet-Weiser 2014; Currie, Kelly, and Pomerantz 2009; García-Gómez 2018; Harris 2004b; Kennedy 2018; McRobbie 1990). These negotiations and implementations are entangled with aspects of identity including race, ethnicity, size, ability, and gender expression. Certain markers of tween girlhood can be recognized and emphasized across identities, but how a tween girl's body and behavior is understood, surveilled, and policed depends greatly on how she is categorized—as a can-do girl or an at-risk girl (Harris 2004a), as prude or promiscuous, innocent or unruly. Social conditioning and disciplining of girls rely on the continual construction and reproduction of an elusive feminine ideal, and girls are expected to maintain pursuit of that ideal over the course of their entire lives or face the consequences of subversion and resistance.

Girls, however, have historically been pretty spectacular at challenging the status quo, both publicly and privately, from embodied resistances to launching protests (Kahn 2023a). There is a distinct and crucial difference between what girls' empowerment is manufactured to look like via individual consumption (i.e., "The Future Is Female!") versus what it can look like in practice. But what has become strategically more complex and confusing in recent years is how the feminine ideal of successful girlhood in the United States has become directly tied to empowerment narratives, confidence culture, and consumption (Banet-Weiser 2018; Kennedy and Coulter 2018; Favaro 2017; Orgad and Gill 2022). The decades-long cultural model of "Girl Power!" endures and makes it seem as though tween girls today have every opportunity laid before them, like they are valued beyond what their bodies look like and what makes them attractive to boys and men. And indeed, we are queering girlhoods (Brickman 2019; Driver 2007; Gonick 2006; Kearney 2011; Monaghan 2016). We are starting to see a broader range of tween girl bodies in representation. Even in the midst of significant social and political change and greater recognition of the power and agency of tween girls across identities, the reality remains that notions of "Girl Power!" are discordantly bound up with a society that insists on playing by patriarchal, White supremacist, classist, cis-het normative rules, and all the woke femvertising and emphasis on individual empowerment (i.e., improvement) do little to disrupt and subvert these power structures.

Contemporary "Girl Power!"—expressly related to a resurgence in popular feminism and consumer feminism—positions the body as not only a project but a marketed product, particularly with the continued growth of social media and emphasis on digital corporeal expression and visibility in recent years (Banet-Weiser 2018; Brumberg 1997; Orenstein 2016; Zeisler 2016). Postfeminist digital culture (Shields Dobson 2015) complicates the tween girl subject—who and what a girl is supposed to be (Kennedy 2018) and how she is supposed to behave. And until the onset of social media at the beginning of the twenty-first century and tween girls' prolific use of these platforms, narratives of girlhood in the United States were understood primarily via recognizable tropes depicted in public and popular media.

Princesses, Mean Girls, and Troubled Teens

In a 2004 review of the teen smash film *Sleepover*, famed movie critic Roger Ebert wrote, "I take it as a rule of nature that all American high schools are ruled by a pack of snobs, led by a supremely confident young woman who is blonde, superficial, catty, and ripe for public humiliation" (Ebert 2007). The trope of the popular girl, placed on a pedestal while covertly disdained precisely because of her enviable status, has occupied popular culture and the American public imagination for decades (Oppliger 2013). The popular girl is both villain and superhuman, the simultaneously loved and hated version of the feminine ideal (Blaikie 2018). She is most often White, definitely thin, certainly able-bodied, generally wealthy, and absolutely heterosexual. She hovers between girlhood and womanhood and is afforded privileges of both. She is sexually active, or at minimum *assumed* to be sexually active by her peers. Above all else, she is pretty, sexy, and embodies ideal beauty, and indeed her popularity is rendered impossible without the celebration of her aesthetic. The popular girl trope is the classic case of the media perpetuating the hypersexualization of girls while reifying the cultural anxiety of girls losing their presumed innocence (Vares, Jackson, and Gill 2011).

In her seminal work on Black feminist thought and intersections of institutional oppression, Patricia Hill Collins conceptualizes controlling images as "designed to make racism, sexism, poverty, and other forms of social injustice appear to be natural, normal, and inevitable parts of everyday life" (1990:69). Mainstream media and popular culture generate controlling images of discernible girl character tropes that are geared toward tween girl audiences but also influence the broader public imagination of who a girl is or should be. Girl characters across film and television are notably represented as older and frequently portrayed by older actresses (Smith et al. 2017). Girlhood and media studies scholar Sarah Projansky writes that

> Girls who are large, differently abled, queer, of color, and/or poor; make "bad" or "dangerous" choices; feel depressed; or even just act silly (1) simply do not exist in media culture; or (2) appear in marginalized representations, on the periphery, with sidekick status; or (3) populate ubiquitous disparaging, disdainful, anxious, and/or protectionist depictions that shore up a narrow version of acceptable girlhood: the impossibly high-achieving heterosexual white girl who plays sports, loves science, is gorgeous but not hyper-sexual, is fit but not too thin, learns from her (minor) mistakes, and certainly will change the world someday (2014:1).

Some of these well-trodden but persistent tropes include the popular mean girl and the funny, quirky, often "ugly" girl who ultimately triumphs in love (and therefore life), but usually only after a makeover and almost always in a context of heterosexual romance. There are reality tropes of teen mothers, bad girls, and other girlhood "cautionary tales" specifically marked by raced and classed connotations. These enduring tropes align with the competing cultural models of innocent girls who need protection and "Girl Power!"

Only in the most recent years has popular media produced films and television series targeting teens that might swerve from conventional narratives and champion storylines of the underdog. In those representations, however, the girl in question can only be diverse in her representation along one intersection of identity at a time. If she is fat, she is White and able-bodied (*Sierra Burgess Is a Loser*, 2018; *Dumplin'*, 2018). If she is non-White, she is thin and otherwise traditionally pretty or viewed as a model minority (*To All the Boys I've Loved Before*, 2018). If she is queer, she is thin and femme presenting (*Crush*, 2022). Narratives of physical disability in popular media are tremendously rare, and it is exceptionally difficult to find a film or series that positions a girl with a physical disability as the protagonist or romantic lead (and most often, able-bodied actors inhabit these roles) (Smith et al. 2017). Invisible disabilities such as anxiety, depression, or chronic pain, just to name a few, may be represented in girlhood narratives in popular media but are often not critically, politically, or relationally positioned as disabilities; they are rather shown as dramatized gendered afflictions that are the fault of the individual girl in question and/or situated as tragic.

More dramatic series of late, including the revamped *Gossip Girl* (2021), *Pretty Little Liars* (2010), *Riverdale* (2017), *13 Reasons Why* (2017), and *Euphoria* (2019), feature thin, White, rich teenage girls with trendy clothing involved in devastating mishaps with drugs, sex, betrayed friendships, criminal behavior, suicide, and intimate violence. These dramatic representations of teenage girls demonstrate the hypervisibility of the oversexualized girl set against the middle-class norm of appropriate (hetero)sexuality (Renold and Ringrose 2011; Rossie 2015).

Given their Whiteness, cis-ness, heteronormativity, classism, and ableism, these tropes reify the image of the can-do girl and uphold the innocent girls in need of protection cultural model. Set against them are different girl tropes that reify the "Girl Power!" model, all intrinsically entangled with popular feminisms, consumer culture, and the empowerment marketplace for tween girls. In the last decade or so, corporations such as Disney have created strong female protagonists such as Merida from *Brave* (2012), Elsa and Anna from *Frozen* (2013) and *Frozen II* (2019), and Moana from *Moana* (2016). These female characters are all animated and created without the primary heteronormative end goal of marriage to a prince (an important departure from representations in the past), yet they are marketed alongside every other character produced by the Disney machine, whether villain, victim, or victor. The challenges they face relate to being different and going against the grain while having extreme privilege as royal princesses positioned within fantasy. They are represented as traditionally pretty, thin, able, and generally constructed within conventional notions of ideal femininity even as they become empowered by overcoming individualized obstacles. While these characters prioritize internal traits such as goodness, fairness, and following your heart, these traits are channeled and made legible through the characters' conventionally desirable appearances. Historically, goodness has been represented via beauty, Whiteness, and thinness, and evilness via ugliness, fatness, Blackness, and deformity (Alter et al. 2016; Erdman Farrell 2011; hooks 1992; Laine Talley 2014). The empowerment marketplace targeting tween girls, "Girl Power!" and popular feminist rhetoric, and contemporary representations of girls in mass media and popular culture have all contributed to shaping an era in which girls are positioned in a very specific way—at the nexus between empowerment and disempowerment.

Postfeminism, Popular Feminism, and "Girl Power!"

The past two decades have produced feminist scholarship centered on gender, power, and the neoliberal characterization of the relationship between them (Banet-Weiser 2018; Gill and Scharff 2011; McRobbie 2008; Tasker and

Negra 2007; Zeisler 2016). Postfeminism has given way to a resurgence of popular feminism, and we cannot dismiss how much consumption and emphasis on individualism play into the contemporary feminist landscape. Postfeminism endures as a framework for understanding a social epoch defined by individual identity, empowerment via consumption, and performing femininity (and now feminism) in ways that align with hegemonic gender expressions. Where postfeminism rendered feminist principles common sense and thus no longer necessary to fight for, resurgence of popular feminism has put second wave feminist principles of fairness and equality squarely in the spotlight. But that spotlight signals feminist identity for purchase. People can still march for what they believe in, but now more than ever, they can also purchase and wear something mass produced that demonstrates a feminist belief system on the body, literally. Gonick et al. write,

> While girl power emerged within the economic, socio-political context of the 1990s where girls could be active, in the 2000s they are now expected/demanded to be fully self-actualized neoliberal subjects. However, the constraints of heteronormative white ableist femininity are also firmly entrenched, though not necessarily in exactly the same old versions. Herein lies the paradox that underpins depoliticized notions of agency and girl power; girls are still bound by the body and sexual difference (2009:2).

Demonstrative of this paradox is how tween girls can readily articulate "Girl Power!" ideology (something that revealed itself time and again in my interviews) and wear these messages on their clothing while still experiencing limited economic, cultural, and political freedoms and internalizing protectionist discourses that manifest in tween girls policing their own, as well as other girls', behaviors, whether online or in physical space. The tween girls I interviewed judiciously recognized these contradictions and constraints, taking in much of the adult-centered fear and anxiety related to their bodies and sexualities and frequently expressing annoyance toward the expectations projected onto them to look and behave in certain ways, especially because, in their view, tween boys are not subject to the same kind of expectations.

As Bulger et al. find in their 2021 report *The Missing Middle: Reimagining a Future for Tweens, Teens, and Public Media*, "tweens and teens are accustomed to having a great deal of control in how and when and where they express themselves online. By contrast, when they encounter content that is developed by adults without youth input, it often strikes them as perpetuating stereotypes about teens or as being out of touch" (6). Tweens desire more authentic representation of their experiences from public media, but public and popular media are often stereotyped and may not land with tween audiences as intended. One way around this? Tween girls make the media themselves.

Tween Girls Go Digital

Tween girls making themselves visible on social media is now a central part of the extant body project. Shields Dobson writes that "scholars of girlhood and culture have theorized the kind of youthful 'new femininities' that have come to prevail as centered around energy, vitality, capacity, and entrepreneurial spirit, along with public visibility and self-exposure" (2015:159). For tween girls, visibility on social media has become paramount to self-expression, and to facilitate the call to be visible, routine digital participation has become the norm for a large majority of American tween girls. An interesting element that makes tween girl social media participation especially difficult to pin down in terms of broader implications and potential impacts is that girls under the age of thirteen are not technically allowed to be on social media platforms, as invoked by federal law (COPPA) and platform policies, yet these rules are not strictly enforced. Tween girls are a simultaneously hypervisible/invisible demographic on social media platforms, in particular on platforms that hinge on visual content.

American youth are now living fluidly between offline and online spaces and engaging in self- and social development in ways specific to their generation (boyd 2014; Buckingham 2008; Farman 2012; Kennedy 2020; Palfrey and Gasser 2016). The transition from adolescence to adulthood and processes of becoming and embodying tween girlhoods are facilitated by social media participation. Social media is not set apart from reality for tween girls; it *is* their reality (Underwood and Ehrenreich 2017). They are building this reality and participating in novel dimensions of what constitutes public space, using social media as a primary vehicle of communication.

Reckoning with the colossus social media has become, the social sciences are continually working out ways to effectively study social media platforms and other digital spaces (Lupton 2014; Marres 2017; Orton-Johnson and Prior 2013; Selwyn 2019; Sloan and Quan-Haase 2016). Changes in platform popularity move fast, and we have barely scratched the surface of measuring the overall impact of social media on youth and at different intersections, exploring different variables. One recent study that looks across several large datasets to measure various elements of Internet use among youth finds very little impact, negative or otherwise, between digital technology use and adolescent well-being (Orben and Przybylski 2019). A Pew Research report from 2022 finds more of the same, with most respondents (ages thirteen to seventeen) indicating either a positive (32 percent) or neutral (59 percent) over-all effect of social media in their lives and 9 percent reporting a negative effect (Anderson et al. 2022).

Taking a more gendered approach, some topical studies suggest that there is no significant correlation between social media use and body dissatisfaction (Burnette, Kwitowski, and Mazzeo 2017; Maes and Vandenbosch 2022). Still others indicate that it is the type of social media engagement and content that matters most in determining health outcomes for adolescents online (Markey and Daniels 2022; Steinsbekk et al. 2021). Two earlier Pew Research studies (Anderson and Jiang 2018a, 2018b) surveying American youth (ages thirteen to eighteen) on their feelings about social media find that young people have mixed feelings about it, with most respondents indicating social media having a positive impact (31 percent) or neutral impact (45 percent) on their lives; 24 percent of respondents indicated it has a negative impact. It is interesting to see from the 2022 Pew Research study that the percentage of respondents reporting net negative impact dropped substantially, from 24 percent to 9 percent. Further studies consider tweens and the specific matter of privacy on social media, finding mixed and nuanced results on its importance in how young people use and navigate platforms (De Leyn et al. 2021; Kim and Davis 2017; Shin, Huh, and Faber 2012).

By talking to tween girls about social media and analyzing examples of gendered embodied performances on YouTube, I seek to expand sociological knowledge of how the realities and complexities of new media cultures intersect with the realities of tween girls' coming of age in contemporary American society. Tween girls today toe an increasingly blurry line between adolescence and adulthood and the physical and digital. Their experiences of "growing up girl" in online space and navigating those choppy waters involve risk and opportunity, regulation and experimentation (Ringrose 2011). It is important to explore these subtleties of experience. As Shields Dobson writes,

> The question of how and to what extent girls and women are able to challenge gendered representational conventions of visibility and the gaze via self-representation and other kinds of digital media production within patriarchal and capitalist systems, is especially important to keep in mind in the context of widespread availability of media production technologies, and prominent calls toward visibility and self-exposure for girls and young women (2015:50).

This research expands on conceptualizations of gendered power relations and body politics through the lens of the digital, situating tween girls as the experts in their own digital narratives and exploring how online body performances reflect the competing cultural models of innocent girls who need protection and "Girl Power!" The reflection of social life for tween girls via social media participation is essential in conceptualizing and understanding contemporary American girlhoods. And because gender identities for women and girls are underpinned by work on and performance of the individualized, neoliberal body project, the roles of the body and corporeal visibility on social media have become crucial to the theoretical and empirical investigation of American tween girlhoods today.

3

She Has the Juice

Tween Girl Visibility and Social Capital on Social Media

"What makes you different might just be your greatest strength."

—Barbie
Barbie in a Mermaid Tale, 2010

I meet Starr at her after-school program on a late November afternoon. When I arrive, Starr, a twelve-year-old Black girl with braided hair, an oversized T-shirt, and Nike sneakers, is shooting hoops with a group of friends in the gym. The club supervisor walks over to get her, and I hang back, watching as I wait for Starr to come over. The half dozen girls in the group interact with one another; they dance around, dribble and shoot the ball, play with each other, and take selfies. Each one either has a phone visible in her hand or hops off the court to check her phone every few moments.

A handful of minutes later, Starr comes bounding across the gym and shakes my hand, a big grin spread across her face. I can tell she is excited, and she tells me it is the first time she has ever gotten to do something like this, give an interview. Of the twenty-six girls I talk with over the course of conducting my research, Starr is among the most forthcoming. During our interview, she talks to me as though we have known each other for a long time. She tells me about her family, her friends at school, the track team she joined, and how she loves to read and write poetry. Part way through our conversation, I direct the topic toward social media.

> KP: What kinds of social media sites are you on?
> STARR: Oh, I'm on Instagram and Snapchat, and sometimes I use You-Tube to, like, watch and make videos and stuff.
> KP: Do you go on social media a lot?
> STARR: Yeah, I'm on it every day.

KP: Can you tell me more about what you like to do on social media specifically?

STARR: Well, like on Snapchat, I can use funny filters, and I can text my friends. Because most of us don't see each other all the time, so we can just snap each other, and we're all good. So, Snapchat is about seeing those friends.

Without my prompting, Starr takes out her phone and shows me some of the Snapchat images she has sent to friends. There are selfies of all kinds, and Starr clearly enjoys using a variety of filters that change her appearance, especially the dog filter and flower crown filter. She puts text over a lot of the images she shares, mostly hashtags that use tween girl lexicon such as "#swag," "#selfie," "#icute," and "#goals." She is clearly adept at taking pictures on her phone, editing them, and sharing them with her chosen Snapchat circle.

KP: And what about Instagram?

STARR: So, on Instagram you can post pictures, or like, you can take pictures, and you post them. And people can comment on them and like them. I get a lot of nice comments on what I post.

KP: How does that make you feel?

Her eyes brighten and she laughs.

STARR: It makes me feel good!

KP: Can you tell me why?

STARR: Well, I think just because, if you post something, and someone likes it or wants to share it or something, it shows that I have done something good. Like, I made something that people like. I have posted something and good people like it. My friends like it . . . (pauses) [For] me, social media is a little, whole other world. Because no one knows who you are on the Internet.

Starr mostly uses social media to communicate with her friends, but she also sees the draw of social media as providing some semblance of anonymity, or at least the possibility of playing around with identity while creating and sharing content. For Starr, social media is a whole world, one in which she can control what she posts and where and play around with who she wants to be and how she wants to present herself.

Today, tween girls use social media as a tool to make themselves visible (Banet-Weiser 2015; Farrell 2022; Shields Dobson 2015). This visibility is underscored by the conditions of tween girlhoods as paradoxical, operating in the liminal space between childhood and adulthood, public and private, and the innocent girls who need protection model and "Girl Power!" model. Tween girls are supposed to be responsible and protect themselves online, but they are also expected to make themselves visible, specifically in ways associated with successful or ideal girlhood.

As Orgad and Gill argue (2022), seeking confidence and being confident are now so embedded in American culture for women that they are beyond reproach. Do we expect the same kinds of performances of confidence from tween girls? In some ways, yes. The "Girl Power!" cultural model is predicated on empowerment as a consumer product and visibility as a conduit for empowerment for tween girls specifically. The thrust toward authenticity and girls being themselves has also found tremendous success in the marketplace. Barbie encapsulates this ethos in the 2010 film *Barbie in a Mermaid Tale*; she learns she is a mermaid, and though she faces challenges, in the end, her difference demonstrates her strength as she embraces who she truly is, saves Oceana, and wins the surfing competition. Disability and girlhood studies scholar Sarah Hill writes that "postfeminist girlhood increasingly calls on these seemingly confident girls to 'make their private selves and "authentic" voices highly visible in public' (Harris 2004:125), and as such, girls and young women are particularly prominent creators of, and participants in, socially mediated online content such as blogs and social networking sites" (2017:117).

But when a tween girl presents herself as confident on social media via the digital girlhoods she creates, she may get bifurcated reactions that either bolster and affirm that confidence or view it as suspect. Indeed, when tween girls do not present themselves as suitably self-effacing, they may be read as attention seeking, roundly understood among tween girls to be a negative character trait. Is girlhood itself a process in which confidence can be built in earnest? How does *tween* as a consumer category factor into confidence building when girls are clearly being sold empowerment and a "be yourself" ideology but are routinely policed and sanctioned when they demonstrate confidence? What potential does social media have to disrupt the consumption imperative toward the empowered self? Can the kind of confidence tween girls articulate feeling when they create digital content be separated from broader confidence culture (Banet-Weiser 2018; Orgad and Gill 2022)?

The tween girls I interviewed emphasize the importance of being able to exercise control over self-representations on social media, which helps enhance their self-esteem, build social capital, engage their interests such as art, dance, and computer coding, and associate their content and, thus, selves with those interests in digitally networked publics (boyd 2010). Content creation, and how and where to share the content they create, matters a lot to tween girls. They can reach audiences of myriad sizes by choosing to post content publicly, privately, or on specific platforms (e.g., YouTube vs. TikTok vs. Snapchat). They can play with identity and present themselves in different ways on different days if they choose, though this choice brings up questions of surveillance and authenticity (explored in more depth in the next chapter). Tween girls also demonstrate creativity and humor with how they edit and share content.

Additionally, tween girls use social media in part to perform their bodies in ways that both align with and resist conventional ideals of femininity and what it means to be a pretty girl. These nuances of body performance offer relevant insight into how tween girls balance contradictory expectations placed on their bodies in relation to protection, privacy, visibility, confidence culture (Orgad and Gill 2022), aesthetic ideals of femininity, empowerment, resilience, and authenticity. Participating on social media platforms plays a significant role in how a girl sees herself, as well as the agency she feels in managing how others see her. In addition to control over self-representation being a boon for self-esteem, the tween girls I interviewed emphasize how visibility on social media is used to accumulate likes and followers, understood as a modern, meaningful form of social capital. These are virtual resources, a form of currency girls can accrue to gain visibility and recognition.

Tweendom is not only a consumer demographic but also a time marked by burgeoning interest in celebrity—yet another marker of the "growing up too fast" moral panic that presupposes and fears tween girls as on the cusp of becoming sexual, a fear that is not entirely misplaced, as young girls are routinely sexualized in all manner of media (Durham 2008; Jackson and Vares 2015; Levin and Kilbourne 2008; Oppliger 2008; Renold and Ringrose 2011). My own interest in celebrity as a tween revolved around boy band phenomena such as NSYNC and the Backstreet Boys. I salivated over lead singers and giggled shamelessly with friends while we performed provocative dances in our bedrooms and basements. We took pictures of each other and of ourselves with disposable cameras. We pored over *17* magazines, eager to emulate whatever trends we could. I felt myself awakened to something intangible but palpable when I watched Kate Winslet pose for Leonardo DiCaprio in the now iconic scene from the blockbuster film *Titanic* (1997). My friends and I fast-forwarded the VHS tape to that specific scene in the after-school hours before our parents came home from work. We were desperate to be teenagers, to be seen as older. We were desperate to be seen. That propulsion toward visibility was my understanding of celebrity and why I felt drawn to it.

Becoming visible was rarefied air (Hamilton 2008; Jerslev 2016; Turner 2004). It belonged not to the many but the few. It would be several more years until Myspace, my foray into online visibility and digitally networked publics, came out in 2003. Social media actuated a seismic shift in the politics of visibility, popular culture, and notions of celebrity, including the idea of "micro-celebrity" (Abidin 2018; Abidin 2020; Banet-Weiser 2017; Jerslev 2016; Marwick 2013b). Citing the work of Alice Marwick, Anne Jerslev writes,

A distinctive "Internet-enabled visibility" (Marwick 2013a:114), microcelebrity implies an online following but may, nevertheless, be micro in scope (Gamson 2011). Microcelebrity is, first and foremost, a particular online performance designed for self-branding, "the presentation of oneself as a celebrity regardless of who is paying attention" (Marwick 2013:114) (2016:5239).

Microcelebrity can also be understood in conversation with the current vernacular of the social media influencer (Bishop 2021).

Being Seen: Digital Girlhoods as Normal Routine

Along with the politics of microcelebrity, social capital, and gaining followers (explored in more depth in subsequent sections), social media participation and visibility have become routine, daily aspects of tween girls' lives. Visibility on social media is complex and distinctly gendered. Politics of visibility are influenced by racialized identities, sexual expressions, and ability. There is risk and reward associated with visibility on social media for tween girls. They must navigate and negotiate protectionist discourses that manifest as both a fear for girls and a fear of girls while contending with the push for individual empowerment via online visibility.

The crucial difference between popular culture representations of tween girls and the content tween girls are creating online is that in the latter, tween girls themselves are doing the representing. Self-representation has always happened among the tween girl demographic, whether through diary entries, art, music, or the subcultural fan zines of the girl-powered 1990s feminist third wave. But for the first time in history, girls and women are consuming, creating, and distributing content on online public platforms at higher rates than boys and men (Ahn 2011; Kennedy 2020; Salter 2016), and the matter of making content public is something that tween girls think about strategically. Bulger et al. write in their *Missing Middle* report that "tweens and teens fluently described deploying different apps for specific purposes and seamlessly moving across various media environments depending on their interests and needs" (2021:6).

Self-representation on social media has become exceptionally normalized and is embedded in the daily routines of American tween girls. Many of the girls I interviewed are active on three, four, or more social media platforms even though most were under thirteen years of age, the current legal minimum age required to create an account on these platforms. Circumventing COPPA restrictions, this demographic is among the most prolific when it comes to content creation and sharing online. Girls spoke emphatically about how social media punctuates their day-to-day lives, and they are not exactly sure what they would do without it (Anderson et al. 2022; Bennett 2023; Vogels, Gelles-Watnick, and Massarat 2022). Making digital girlhoods, whether selfies, videos, snaps to send to friends, pictures, stories, or TikToks, has become a normal part of everyday life for tween girls. An aspect of this normalization is certainly feeling a sense of fitting in and not wanting to be left out or miss anything (Barry et al. 2017; Schmuck 2021). Some of it seems remarkably subconscious.

Each part of the day is ripe for documentation, from when a tween girl wakes up to when she gets ready for bed. I asked each girl I interviewed how much she posts on social media, and most post at least once a day, if not several times, on various platforms. Some of the girls name strategies in how they think about what they post and where and how often depending on the platform in question (e.g., Instagram vs. Snapchat vs. Musical.ly). They closely consider what kind of audience they are posting for, whether a private group of friends or the broader public.

Noelle is a thirteen-year-old Black girl who loves nail art and wants to open her own salon one day. During our interview, she leans over the table to show me her Instagram account. Noelle explains to me the difference between a profile picture and new pictures posted on her account. She flips through photos she has posted to Instagram (many of them showing off intricate nail art), and says,

> See? I have a profile picture up here, and I can, like, edit things to show more stuff about me or not for the people that follow me. And I can change my profile picture. That's what people see first if they come to my profile. And then you can post other pictures to your Instagram account, and if someone follows you, they can see what you post and like it or comment. You can decide whether you want someone to follow you or not.

Noelle tells me how she can edit her profile and control what she puts out to her followers, offering and sharing content as she chooses. Profiles are specialized, unique glimpses into tween girl selves (boyd 2007; de Ridder and van Bauwel 2015; Farrell 2022; Herring and Kapidzic 2015). Tween girls choose specific profile names, pictures, and taglines that reflect their interests and demonstrate who they are, and they further shape self-representations through what they routinely post to their profiles (what would show up on a follower's feed). Many of the girls I met took out their phones to show me exactly what they were talking about. I got a distinct sense of how tween girls' social media participation is ingrained in daily routines.

Brooklyn is a tall and quiet thirteen-year-old Black girl I meet on a chilly October day. Unlike Starr, who was very open during our interview, Brooklyn seems a bit hesitant at the beginning of our conversation. She becomes more animated when we start talking about selfies. A small smirk on her face, shrugging her shoulders, she says,

> BROOKLYN: I post a picture of myself every day. Just every day, every morning, I take a picture of myself and post it. I don't know. It's just what I do.
> KP: Why do you think you do that?
> BROOKLYN: Well, I just like to take pictures! (laughs) And I like my friends to see. [When] I take pictures on Snapchat, I save them to my phone, and then I post it on Snapchat, then I post it on Instagram, then I post it on Facebook . . .
> KP: Wow! So you post to a lot of different social media sites?
> BROOKLYN: Yeah, I post the most stuff on Snapchat. Like, a lot throughout the day. On Instagram, I post stuff like twice a week and on Facebook twice a week.

I am struck by the seeming nonchalance that Brooklyn attaches to this part of her day. Brooklyn tells me that she likes talking to her friends over the course of the day, especially her friends who go to a different school. Posting on Snapchat is her way of communicating with that circle of friends, since she does not get to see them every day. She posts less on Instagram and Facebook because she sees those sites as less intimate. On Snapchat, she shares content with her close friends almost constantly. They are hyperconnected throughout the day, and she knows exactly who she is sharing to. Managing relationships and facilitating communication with friends in physical networks is a meaningful shared motive among tween girls surrounding daily social media use and the production of digital girlhoods (Dunne, Lawlor, and Rowley 2010; Farrell 2022; Ging and O'Higgins Norman 2016; Wade 2019a).

Pepper, a White ten-year-old with thick-framed glasses and shaggy brown hair, wears a unicorn hoodie and fidgets her hands inside her sweatshirt pocket while we talk. She seems a bundle of pent-up energy, constantly moving her legs and shifting around in her chair. Even though she conveys a nervous energy, she seems clearly excited, even confident, in telling me about how she uses her social media accounts.

> PEPPER: For Snapchat I usually post a lot of selfies with my brother and my sisters and stuff, and if we're doing anything fun that day, like rollerblading, then I'll post that. My baby brother is really cute, so I post a lot of selfies with him. And Instagram, like every day I post like one thing on average, and for Snapchat I post like two to three things on average.

KP: What kinds of things do you post on Snapchat?

PEPPER: If I see something funny, like a funny meme or something, I share that with my friends. Or I just take pictures of what I'm doing. I share what I'm interested in. If I'm doing something fun or cool, I share it so other people can see it.

Sierra, a shy Black girl age ten, talks quietly to me, her beaded braids dangling in front of her eyes. She smiles more as our interview goes on, and when I ask about her daily social media use, she gives me the rundown of what she posts, on which platform, and how often.

SIERRA: I post like five things a day on Musical.ly and like, twice a week on Instagram . . . [I] post singing videos, pictures of me, or pictures of something I went to. Or like, if there was something that looked really good that I ate, I would take a picture of it.

KP: What's Musical.ly?[1]

SIERRA: There's all these songs you can choose from. And you make these short videos where you sing along or dance along with the song and then post it. It's kind of like Snapchat, but the video doesn't disappear unless you delete it. It can be private or non-private.

KP: Are your accounts private or do you make them public?

SIERRA: Mine is public. People can see it. Like, if I post a Musical.ly video, anyone can see it and like it, or comment and stuff.

My interviews with Brooklyn, Pepper, and Sierra reveal how tween girls can be strategic and deliberate in controlling what they post, how often, to which sites, and who can see the content. Pepper posts a lot of content and images related to what her family is doing and her immediate interests, primarily focused on fun and recreation (Coulter 2021). Brooklyn emphasizes in our interview that she mainly wants to be connected to friends. She likes seeing what her friends are doing online, and she likes her friends to see pictures she posts. The benefits of social media in this scenario feel obvious. For Brooklyn, it seems a simple and straightforward social exchange. Snapchat is more about daily use in staying connected with friends, and Instagram and Facebook are used with less frequency, but she still posts new content multiple times a week as part of maintaining an online presence and a certain level of visibility.

Sierra, on the other hand, chooses to make much of what she posts available to a wider audience. This surprised me a little, as during our interview, Sierra is quieter and more reserved than many of the other girls I talked to. Her body language is more closed off, and in the beginning of our conversation, she answers my questions in a succinct, matter-of-fact way. This could very well be because of my role as interviewer and the fact that she does not know me and maybe does not feel like revealing too much. But it was interesting to learn that Sierra posts public videos of her singing and dancing on Musical.ly upward of five times a day. It feels discordant with how I perceived her during our conversation, but it goes to Starr's point at the beginning of this chapter—that social media can be this whole other little world in which girls get to try on different selves for size and play around with different aspects of expression and performance (Davis 2012; Farrell 2022; Kennedy 2020; Shields Dobson 2015). Social media platforms are spaces where tween girls can feel a sense of freedom of expression, where there is potentially more opportunity to explore various sides of themselves against the limitations they feel in their physical worlds.

After talking with twenty-six tween girls about what social media means to them, I learned that, just like many adults, tween girls have a love/hate relationship with social media and espouse a "can't live with it, can't live without it" mentality (Bennett 2023; Burnette, Kwitowski, and Mazzeo 2017; Vogels, Gelles-Watnick, and Massarat 2022). Part of the normalization of digital girlhoods becoming a daily routine manifests in how tween girls sometimes post content without thinking too much about it—it is just something to do. But there is a difference between taking a selfie and keeping it in your photo library and taking a selfie and posting it to social media: *someone else* (or many others) is going to see it, and that is a distinct feature of content creation and how it precipitates a richer understanding of contemporary tween girl digital cultures. As Tiidenburg and Gómez Cruz suggest, "posting or exchanging selfies is seen as frivolous and self-absorbed, but the relationship between subjectivity, practice, and social use of those images seems to be more complex than this dismissal allows" (2015:2). Selfies are laden with meaning, and this interplay between "subjectivity, practice, and social use" is ripe for further inquiry.

I wanted to learn more about and try to understand this important difference between keeping a selfie private in a photo library versus posting it to social media, especially regarding possibilities of resistance to dominant narratives, creation of counternarratives, and potential for social and political change for tween girls via social media participation (Hart and Mitchell 2015; Keller 2019; Phelps-Ward and Laura 2016). I wrote about this in the 2019 edited volume *Body Battlegrounds* (Bobel and Kwan), in a piece titled "Am I Pretty Enough for You Yet? Resistance through Parody in the Pretty or Ugly YouTube Trend." While that piece examines the trend through a lens of parody and analyzes Pretty or Ugly videos in which girls are clearly mocking the trend and creating a counternarrative, elements of the Pretty or Ugly trend more broadly illuminate key themes of pressure to be seen, the meaning of gendered visibility in this context, and microcelebrity.

At times, girls bemoan feeling distracted by social media and the compulsion to be constantly "plugged in" for fear of missing out on something, especially regarding dynamics and goings-on in immediate friend groups and popular culture or celebrity news. Some interviewees mentioned that they see and feel a certain amount of pressure for girls to present themselves in particular ways, especially in comparison to other girls their age (Choukas-Bradley et al. 2022; Fardouly et al. 2015; Fardouly, Willburger, and Vartanian 2018; Farrell 2022; Feltman and Szymanski 2018).

I ask Pepper whether she thinks social media is a good or bad thing. I can see her struggling with the question, but she finally says,

> I think social media has maybe made things worse. But like for me, it's not a big deal because I use it for communication, you know? But it probably made things worse because of all of the pictures that girls see online and like really, really, really pretty girls and they want to be like that, or they'll see really, really, really pretty girls with cute boys and then they'll want to be like that, so they can get a guy. I just think it made it worse.

Pepper sees how girls are impacted by the compulsion to compare their bodies to other girls' bodies, especially when it comes to attracting attention from boys (Burnette, Kwitowski, and Mazzeo 2017; Choukas-Bradley et al. 2022; Nesi and Prinstein 2015). Though Pepper uses social media primarily to communicate with family and friends (which I found to be the case for many of the tween girls I interviewed), she also demonstrates a set of shared gendered knowledges, recognizing the stringent expectations associated with tween girls needing to look a certain way online and "get it right" in terms of how they post images or videos of themselves online (Gill 2021). Pepper emphasizes interacting with images of other girls' bodies as potentially harmful to girls and their self-esteem. Research and resultant scholarship drawing connections between media and impacts on body image suggest that girls in particular may be influenced by their social worlds, peers, and external feedback, which in turn influence how a girl may represent herself in digital space (Fardouly, Willburger, and Vartanian 2018; Tiggemann and Barbato 2018). As Farrell points out, existing literature "suggests a link between the need to seek affirmation and self-presentation, and how teenage girls are exploring self-presentation and sense of self online" (Farrell 2022:11).

Dominique, a Black eleven-year-old, is on the quiet side but has a very warm demeanor. She echoes Pepper's complicated feelings when reflecting on her own experiences on social media during our interview. When I ask Dominique what she likes and dislikes about social media, she says,

> I feel like sometimes it is hard because I see what other kids in my grade post. And I'm like, bigger than all the other kids in my grade. So my friends told me, don't be down on yourself, you're not that much bigger than us. I still say, yeah, I'm bigger than all the other kids in my grade. I see what my friends post, and like, it feels like all of the kids in my grade are skinny so I'm like one of the biggest ones. So sometimes I feel sad because I feel bigger, or some people might call me fat when I post a picture, and I say, "Okay, I'm going to take it as a compliment." Like some people comment and call me brave because when people say I'm fat I just say, "Thank you, I know I am, but I stay healthy." I'm just big. I eat healthy and stuff, but I'm just big. So sometimes I take it as a compliment, and I'm like, okay, I'm a big girl. That's good. That means I'm growing. I'm okay with it. But sometimes it does hurt. Sometimes I just say that even though it really hurts inside.

I feel emotional when Dominique shares this with me. On the one hand, as a fat studies scholar and educator, I feel emboldened by more mainstream fat acceptance dialogue and the calling out of antifat stigma and prejudice that seems to be occurring more frequently in American pop culture and media these days (Hobbes 2018; Gordon 2020; Gordon 2023; Harrison 2021; Mercedes 2020; Sole-Smith 2023; Strings 2019). There is clearly more cultural interest toward critique of the thin imperative. Fat studies scholars and fat activists have made strides in differentiating between body positivity as individual, neoliberal project and fat liberation, which has its roots in intersectional critical thought and grassroots social justice organizing (Cooper 2016; Dionne 2019; Gerhardt 2020; Harrison 2021; Mercedes 2020).

On the other hand, the fat liberation framework has not been absorbed into mainstream public media or popular culture. Antidiet rhetoric is broadly co-opted by straight-sized White cis women. It remains tenuous how effectively fat acceptance ideology—or even a diluted, adjacent version of fat acceptance as body positivity—is being internalized by a younger demographic, especially in a culture defined by hyperconsumption. Antifat sentiments and antifat discrimination endure as deeply entrenched in our society; young girls become keenly aware very early on that being pretty is important to their perceived value, and a predominant component of being "pretty" means being thin. *Fat* is still a loaded term often used as a synonym for *ugly*, and the stakes are high for girls to be characterized as pretty. Fat embodiment is also often read as a personal moral failing indicative of a lack of self-discipline or low sense of self-worth (Erdman Farrell 2011; Gordon 2020; Griffith 2004; Murray 2007).

As a fat person myself, I feel that twinge and ache for Dominique and the pain she expresses as I recall similar experiences from my own adolescence. I share some of those experiences and the feelings they bring up with Dominique during our conversation. I remember cruel moments during middle school when people would make fun of me or comment on my size. One comment stands out in my memory: a thin, White, conventionally pretty, popular girl (the paragon "mean girl" trope) maliciously said in front of a large group of peers that if she punched me in the stomach, it would be like punching a pillow. This memory lands differently now, as I have centered my own critical thought and scholarly interests in body politics, girlhood studies, and fat studies, but it still shaped how I thought about my body and my worth for quite some time. On reflection, I wonder what it might have meant to have an outlet such as social media to explore that experience and share it with an audience.

My Whiteness also necessarily informs my experiences of privileged embodiment, and my fatness is critiqued in relation to that Whiteness. Pervasive antifatness within all social institutions cannot be separated from anti-Blackness, as the two are mutually constitutive (Cox 2020; Harrison 2021; Mercedes 2022; Shackelford 2021; Strings 2019). Though I cannot project Dominique's experiences and expressions beyond what she shared with me during our interview, her embodiment as a fat Black girl matters in a context of the politics of tween girl digital visibility—especially as racist, classist, and ableist notions of health and a healthism imperative (Crawford 1980) have been conflated with a White, thin, young, able, cis-het aesthetic and continually weaponized against marginalized communities, particularly fat Black, Brown, and Indigenous women and girls (Bowen 2021; Cox 2020; Harrison 2021; Kirkland 2011).

Dominique not only encounters peers at school but also engages with what her peers post on social media: often selfies, pictures of friends, and social media influencer bodies. Dominique articulates having a strong system of support around her, and she responds to online criticism in admirable ways, demonstrating strong self-awareness and digital literacy (Burnette, Kwitowski, and Mazzeo 2017; Meyers, Erickson, and Small 2013).

Her size does not keep her from making herself visible online and participating on social media in the same way her friends and peers do, but her feelings about this visibility and participation are, unsurprisingly, complicated. Dominique sees the good in her size as evidence that she is strong and healthy and growing. Yet she also sometimes feels hurt by what she sees, what she compares herself to, and the negative comments she gets on her pictures.

Her comment about people calling her brave is an experience shared by many fat content creators across social media sites. Actress and comedian Nicole Byer published a memoir and self-help guide to wide fanfare about this very phenomenon titled *#VERYFAT #VERYBRAVE: The Fat Girl's Guide to Being #Brave and Not a Dejected, Melancholy, Down-in-the-Dumps Weeping Fat Girl in a Bikini* (2020). Because of the widespread acceptance and capitalist co-optation of body-positive language and ideology, lauding fat people on social media (especially female and feminine identifying people) as brave for "putting themselves out there" has become a discernible reverberation and particularly gendered curiosity. Casting the action of making one's fat body visible on social media as brave presumes that there is the chance, the significant chance, that doing so is potentially dangerous or risky and may result in pain. Fear often accompanies brave actions. To frame bravery as showing courage infers that there is something to fear, a reason courage is necessary.

Calling fat women and girls brave for making their bodies visible on public platforms does the insidious work of reproducing a system of body politics that Others certain bodies: bodies that are fat, Black, queer, gender nonconforming, disabled, and aging. By extension, this system can make individuals at various intersections of identity hypervisible, which can have (perhaps unintended) negative impacts. Fat individuals who post pictures of themselves online are often the targets of violence, bullying, and other negative consequences simply for making their bodies seen. The response of "you are so brave" codes the possibility of danger and violence toward and against these bodies, in various forms, as likely or expected.

While digital self-representation certainly has positives in the sense that tween girls have a lot of choice and can wield some control over how they present themselves online, it is necessary to reckon with the reality that American tween girls are now living in a time when airbrushed images of models in magazines are not the only influence on their sense of self by process of comparison. Now, with advancements in digital editing software and the onset of endless applications for altering images, tween girls themselves can *be* the models. While the girls I interviewed used "Girl Power!" and empowerment language quite often and expressed a spirit of "it's not what's outside but what's inside that counts," it is crucial to consider that tween girls are consuming more digital images of other girls on a daily basis than ever before. We are still attempting to understand the impacts of this consumption. Some existing scholarship suggests that high levels of social media consumption may lead to increased processes of bodily comparison, which can have negative impacts on body image and self-esteem (Choukas-Bradley et al. 2022; Holland and Tiggemann 2016; Knorr 2017; Maes and Vandenbosch 2022; Salomon 2017; Simmons 2018). Other literature suggests that form or type of engagement on social media matters most (e.g., engaging with body-positive or size-inclusive content has positive correlations with heightened body confidence and increased self-esteem), support networks can help mitigate negative impacts of body comparison on social media, and feminist sensibility may disrupt experiences of self-objectification and surveillance, offering a protective layer from internalizing damaging messaging surrounding body image and negative self-esteem (Burnette, Kwitowski, and Mazzeo 2017; Cohen, Newton-John, and Slater 2021; Feltman and Szymanski 2018; Markey and Daniels 2022; Mingoia et al. 2017).

Even though making digital girlhoods has become an important and recognizable part of tween girls' daily lives, tween girls' feelings about social media are not straightforward. The control girls feel about what they put online is mediated by the reality that these platforms are owned by corporations and that the content they are producing is social—it is designed to be seen, whether by large or small audiences. The audience is certainly an important aspect of tween girls' social media use, as likes and followers are recognized among peer groups as a meaningful form of social capital (Farrell 2022).

Visibility and Social Capital

Dani is a thirteen-year-old Black girl who gives off an air of total confidence when I meet her. She holds herself in a noticeably comfortable way. I get the sense that this young person really likes who she is. A self-proclaimed tomboy, she wears a backward cap and basketball jersey and sits backward on her chair. Dani is quite indifferent when it comes to defining the role social media plays in her life, which sets her apart from most of the other girls I interviewed. She tells me she uses Facebook to connect with friends and family members who live farther away. She uses Snapchat to stay in touch with friends during the day but rarely posts anything publicly. But while Dani produces less of her own digital girlhood on social media compared to many of my other interviewees, she has plenty of perspective and opinions to offer in terms of how girls use social media, especially when it comes to making themselves seen. She tells me,

> So, okay. Like you know how people on Instagram and Facebook and all that stuff, they have "likes"? So, if you get a certain amount of "likes," it's like you are popular or have cloud, is what they say. Cloud is like popularity. So, if you got that then everybody knows you. You know, like you have this cloud, you have this popularity. So, you're the person that has the juice, is what they say.

Cloud and juice are brand new lexicons for me. According to Dani, cloud and juice are only attainable by building a clear presence on social media and require tween girls to engage in frequent posting to promote visibility, build their image or brand, and gain likes and followers (Banet-Weiser 2014).

In contemporary America, being pretty is still very much equated with girlhood success and achieving the ideal feminine. When I was doing textual analysis of the Pretty or Ugly YouTube trend, a theme came up of tween girls asking the pretty or ugly question and, in the very same breath, articulating some version of "I want to know if you like me." Girls seemingly conflate the answer to the pretty or ugly question with their overall worth and value or, more to the point, their likability. This conflation is not surprising, considering how everything—from religion to philosophy to medicine to popular media—has situated being pretty as good and being ugly as bad. It stands to reason that much of the social media content tween girls post deals directly with physical appearance and making their bodies visible and consumable, because developing a sense of self in a society that values aesthetic capital is necessarily attached to what you look like (Burnette, Kwitowski, and Mazzeo 2017). The pretty or ugly question is a century old, at minimum, in terms of how it structures and influences how girls develop a sense of overall self-worth (Brumberg 1997; Driscoll 2002). That said, self-representation and "doing girlhoods" in the digital age are differentiated by emphasis on the potential for empowerment via visibility (Banet-Weiser 2015). Peggy Orenstein writes that "the body has become even more entrenched as the ultimate expression of the female self, evolving from 'project' to consciously marketed 'product'" (2016:17). Dani illuminates this point.

> Social media is a place where more people can notice you. And if more people on social media think you are pretty, then maybe you are pretty... [People] take Instagram so serious. Like how many "likes" they get, how many people follow them and stuff like that. I guess more people on social media saying you are pretty matters more than you believing that you're pretty.

Dani separates herself from girls who post this kind of appearance-related content. Her tone comes across as disparaging. She even shakes her head when she says, "I guess more people on social media *saying* you are pretty matters more than you *believing* that you're pretty" (my emphasis). Even as Dani distances herself from taking social media too seriously, she clearly recognizes the gendered phenomenon of girls' putting their bodies front and center online to be seen and noticed. I picked up on this relationship in other interviews as well; gaining likes and followers on social media in response to appearance-driven content is viewed as an important form of social capital.

Girls blur the line between physical and digital worlds when they talk about gaining popularity, being seen and recognized on various platforms, and garnering the social capital currency of likes and followers. In my interview with Michelle, a soft-spoken Black eleven-year-old with a smile full of braces, she vocalizes what she sees as a significant difference between girls and boys in how and why they use social media.

> MICHELLE: I think boys kind of, well, what girls do is like, they'll say, like, "Maybe I should wear this outfit tomorrow." Like, [boys] use social media differently than us because they don't care about what they wear to school.
> KP: Do you think girls care about that?
> MICHELLE: Oh yes. Because, um, well, they want to look their best. It's kind of like the thing in middle school. You're like, "Oh he's cute, I should totally wear something that makes him notice me more because he doesn't notice me" or something like that.

Whether at school or online, tween girls put emphasis on getting attention and getting noticed for being pretty and further heteronormative emphasis on getting this attention from boys specifically. From tween girls' perspectives, it is complicated, which also comes up in Pretty or Ugly videos. Some of the girls participating in the trend lament childhood being over, entering a period of life when they need to care more about what they look like. One video stands out in particular: video subject Kelly, a White girl with brown hair and glasses, approximately eleven or twelve years old, sits in front of her bed on the floor, her shoulders slumped and hands clasped under her chin. She sighs emphatically into the web camera.

> I guess I am making one of these videos now, because, well, everyone at school cares more about what each other looks like now. And I've seen other people making these videos. So, tell me, am I pretty or ugly? (sigh) I didn't think I would have to deal with this stuff yet.

Tween girls grumble about how they must put more effort into appearance to be liked or even listened to; at the same time, they frame caring more about appearances as a natural part of what it means to be a girl.

My interviewee Michelle uncritically positions girls' caring about their appearances with a sort of "of course" response to navigating this middle school stage of existence. From her perspective, of course girls care more about their appearances. Why would they not, when they live in a society that places such significance on female and feminine aesthetics as attributable to broader qualifications of worth? This status quo is hardly the fault of social media, which has been around for only about two decades. What begs further analysis is how social media magnifies such feelings of pressure, comparison, and body dissatisfaction—and how it might be a useful tool in resisting and challenging demanding ideas of what feminine beauty looks like and how to achieve it. An intersectional approach to girlhoods is vital to understanding how such magnifications are experienced across and within identities, as well as how multiple modes of resistance via social media participation might serve toward more nuanced understandings of American girlhoods.

I spend a long time talking with Genie, a sharp and funny ten-year-old White girl. We talk about why and how tween girls seem to use social media more than boys. Genie tells me she notices that girls are frequently attached to their phones.

> KP: Why do you think that is, that girls are more attached to their phones?
> GENIE: Well, it's mostly girls that are popular at school, like, and they want to change their self so they can be popular. Because like, everybody wants to be popular and be swarmed by . . . boys, I guess? And like, middle school is the worst. If you're not popular, no one is friends with you. If you're popular, then everybody's friends with you. So they want to have more friends, I guess.
> KP: Hmm. Why do you think being popular and having friends might be important to girls?
> GENIE: Well, girls think it is going to affect their future.
> KP: Can you tell me more about that?
> GENIE: So, if [a girl] is popular, they're going to get a good boy, and they're going to get married to him, and it's just going to go on from there. And posting on YouTube can help with that, because you can get followers and subscribers and stuff. You can be more popular.

I was really surprised and intrigued by Genie's sense of conviction when she shared this idea. She thinks about popularity in the physical context of being at school and having friends and aligns it with being liked. But more than that, she sees the process of posting on social media as having long-term impacts, outcomes, and potential consequences, and she points to YouTube specifically. As Burgess and Green write in their book *YouTube: Online Video and Participatory Culture,*

A common assumption underlying the most celebratory accounts of the democratization of cultural production in the mid 2000s (Grossman, 2006a, 2006b) was that raw talent combined with digital distribution could convert directly to legitimate success and media fame—if only the right platform were provided. This assumption was especially noticeable in the early mainstream media discourse around amateur video, usually invoking individual success stories that appear to realize this promise (2018:33).

Whether or not becoming a YouTube star or social media influencer is a tangible reality for tween girls, the *potential* of that reality is felt, as tween girls consume and create tremendous amounts of content on YouTube. The premium placed on visibility and changing meanings of celebrity amid an uptick in influencer culture (Abidin 2020; Marwick and boyd 2014; Bishop 2021) contribute to how tween girls situate themselves in relation to gendered performances in digital space.

For Genie, publicly posting on YouTube can serve to ensure a good future—especially in terms of the marriage market and the conditioned heteronormative response that girls should attract a boy and eventually get married. This goal of being viewed as attractive or pretty is an essential component of tween girl popularity and being liked, mapping onto contemporary notions of neocelebrity and visibility in digital space. Within pop culture and public media, a popular girl is almost always conventionally pretty and ascribes to normative notions of ideal femininity, and if a girl who falls outside of these parameters *is* popular, there seems to be a need to justify that popularity to make it legible or believable. Banet-Weiser speaks to the gendered parameters of online influence and girlhood when she writes,

> The presence of girls producing media online gives us something important to celebrate, given the historical exclusion of girls from fields in technology, media production, and science. Yet, the spaces where girls are being encouraged to produce and make media are also conventionally feminine; as Brooke Duffy has argued, the genre of make-up tutorials, fashion blogs, haul videos, fitness tutorials, and so on are clearly feminized spaces, with many producers garnering contracts with corporations and media companies and creating economically successful careers from these entrepreneurial endeavors (Duffy 2015) (2017:271).

All this considered, insofar as social media and the production of digital girlhoods are reifying certain tropes and gendered expectations of tween girl interests and embodied gendered performances, social media is also changing and challenging a pretty-equals-popular equation. My findings demonstrate that a tween girl can strategically use social media to make herself more visible and gain likes and followers in ways that go beyond appearance-related content. Having juice on social media does not necessarily require a tween girl to be conventionally pretty. Using social media platforms to perform *authenticity* (explored further in the next chapter), to be funny, demonstrate expertise, make art, offer social commentary, and much more, can contribute to increased social capital and increased resources and rewards in a shared values system among tween girls (Bulger et al. 2021). While in many ways, being pretty is still of significant importance in contemporary tween girlhoods in America, there are emergent, novel forms of garnering visibility, popularity, and influence that do not necessarily rely on assimilating to or accommodating rigid standards of ideal feminine appearance.

Self-Representation, Popularity, and Passionate Pursuits

Some of my interviewees frame the matter of building social capital on social media in particularly gendered ways, while others frame social capital online as an intrinsically embedded desire that just exists for people growing up in this digitally affixed generation. My interviewees Dominique and Ariel explicitly mention this desire during our interviews. Dominique, Black and eleven years old, tells me, "I don't have my own [YouTube] channel yet, but I want to when I get older. I would post stuff going on in my life. I would make it public. That's the whole point of having a channel, like so you can have viewers and subscribers." Ariel, a White ten-year-old with a purple sweatshirt and thick-framed glasses, offers a comparable perspective. She explains,

> ARIEL: People my age usually want to, like, use social media to get out there. Like a lot of people in my class, they just want to be out there.
> KP: Can you tell me what you mean by "out there"?
> ARIEL: Like, they want people to get to know them, who they are, and they want to get followers and that sort of thing.

Dominique and Ariel both highlight how social media is used as a tool for self-representation and sharing who you are with a broader audience. Dominique would use her YouTube channel to share aspects of her day-to-day life, and she would allow people to view it publicly. YouTube began as a basic video-sharing platform (Burgess and Green 2018). Within a handful of years, its popularity soared, and the site added the option for people to create personal profiles, also known as channels. Channel pages allow for friending and following, and users can share videos and decide who sees what content by sharing publicly or privately (Burgess and Green 2018). Dominique sees YouTube's public nature as its central purpose; she hardly sees the point of having a YouTube channel if she is not going to make it public. Ariel speaks for herself and her peers, relating self-representation to social capital and describing how people her age want to share who they are online, taking advantage of this new medium of public space and opportunity for building networks, expanding social connections, and exploring self and identity.

Tween girls must learn how to navigate the digital landscape and balance the desire for and importance of visibility on social media in a climate marked by a resurgence of popular feminisms, "Girl Power!" ideology, empowerment via consumption, and cultural imaginings of the tween while keeping themselves protected in online space. The tween girls I interviewed tend to keep content private on their accounts but will strategically post publicly on certain platforms if they see it as increasing their social capital. Tween girls also learn, sometimes through trial and error, the risks associated with posting public content. As White, ten-year-old Samantha tells me, "Like, if you have YouTube, you have to know that people will criticize you or like, say mean things about you. Like, if you don't like it, well, that's just part of having a YouTube account." Samantha speaks very plainly about the dissolution of private and public on YouTube and has a strong sense of the associated risk and reward. If someone is going to make content public, they must be prepared for a wide range of outcomes, including criticism and potential harmful commentary and response to videos. A smaller subset of the girls I interviewed do make much of their content public, especially on platforms such as YouTube and Musical.ly (now TikTok); these platforms are meant for gaining followers and garnering likes from a larger audience rather than circulating private or personal content among an intimate group of friends.

Tween girls can also serve their passions and interests through controlling self-representation and building social capital online. I have my interview with Jessie, an energetic, intelligent Black twelve-year-old, on a cold February afternoon. When the topic turns to YouTube, she absolutely lights up. She exclaims,

> I just started my own YouTube channel last night! My mom said I could start a dance channel where it could be me and my friends doing my dances that I made up. My goal when I grow up is to become an entrepreneur to build my own dance building, my own dance business. And I've been talking to my mom about that, and I feel good that I can talk to my mom, because she said when she was younger, she used to love dancing too. So, I asked, can I start a YouTube channel? Since that's how most other famous dancers started. Because before you know it, somebody famous will see it and then it will just build on that. [I] just feel like that would be a good way for me to start pursuing my dream of becoming a professional dancer and choreographer.

Jessie has a keen sense of how YouTube can be used to foster visibility and how that visibility can be leveraged into influence and celebrity (Abidin 2020; Bishop 2021). She sees it as a very practical conduit to establishing herself within her interest of dance, creating content to build on that dream. Though new to the experience of building and posting on her own YouTube channel, Jessie clearly understands strategies of controlling and curating her YouTube content to be specifically geared toward dance and choreography so she can create opportunities to be associated with those distinct interests. Jessie correlates her sense of self with dance, as she mentions it frequently during our interview. She talks about how she could potentially be seen by someone famous or connected to the industry and suggests that this is how dancers get their start these days—by building digital content and making themselves visible on a public platform.

Jazz, a Black ten-year-old, is a self-described artist. Her energy and smile are infectious. She sits up on her knees in her chair and leans far over the table. Her body seems ready to burst, constantly moving, like she could bounce all over the walls. Yet she is mature for her age in how she speaks; there is perceptible wisdom and thoughtfulness in how she answers my questions. We talk for well over an hour about school, friends, bullying, social media, and how she loves creating art. She draws animations on her iPad. Her mom tells her she is too young to have a YouTube channel, but she frequently uses Snapchat to show off her artwork to friends and family. She has her sights set on YouTube because of its public nature. She tells me that her mom will let her start her own YouTube channel when she turns thirteen. She says, "I'm excited about getting a YouTube account because I can get fans that support me and like, I can know how I'm doing in my drawing and everything, and like, what I need to improve on." Jazz sees YouTube not only as an avenue to build a following and gain fans but also as an online community that can provide feedback and support so that she might get better at what she enjoys doing. In either case, it is a tool she can use to her advantage.

There is an interesting parallel between Jazz using YouTube as a platform to get feedback on an artistic interest such as drawing and tween girls using YouTube as a platform to get feedback on their appearances. One scenario feels intrinsically easier to support (art) than the other (appearance), and both are imbued with a certain set of social values that leave adult stakeholders either encouraged or appalled. But this again demonstrates the paradox of American girlhood. We want Jazz to foster and nurture her artistic interest, yet structurally and institutionally, we are more likely to devalue artistic pursuits in favor of more "practical" enterprises. And we see clearly where and how emphasis on meeting particular ideals of aesthetic and appearance has delivered success for women and girls. The Pretty or Ugly trend is complex and should not generate straightforward disdainful responses that lament tween girls' apparent narcissism and attention seeking for asking the question on YouTube. Rather, we should consider critically the social and cultural contexts that incite such inflammatory responses to the Pretty or Ugly YouTube trend. Clearly, when it comes to the production of digital girlhoods, not all content is created equal.

Tween girls conceptualize visibility and social capital on social media through multiple lenses, not only in notably gendered ways but also in ways that serve their specific passions and interests. This echoes findings from Bulger et al., who write,

> Whether younger or older, living in rural or urban areas, and regardless of interests, tweens and teens told us of the many ways they turn to how-to videos to learn new skills, support creative interests, and solve problems. Videos for supporting artistic pursuits appeared to provide an especially important outlet in the absence of after-school activities and in-person lessons [during COVID-19 lockdown] (2021:15).

Gaining likes and followers is not always about being pretty or popular but rather about engaging interests and passions and being visibly linked to those things. Regardless of the lens, tween girls characterize gaining likes and followers as a fundamental intention of making online content available to wider audiences, and they recognize it as a meaningful, modern form of social capital. Tween girls use social media as a tool for exploration and to seek validation and affirmation, whether that validation be about physical appearance (as in the case of the Pretty or Ugly trend) or about their passionate pursuits (Farrell 2022).

Girls describe having to constantly work at maintaining their online personas, leading some to express feelings of emptiness, loneliness, and stress associated with conformity online (Brandes and Levin 2014; Jong and Drummond 2016). Malvini Redden and Way's (2017) qualitative study proposes that girls make significant links between online affirmation and concepts of self, whereby likes online are viewed as reaffirming and providing social approval. Seeking validation from peers and family is a normalized aspect of female adolescent development (Aberg and Koivula 2022; Brown and Gilligan 1992; Farrell 2022; Orenstein 1994), especially given the broader social conditions of American girlhoods that underpin this normality. While there are potentially negative impacts associated with sharing content publicly, consuming too much appearance-related content, and engaging in bodily comparison, tween girls resolutely argue the importance of being able to represent themselves on social media platforms via the digital girlhoods they create, especially as this self-representation correlates with increased self-esteem and positive sense of self (Valkenburg et al. 2021). Maintaining control of self-presentation is a route to building self-esteem, especially among demographics that have historically been situated as having lower levels of self-esteem and self-efficacy; tween girls are certainly understood as a key demographic in this case (Hill 2017; Wade 2019a).

Posting on social media to gain likes and followers is a form of social capital that, for all its potential pitfalls, serves to affirm tween girls and boost their self-esteem. My interviewee Tessy, a White ten-year-old, says, "Getting 'likes' and giving 'likes' are just like getting compliments. You can make someone else feel good, and if someone 'likes' what you post, then you feel good too." Again, the boundaries of the physical and digital are blurred here. Tessy sees the role of the like button across platforms as akin to giving or getting praise from someone in a face-to-face interaction in physical space. Constance, a bright and funny Latina girl, also ten years old, explains to me,

> Getting comments and likes are really important to me because it gives me the self confidence that I need to grow up and be a good woman . . . [It's] not just about interacting with friends. It's about opening up to the world.

Constance's words "grow up and be a good woman" and "opening up to the world" project into the future, moral harbingers emphasizing a function of social media in steering the passage from girlhood to womanhood. Her words are hopeful and suggest that tween girls feel that a world afforded by social media participation is waiting for them and that they have a powerful part to play in shaping how the world views them via their participation— that social media, as a reflection of social life, the good and the bad, is there for them to explore (boyd 2014). They do not need to be restricted from it or suppressed within it. Rather, they need to be given tools to navigate social media in ways that keep them safe, certainly, but also that emphasize its positive possibilities, the aspects of social media most beneficial to them.

Constance brings up confidence in direct articulation during our interview. In their 2022 book *Confidence Culture*, authors Shani Orgad and Rosalind Gill question why the culture of confidence has emerged in recent years, suggesting that a gendered confidence imperative is ramping up in part because of the discernible increase in representation of popular feminisms. Though Orgad and Gill speak to confidence culture as it relates to the market for self-esteem (Banet-Weiser 2014) and tween girls as a target demographic for that market, they mainly consider the role of mothers as the purchase power behind empowerment products geared toward their daughters. I am curious about how the confidence imperative maps onto tween girls' social media consumption and participation, especially as current literature on the impacts of social media along lines of empowerment and disempowerment is split and enigmatic in its findings.

Some situate social media as a principal cause of low self-esteem and body image concerns among female adolescents (Fardouly and Vartanian 2016; Tiggemann and Miller 2010; Tiggemann and Slater 2013), while others emphasize social media's potential for empowerment and embodied resistance (Aberg and Solonen 2021; Barnard 2016; Kedzior and Douglas 2016; Tiidenberg and Gómez Cruz 2015; Wade 2019a). Because understandings of girlhoods and the impact of social media are not created equal across identity categories of tween girls, further intersectional inquiry is necessary to recognize where and how there are opportunities for embodied resistance and creation of counternarratives via digital girlhoods. That said, my findings align with recent literature (still scant but growing) that finds increased self-esteem as a motivation for posting content online as well as an outcome of doing so (Aberg and Koivula 2022).

In my conversation with Ariel, she talks about how important it is that people "like" the YouTube videos she creates with her sister because those likes indicate to her that she is "doing a good job." She tells me,

> The thought of me making [a video] gives me a kind of happy feeling . . . [When] you watch your own videos, it kind of makes you feel happy because if it's funny to you, then you think it could be funny to other people. And then you're always like, happy about watching your video because it's the thought of you making it . . . [Like] it kind of makes you confident that it's going to get some likes or whatever.

In a significant departure from how my interviewees Dani and Genie talk about social media visibility and social capital as primarily related to appearance, being pretty, and needing popularity to attract boys, both Constance and Ariel articulate an ethos of and reason for garnering social capital centered on self-esteem. Constance sees getting likes on social media as a direct avenue for building self-confidence, exposing herself to new ideas, and, as she puts it, "opening up to the world." And in the earlier interview excerpt, Ariel does not automatically equate getting likes on her videos with feeling good about herself. Rather, her reasoning happens in reverse. Ariel watches her own videos after making them, and the act of watching them back makes her feel good. The literal act of making the video, of creating the content, is what brings her joy and satisfaction. And she centers what *she* thinks about it as being of primary importance. When she feels good about what she creates, she feels confident that other people will like it too, and that viewers will validate her by clicking the like button.

The tween girls I talked with emphasize feeling a sense of accomplishment and pride when viewers like or offer supportive or affirming comments on the content they create. Ten-year-old Genie, the interviewee who talked at length about social media visibility, popularity, finding a boy, and getting married, is a frequent poster on YouTube. She enjoys making videos that offer commentary and her personal reviews of video games she plays. She also makes videos that teach people how to do computer coding.

> KP: How does it feel when people respond to your videos?
> GENIE: It makes me feel really good. It shows that people have seen what I have worked hard to do. It's like, "Yay! Somebody noticed what I have done!"

Similarly, Taylor, a ten-year-old White girl brimming with energy, tells me, "I like to sing and dance and stuff like that. So, I'll post on Snapchat of me dancing or talking or telling people what I'm doing. It can be creative! It brings me joy, like, having somebody say, 'I really like this video' if I post one."

Positive reinforcement has widely recognized psychological and emotional benefits, and it is useful to consider how likes, subscribers, and followers contribute to novel understandings of girlhood development and avenues of increased self-esteem in the online context as tween girls create and produce digital girlhoods. Author Amanda Rossie speaks to this relationship in her work on girls' visibility on social media when she writes, "The link between visibility and girls' empowerment is an important one, especially when thinking about girls' online self-representations" (2015:231). She argues that the onset of digital participation as a norm has catalyzed increased use of social media as a vehicle for visibility, and within a postfeminist digital cultural context, visibility can operate as a meaningful route for building self-esteem.

Conclusions: The Politics of Being Seen

Tween girls are no longer just looking at themselves being represented in popular media; they are *doing* the representing. They are creating content—digital girlhoods—through which we have an opportunity as a larger society to understand more about contemporary American girlhoods if we take the time to engage. There is still constrained agency to reckon with, as tween girls do not exist in a vacuum. Gendered, raced, and classed power dynamics exist online as they do in physical space. Tween girls internalize dominant narratives of girlhood that often center on fear of what can happen to them if they make themselves (and their bodies) seen, but they must also reckon with distinctly gendered, raced, and classed expectations of visibility that have become a central component of personal empowerment narratives in the post-feminist digital landscape (Banet-Weiser 2015; Orgad and Gill 2022; Shields Dobson 2015).

Tween girls are expected to make themselves seen as they maneuver in the liminal space between childhood and adulthood, and all the while they must take full responsibility for their bodies and make good choices about how they represent their embodied selves in the digital landscape. Navigating this tricky terrain necessarily carries over into how tween girls engage with and respond to each other online, especially related to the digital girlhoods they produce. Tween girls grapple continually with competing cultural models of girlhood that frame their social, cultural, and political realities. The contrast and tension between protectionist discourses around innocent girls and "Girl Power!" ideologies, narratives, and embodiments play out in endless ways online.

During my research, I discovered that tween girls will at times set themselves apart from certain kinds of content creation, Othering fellow tween girls, especially those who post more appearance-related (i.e., attention-seeking) content, in the process. Pursuit of likes and followers in this context of creating appearance-related content is sometimes interpreted as suspicious or off-putting. Many girls I interviewed see this kind of content creation as shallow, inauthentic, or blatantly attention seeking. My interviewees demonstrate a sense of "I'm not like other girls" in how they position their own creation of digital girlhoods.

Popularity on social media is multifaceted, and as I demonstrate, tween girls make a distinction between the goal of popularity based on being pretty and attractive to boys and popularity and social capital garnered via recognition of interests and passions, such as dance, art, or gaming. Some girls producing digital girlhoods very clearly resist and reject conventional notions of femininity, eschewing appearance-related content, while others embody conventional femininity in culturally specific ways. Most often, however, this push-pull between resistance and accommodation happens all at once, in conversation and contradiction. Indeed, tween girls' social media presence today is defined by tensions between empowerment and disempowerment, privacy and publicity, and authenticity and affectation.

4

Am I Pretty or Ugly?

Being "Authentic" Online

"Beauty begins the moment you decide to be yourself."
—Coco Chanel

"All little girls should be told they are pretty, even if they aren't."

—Marilyn Monroe

"Happiness and confidence are the prettiest things you can wear."

—Taylor Swift

Sally stands in front of a web camera, shifting her weight back and forth. A White tween girl nine or ten years old, Sally has long brown hair, wears a bright yellow tank top, and has on a noticeable amount of makeup, including eye shadow, blush, and lipstick. Smiling into the camera, she bounces up and down on her heels and plays with her hair, emanating nervous energy. She says,

> Hi guys . . . I wanted to make a video to ask if I was pretty or ugly. Now, be honest. 'Cause a lot of people say that I'm ugly, and I just wanted to know the truth. Am I pretty or ugly? And another thing, be honest, it's okay what you say. I don't really care if I'm . . . pretty or ugly. Well, I care. I mean . . . so like, people call me ugly at school, and then other people call me really pretty. And a lot of people call me ugly too. But I just want to know, am I pretty or ugly? So please just write comments if I'm pretty or ugly. So yeah. Um. (laughs nervously) Yep, that's all. And also look at my other videos. Yeah never mind. Don't look at my other videos. Thanks. Bye!

Sally's Pretty or Ugly YouTube video encapsulates the overall formula and ethos of the Pretty or Ugly trend. She represents the most common demographic of tween girls found in the videos: White, young, has access to a digital device (laptop, tablet, or phone), and makes the video by herself. The vast majority of Pretty or Ugly videos I analyzed feature one subject, somewhere between the ages of ten and fourteen, White, who films herself in a bedroom, bathroom, or shared household area such as a living room or den, asking viewers to comment on whether she is pretty or ugly. Though not entirely absent in my sample, videos made by groups of girls are rare. It seems to be most commonly an individual enterprise. Videos last anywhere from a few seconds to several minutes but on average tend to be about thirty seconds long.

In some of the videos, the pretty or ugly question is posed clearly and immediately. In others, the question is couched well within the script, maybe hidden, only arriving in the final moments of the video. Yet the titles of the videos necessarily align with the trend, or they would not have been included in my sample for analysis. Sometimes the subject in the video does not verbally ask the question at all, and the only indication of her participation in the Pretty or Ugly trend—and of her desire to learn the answer to the question—rests in the name of the video and the tagline underneath. Most of the videos I analyzed include spoken words, but several feature girls who do not speak at all. While there is discernible variation in how tween girls present themselves in these videos and how they ask the pretty or ugly question, there are certain intelligible markers and modes of language and performance that render the trend very recognizable.

In this chapter, I unpack the Pretty or Ugly YouTube trend and the reactions of my interviewees to the videos I showed them from the trend. Tween girls contend with performing "can-do" girlhood and ideal femininity in their Pretty or Ugly videos. As the epigraph quotes in this chapter demonstrate, gender, femininity, beauty, prettiness, confidence, happiness, and "being yourself" are all bound up with one another. Famed fashion designer Coco Chanel, mega–movie star and model for sultry American beauty Marilyn Monroe, and stratospheric ultracelebrity Taylor Swift each made perennial statements on the connection between girlhoods, feminine aesthetic, and exuding confidence. I noticed that when the tween girls I interviewed watched, reacted, and responded to the Pretty or Ugly videos, they often enforced a values system of digital authenticity. Tween girls emphasize realness and vulnerability in self-presentation and performance while also finding themselves caught within competing cultural models of contemporary girlhood—girls as both empowered and disempowered—and the confusion that results from circuitous demands. Interviewee responses to the Pretty or Ugly videos reveal important questions about a digital authenticity values system (what constitutes being real or fake in online space) and about bullying in physical space as a perceived motivation behind tween girls posting these videos—and how making the body visible on social media is a markedly gendered and raced practice.

Scholar Sarah Banet-Weiser theorizes that authenticity is not only viewed as "residing inside the self but is also demonstrated by allowing the outside world to access one's inner self" (2012:60). After showing a series of three Pretty or Ugly videos to each tween girl I interviewed, a pattern emerged among interview participants highlighting and policing a right way and a wrong way to present and post a Pretty or Ugly video (Gill 2021). They approach the trend with a certain level of suspicion and irritation, as though preconditioned to read the girls making Pretty or Ugly videos as fake or phony from the outset. According to the girls I interviewed, the tween girls who make and post these videos in the "right" way are read as authentic in their performances; this authenticity is only legible as authentic if the girl(s) in question suitably self-deprecates and does not come across as obviously attention seeking.

Also compelling was how the tween girls I interviewed distanced themselves from the tween girls in the trend after watching the videos. Most of my interviewees articulate some version of "I would never post a video like that," often voicing "Girl Power!" rhetoric and policing the girls in the videos using language such as "It's what's inside that matters" or "They already know they are pretty, so why would they post about it?" They emphasize a belief that a tween girl who chooses to post a Pretty or Ugly video must already understand herself as pretty, or she would never post it in the first place, rendering her fake and attention seeking.

Paradoxically, even as interviewees distanced themselves from the trend and/or policed the girls in the videos, they also see the practicality of posting a Pretty or Ugly video to get answers, particularly if the girl in the video indicates she is being bullied or receiving mixed messages about her appearance from peers at school, friends, or family members. Contradictions within interviewee reactions to the videos further indicate the nuance and complexity of how tween girls navigate protectionist discourses and compulsions, "Girl Power!" ideologies, and the pull toward digital visibility. Girls' responses demarcate clear gendered approaches to using social media and offer key insights into the politics of appearance surrounding gender and race and the practice of making the body visible on social media.

The Formula of Pretty or Ugly

Sally's video script is emblematic of numerous themes that came to the fore in the textual analysis portion of this study: tween girls facing confusion and uncertainty, desiring truth and honesty from viewers, balancing performances of empowerment and disempowerment, feeling pressure to perform perfection and realness, and reflecting on experiences of being called pretty or ugly in physical social settings (e.g., at school and among peers/friends). What follows is a glimpse of a handful of other Pretty or Ugly video scripts from my sample:

> Some people tell me I'm pretty, and some tell me I'm ugly. But I want to know what YouTube thinks of me. So below, please comment if I am pretty or ugly. Please be honest and tell me what you think. I love you! Subscribe! - video by Elodie, White, eleven or twelve years old

> Hey guys, um, I know I haven't made a video in a while but um, the question I want to ask you is, well, basically, am I pretty or am I ugly? And your opinion really means a lot to me because people say I'm pretty, some people say I'm ugly, and I don't know what one I am. So um, like the video if you think I'm pretty and don't like if you just think I'm not pretty and all the other bad things you can think of. So anyway, um, I don't know. Be honest. This is me. - video by Reagan, White, ten or eleven years old

> Hey, um, I'm doing a video about if I'm ugly or not. I had many people say that I am and I just sort of just want to know why that is. A lot of people have been saying it's because of my nose. And um, and I want to know why. I get it's like, but I just, I like to know why you think I might be ugly, or why I might not be to you. So, if you can comment below and just say why or why not and tell me what you really mean please. I think that's it. Yeah. Bye! - video by Peyton, White, thirteen or fourteen years old

> Um, hey everybody. I have a pretty basic question. Um, I just want to know if I'm pretty. Um, all my friends at school are always like "Oh you know you're so pretty, blah blah blah." But I don't have a boyfriend, and boys don't like me. And I don't know I just, I just want to know. So, leave a comment. You can be honest. Um, am I pretty? Am I ugly? I can take it; you can tell me. Alright, thanks guys! - video by Marie, White, eleven or twelve years old

Each of these excerpts demonstrates a sense of confusion on the part of the tween girl making the video, not knowing what she is or how to categorize herself as either pretty or ugly. Reagan and Elodie indicate that people are telling them they are both pretty *and* ugly, and they want viewers to assess their appearances and give them honest opinions. Peyton pinpoints a specific attribute (her nose) that has been the subject of derision and negative feedback surrounding her appearance, but she seems to question the validity of this feedback and seeks further honest opinions from YouTube. Marie is called pretty by her friends at school but doubts this assessment of her appearance, specifically pointing to her lack of boyfriend as suspect and indicative that she may in fact *not* be pretty, even though people at school tell her she is. Her sense of self-worth seems attached to the question of whether she is pretty, which is by extension attached to the social meaning associated with having a boyfriend in this heteronormative context. Marie shores herself up for the truth, assuring her viewers, "I can take it; you can tell me." In all cases, themes of uncertainty and confusion, the quest for honesty, the push-pull between empowerment ("Be honest. This is me") and disempowerment ("Boys don't like me"), and the blurring of the physical and digital are prominent across the Pretty or Ugly videos in my sample.

News media responses to the trend have emphasized how girls in the video are "feigning insecurity" (Waldman 2013) or "feigning nonchalance" (Maldonado 2013). After watching and analyzing hundreds of these videos, I suggest that it is more complex. Tween girls in this trend are not feigning or faking but are sincerely exploring the dynamics of gendered visibility along various axes of identity on a highly visible global public platform. The dueling expectations assigned to tween girls' embodiments and sexualities are evident in the trend, and amid these contradictions, a girl is left questioning what she is (pretty or ugly) and, by extension, *who* she is. Because conventional notions of ideal femininity and achieving girlhood are deeply enmeshed with constructions of pretty as successful and empowering (Azzarito 2009; Banet-Weiser 2014; Brumberg 1997; Harris 2004a; Swindle 2011) and ugly as in need of correction or a manifestation of failing, if a tween girl is unable to identify whether she is pretty or ugly, it may disrupt her process of developing a sense of self.

Politics of Racial Performance

Racial identity is a key element of analysis of the trend, as Black and Brown tween girls navigate a perpetual thrust toward Whiteness as related to a constructed ideal femininity; proximity to Whiteness is historically and intrinsically bound up with girlhood corporeal politics of what it means to seen and understood as pretty (i.e., good) (Azzarito 2009; Carter Andrews et al. 2019; Rosario, Minor, and Rogers 2021). As Mikel Brown notes, "part of being an acceptable girl in a culture so deeply infused with white middle-class values, is to be, or at least appear to be, 'nice'" (2003:6). The tween girls in the video scripts sampled here are all White or White passing, given how I read and categorized their racial identities in my analysis. What it means to be a pretty girl and how prettiness is associated with other values (e.g., being liked, being seen, being good) becomes more entangled when taking constructions of race and racial subjectivities into account, recognizing how Whiteness and proximity to Whiteness is privileged in embodying ideal femininity and can-do girlhoods (Avery et al. 2021; Banet-Weiser 2015; Harris 2004a; Hill 2019; Morris 2015). Renold and Ringrose (2011) relatedly argue that as tween girls navigate contradictory ideals of girlhood such as "sexual knowingness" versus sexual naivete, their performances of femininity are continually shaped and impacted by the raced and classed social contexts in which they exist.

In studying the trend, it became apparent that White girls, who seem to produce the vast majority of Pretty or Ugly videos and are overly represented in my sample, may perform elements of Black beauty and co-opt Black cultures with impunity through consumption and physical expression (e.g., hairstyle, dress, music, language, gestures), always within a safety net of White privilege (hooks 1992; Jackson 2021). In a hyperconsuming culture, there is social and aesthetic capital to be gained from White girls performing Blackness, not unlike how White female celebrities have capitalized on Black female bodies, especially fat Black female bodies, as work sites to reinforce and protect a dominant White beauty ideal (Bailey 2021; Butler 2013; McMillan Cottom 2013).

Some of the Black girls making videos in the Pretty or Ugly trend exhibit elements of performing Whiteness (Carter Andrews et al. 2019; Hill 2019; Mooney 2018). There remain culturally reified characteristics of successful postfeminist girl subjects (Gill 2007); a girl must be pretty, thin, gentle, educated, middle to upper socioeconomic status, and White. Pretty or Ugly videos featuring Black girls often exhibit adherence to these traits in terms of body performance via dress, gestures, and volume of voice (or lack of voice) that read doing successful girlhood (Currie, Kelly, and Pomerantz 2009). This is not to suggest that all Black girls embody Blackness in codified and recognizable ways, or to essentialize Black girlhoods, but rather to emphasize the complexities of how racial embodiments are bound up with and reify gendered performances of ideal prettiness in a context of this YouTube trend and the creation of one specific form of digital girlhoods.

This subset of YouTube videos in my sample—White girls performing Blackness and Black girls performing historically White supremacist, colonialist notions of prettiness and associated embodied behavior—demonstrates how enduring White supremacy, racism, colonialism, and colorism operate both overtly and covertly within a postfeminist and consumer feminist, neoliberal colorblind landscape. Black girlhood studies scholar Dominique Hill writes,

> Due to the construction of Blackness and femininity as antithesis, Blackgirls are burdened with historical stereotypes of Black femi-

ninity and monolithic portrayals of Blackgirl's ways of being. They/
we weave in and out of the homogeneous category Blackgirl to de-
vise choreography that aligns with desirable constructions of self
(2019:281).

The fact that tween girls' self- and social developments now take place on social
media to such a significant degree begs further questions about how social
media participation has the potential to create space and opportunities for
Black tween girls' authentic expressions, resistances, and celebrations of Black
embodiment via digital girlhoods (Barner 2016; Erigha and Crooks-Allen
2020; Hill 2018; Kelly 2018; Lindsey 2013; Tanksley 2016; Wade 2019a).
Ashleigh Greene Wade speaks to this question in her work on Black girlhoods
and social media, arguing that "in some ways, Black girlhood(s) already constitute alternative girlhoods among hegemonic conceptions of the white,
middle-class girl figure, and the digital can function as one tool to visibilize
Black girls as girls and demonstrate the complexities of Black girlhood(s)"
(2019a:20).

I had the privilege of speaking with many Black girls during the interview portion of this study; they made up most of my sample of interview participants. This was not the case for the Pretty or Ugly videos, as most of the
subjects in my video sample are White or White passing. As a White woman,
I cannot embody or fully comprehend experiences of Black girlhoods. Black
girlhoods themselves are expansive and manifold. But I can center what the
Black girls I interviewed shared about their experiences on social media and
their responses to the Pretty or Ugly YouTube trend and offer analysis of the
gendered and racial politics brought to the fore in the videos.

Though beyond the scope of this research in its specificity of Black tween
girl embodiment as identity, transition, and process, this area warrants more
in-depth local and transnational empirical investigation, in particular exploring dynamics of normalizing and celebrating Black girlhoods in digital space,
homosocial relationships among Black girls online, and self-representation
and self-actualization processes on social media platforms. Treva Lindsey
argues there is great potential in "Black girls both creating and being the primary subjects of mass media representations of themselves" (2013:32), and as
Wade suggests, "Black girlhood studies as a field still needs more accounts of
Black girls' experiences in their own words, and these accounts should represent the range of subjective complexities that Black girls embody" (2019a:17).

Am I Real Enough?

As referenced earlier in this project, broad spectrum response to the Pretty
or Ugly YouTube trend has categorized it in a variety of ways. Some news and

popular media see it as evidence of girls in crisis, especially regarding negative body image. Some professional response to the trend has labeled it as normal tween-age anxiety, behaviors to be expected among female adolescents. Academic response to the trend is notably lacking, but the handful of articles that investigate it to varying degrees are equivocal in their take. One analysis sees the trend as reifying control of girls in public space and reproducing dominant gendered narratives (Nurka 2014). Another finds it symptomatic of brand culture and a manifestation of economies of visibilities in a postfeminist landscape (Banet-Weiser 2014). Yet another sees it as a potential conduit for increased self-esteem but that the public nature of the videos arguably functions as disciplinary action to further control and restrain girls, especially through the process of viewers commenting on the videos (Rossie 2015).

A significant number of videos on YouTube itself have popped up in response to the trend. People offer various commentaries and opinions, asking questions such as "Where are the parents?" and castigating video subjects for their ostensible bid for attention and what many considered to be self-esteem failure on the part of tween girls. Popular responses to the trend fortify the competing and contradictory expectations laden on the bodies and behaviors of girls. Those contradictions are readily seen in the performances of tween girls creating and posting Pretty or Ugly videos.

In a culture where tween girls are living their lives online, the question of what is real has become deeply relevant to this demographic. Digital authenticity is an intricate construct of identity performance, of tween girls managing their identities and impressions in digital space via their social media visibility. Garcia-Rapp writes, "Identity, as well as authenticity, is not objective or stable, but rather performative, contextual, and shifting. Both concepts are in practice contingent and dynamic, because people consciously and unconsciously 'work on them,' modify them, and 'learn by doing,' in their various social worlds" (2017:131).

I define *authenticity* using Dubrofsky and Wood's (2014) conceptualization of authenticity as marked by behaviors that do not feel strategic or calculated; it is constructed and contextually bound rather than natural or essential. The notion of authenticity in digital space is already fraught by nature of the digital as inherently mediated. Perceptions of digital authenticity—whether someone is perceived as real or fake online—is a values system mapped onto the digital from the physical. Tween girls have long chided one another within peer groups for overtly seeking attention or feigning niceties (Mikel Brown 2003; Mcqueeney and Girgenti-Malone 2018; Simmons 2002), but because social media has become a normative part of daily life and social development for tween girls, this values system has now found its way into social media participation and homosocial behavior among girls online.

Tween girls continue to police one another and reinforce a hierarchy; it is undesirable for a girl to be seen and labeled as fake or superficial. I found that girls desire, even demand, authenticity and realness in how other girls present themselves and perform their bodies online. The digital landscape as mediated space, however, renders this demand a little more complicated than just expecting girls to be themselves. Insofar as my interviewees were quick to espouse "Girl Power!" rhetoric ("Be who you are!" and "It does not matter what other people think"), they were also quick to decry girls in the Pretty or Ugly trend who came across as overconfident or desperate, which, interestingly, were often understood as the same thing. It seems that the line between being seen as real or fake on social media is a thin one.

I showed three Pretty or Ugly videos to my interviewees, randomly selected from my sample of 260 videos. I showed participants the video from Sally, whose video script opens this chapter, a video by Carlotta, and one by Donna. All three of the sampled videos feature girls who are White and between the ages of ten and fourteen. They all appear to be by themselves, using web cameras on laptops to record the videos. Sally appears to be the youngest in the sample at nine or ten years old; Carlotta appears as the oldest at thirteen or fourteen years old, with Donna falling somewhere in between, approximately eleven or twelve years old. All three are making their videos in bedrooms, blurring the lines between public and private in the digital epoch, as viewers can see into these intimate spaces (Kearney 2007; Kennedy 2020; McRobbie and Garber 2006). Sally wears a significant amount of makeup in her video. Donna also wears makeup, though it is less apparent than Sally's. Donna wears an animal hat on her head and plays music in the background of the video while she speaks. Carlotta has very short hair and thick-framed glasses. She does not appear to be wearing any makeup.

Sally is standing up in her video and moving around as she speaks into the camera. Donna sits on her bed, facing the web camera and leaning toward and away from it so that at various points we can see her whole body and at other points close-ups of her face. Carlotta is sitting in a chair, ostensibly at a desk in her bedroom, and we see only part of her upper body, primarily her face. The commonalities among video scripts are clear, but there are nuances in how the girls perform their bodies (Butler 1990). The way they dress, whether they wear makeup, how they position their bodies in the videos—all these things matter in how the video is read and understood by a viewer.

Carlotta's Pretty or Ugly video is an important example of the push-pull between performing the self in an authentic way and feeling pressure to conform to certain tenets of conventional femininity (Currie, Kelly, and Pomerantz 2009; Gill 2021). She says,

I have seen a lot of these videos that say girls are pretty or ugly. I just want to put myself out there and say what do you think of me? . . . [I] have seen a lot of stuck-up girls who know they're pretty but they want affirmation. They're attention whores. I've seen girls who truly don't know if they are pretty or ugly. I know who I am. I am just me. But I want to know what you think. I want to know if you think I am pretty.

Carlotta also demonstrates how girls in the trend itself often police how other girls have posted their own Pretty or Ugly videos. Carlotta positions herself as authentic in that she knows who she is ("I am just me"), suggesting to viewers that she is not putting them on or being fake. She sets herself apart from other girls in the trend by underscoring her own authenticity. Yet she is still seeking affirmation because she is asking the question and seeking answers from viewers. As she says, "I want to know if you think I am pretty."

Donna's video script goes as follows:

Hello everybody, it's me. Just out of curiosity, I want to know if I'm ugly or pretty. Because sometimes at school I get picked on that I'm really ugly. And sometimes I don't get picked on because they think I'm pretty. But I need your honest opinion. You tell me if I'm pretty or not. I don't have any pictures, but as you know, you can see me right now. So, you comment and you like if you think I'm pretty and don't like if you don't think I'm pretty. Um, thanks! Bye!

After watching these videos from Sally, Carlotta, and Donna during each interview, it quickly became apparent that my interviewees interpret the videos in two primary ways: 1) they feel suspicious of the video subjects, who they believe come across as attention seeking, and 2) they emphasize a practical understanding of why tween girls might post these videos if they are being bullied or picked on by peers. These reactions are not mutually exclusive and are at times expressed in conjunction with one another, which relates heavily to the contradictory demands of contemporary girlhood that tween girls embody through performances of empowerment and disempowerment. I first explore my interviewees' initial interpretation of the trend regarding suspicion and then reflect on the second interpretation regarding practicality and motivation for why tween girls make and post Pretty or Ugly videos.

"She Already Knows She's Pretty": Suspicion and Scorn

During our interview, I show the three Pretty or Ugly videos to Ariel, a White ten-year-old. Her reaction is quick and telling.

ARIEL: People in these videos, they're like, saying that they want honest opinions, but they really won't care if they're ugly because they simply know that they are pretty. They already think they are pretty.

KP: Why do you think they already know that they are pretty?

ARIEL: Well, it's like, they are making this video and asking everyone, and like, anyone can see it. I don't think they would post it if um, like, they really thought people would say "ugly."

The public nature of the videos casts doubt for Ariel. She has a hard time believing a tween girl would post a YouTube video asking this question if there was any chance she would get negative comments or be called ugly in response, suggesting a presumed fragility of girlhood self-esteem (Brown and Gilligan 1992; Orenstein 1994). But rather than see this attitude as confidence in appearance on the part of the video subjects, who, from her perspective, already think they are pretty, Ariel finds it off-putting that a girl who seemingly already thinks she is pretty would seek such validation on social media. To Ariel, the girls in the videos are out for attention and come across as fake, or inauthentic, in their performances.

Other responses echo Ariel's feelings about the girls in the videos. Kendra, a thirteen-year-old Black girl, finds the videos amusing. It is interesting to watch Kendra's body language change when we start the videos. While watching, she rocks back in her chair and smirks, crossing her arms over her chest. When she watches the video of Carlotta in particular, she shows her exasperation in a humorous way and has a hard time getting her words out in response. She smiles, chuckles, and shakes her head, saying,

I mean, it's like, she is saying that she is herself, but then like, why do you want to know [if you are pretty or ugly]? Or like, why ask other people? Ah man, I think, like, it doesn't matter what people think about how you look. It's the way you think about how you look yourself.

"Girl Power!" language is obvious in Kendra's response, but it functions in such a way that Kendra ultimately scrutinizes and criticizes Carlotta for posting the video in the first place. From Kendra's point of view, it should not matter what other people think, only what you think of yourself, so the video, by virtue of its existence on this public platform and within the purview of the trend, is already positioned as inauthentic.

For tween girls today, it is unattractive, even deviant, to come across as somehow desperate for attention. Within the logic of the "Girl Power!" cultural model, a girl should already know her self-worth and that she is good enough as she is. She should be confident—but not obviously so. Much emphasis is placed on charming and self-aware "imperfection" within confidence culture (Banet-Weiser 2017; Orgad and Gill 2022) and on being real in online space, especially as larger cultural discourses reproduce an ethos of social media being manufactured, false, phony, and inauthentic—discursively positioning tween girls' gendered content creation around appearances and aesthetic capital as trivial, immaterial, and even petty.

In an analysis of online commentary surrounding selfies in particular, author Anne Burns posits that "selfies have a regulatory social function in that there is a connection between the discursive construction of selfie practice and the negative perception of selfie takers" (2015:1716). She goes on to suggest that "instead of being a positive tool for self-exploration and for mediating a position relative to one's peers, photographic self-expression (particularly by women) is reframed as a matter of petty and squalid attention-grabbing" (2015:1723). Tween girls are continually disciplined into caring about their appearances because we associate appearance with girls' worth and value in aesthetically driven, White supremacist, capitalist patriarchy. And then we turn around and call this behavior vapid, trivial, attention seeking. We render the question "Am I pretty or ugly?" a shallow concern expressly *because* we associate it with femininity. Indeed, we are most likely to celebrate girls who readily demonstrate a keenly balanced performance of the best parts of masculinity (logic, reason, strength, self-assuredness) while looking and acting suitably feminine. "I'm not like other girls" becomes code for easygoing, cool, carefree, happy, intelligent, low maintenance—a badge of honor in a system that privileges the masculine. Ongoing discipline and surveillance within postfeminist neoliberal confidence culture positions girls as self-disciplining subjects enlisted in the surveilling and disciplining of other girls. A theory of the importance of tween girls' self-representation in digitally networked publics (and how those representations are received and mediated by other girls) matters a great deal. These videos are not shallow; they are a meaningful tussle with and toward selfhood.

Though the Pretty or Ugly videos are not straightforward selfies, they are certainly embodied performances of gender, race, class, and ability, and as artifacts of tween girl digital cultures, they richly demonstrate the constant negotiation of what performing successful girlhood means in a contemporary American cultural context. Further studies support these politics of negotiation and the enigma of conformity and authenticity that punctuates tween girls' experiences of self-presentation on social media. A 2019 study by Yau and Reich finds that girls (aged twelve to eighteen) are influenced by peer approval and strategically configure their content toward entrenched norms more likely to gain them likes. Similarly, Farrell references a study by

Zillich and Riesmeyer (2021) in her doctoral work on teenage girls on social media, echoing findings that teenage girls are "self-presenting in a performative nature, whereby they are adhering to social norms while at the same time balancing their own sense of self and a desire for peer acceptance" (2022:7). Findings from other studies suggest that girls perform the best version of themselves—curating content that is perfectly imperfect, self-effacing, and vulnerable but also full of girl-coded embodied norms and desires surrounding beauty and body work, femininity, and hetero-sexiness (Chua and Chang 2016; Davis 2013; Gill 2021; Jong and Drummond 2016; Van Ouytsel et al. 2020; Weinstein 2018; Zillich and Riesmeyer 2021).

As *influencer* has become a more entrenched part of the American cultural lexicon, the drive toward creating authentic and relatable content has burgeoned (Bishop 2021). My interviewees certainly emphasize this ethos in their responses to the trend, indicating that girls should just be themselves, be real, and not ask whether they are pretty or ugly, especially on a public platform like YouTube, understood in terms of its potential and promise for visibility, dissolve between the public and private, and new imaginings of microcelebrity (Jerslev 2016; Hackley and Hackley 2015; Hearn 2008; Marwick 2013a). Concurrent with this push for authentic visibility, dominant narratives of girlhood and femininity still situate being pretty as of the utmost importance in achieving girlhood success. In her work on girls' visibility on social media and the Pretty or Ugly trend, Amanda Rossie writes, "Girls should be visible online but must not seem too desperate or straightforward while seeking approval" (2015:253). In other words, a girl is supposed to be pretty but not know or demonstrate awareness that she is pretty. Interviewees were clearly enacting a digital authenticity values system when they consumed videos from the trend; they do not like it when they sense that a video subject already knows she is pretty and is seeking validation from viewers regardless.

Twelve-year-old Maya, a quiet and bright Latina girl, is also suspicious of the girls in the videos:

> I feel like they're just showing off because it doesn't matter if you're pretty or ugly, you're just yourself. And that's all you're going to be. It doesn't matter if you want to copy someone else, or do you want to be your own self? I don't really care what other people tell me, if I am ugly or pretty. I'm just myself, and that's what I am.

Maya does not like how the girls seem to be showing off in the videos. The value of being real is prominent in Maya's response, as she separates herself from the Pretty or Ugly trend and articulates a strong feeling that appearance does not, or rather should not, matter. During our interview, I am struck by

Maya's sense of self, the certainty with which she asserts her take on the videos, and the emotionally charged response she has to them.

> KP: Can you tell me a little bit about what helps you feel that way? Just in terms of that confidence you have in being yourself?
> MAYA: Because I know that I have people that really like me, and I have someone to talk to. I know they like me for who I am. And I shouldn't change, even if like, another person brags about what they got or what they don't got. Because I got what I got, and that's all I got.

While still in this vein of discussion, I tell Maya that there are hundreds of thousands of these videos on YouTube of girls asking if they are pretty or ugly, and I ask her to give me her thoughts as to why that might be.

> MAYA: Well, maybe something is happening in school. Or they don't have no one to talk to. Because I have someone to talk to and I know who to trust. And they probably just want to show off, and check, "Oh yeah, I'm pretty. I know that already."
> KP: So, you think it's possible they already think or know they are pretty?
> MAYA: They know already. They just want to show off.

The theme of trust, or of not knowing who to trust, rings pertinent in relation to girls in the Pretty or Ugly trend seeking honest responses from viewers. Maya situates her own self-confidence and self-assurance within the discourse of trusting people and knowing that people like her for who she is. She has people she can talk to, and her perception of why tween girls might be posting these videos is that they might not have that same support structure. Maya's response is a departure from what I saw happening among tween girls making the Pretty or Ugly videos. Again and again, video scripts in the trend expose some sense of not trusting peer groups or friends to tell the truth. Tween girls are likely to not believe what their friends are saying because they position friends as having to lie and not being able to tell you the truth about what you look like. While my interviewees are suspicious of the tween girls making the videos, the tween girls in the videos are suspicious of their peer groups and relationships in physical space, not trusting them to be objective in their assessment of girls' appearances.

Girlhood studies and feminist scholars who theorize on the body and examine how ideal feminine beauty is perceived and felt among female adolescents indicate that girls are socialized to compare their bodies with one another, especially in relation to compulsory slenderness. Choukas-Bradley et al. write of this body of knowledge:

> Western cultural contexts socialize young women to over-value physical attractiveness; to devote substantial cognitive, emotional, and financial resources toward attempts to achieve cultural beauty standards; and to experience body image concerns, shame, and distress when these standards cannot be achieved (2022:684).

Use of "fat talk," which depends on displaying a certain degree of self-deprecation and humility, is identified as a way of building social relationships among girls (Nichter 2000; Reischer and Koo 2004). Girls test the waters with one another by using self-deprecating language about their own bodies to secure affirming responses. For example, if a tween girl says, "I feel fat today," she is likely to hear some version of "You are not fat!" in response.

In the case of the Pretty or Ugly trend, however, there is a rejection of assessment and affirmation by friends and peer groups, as the tween girls in the videos position their friends at school as being inauthentic, lying to them about how they really look. Tween girls seek objective assessments and affirmations from people they likely do not know but who feel like a community—the digital community or networked public of YouTube (Banet-Weiser 2014; boyd 2010; Burgess and Green 2018). Self-deprecation, negative self and body talk, and expressions of low self-esteem are heavily coded feminine and understood as a relational or common experience, referred to as "normative discontent" (Rodin, Silberstein, and Striegel-Moore 1984; Tiggemann and Wilson-Barrett 1998). If a girl is performing in a suitably humble or self-effacing way, she can be read by other tween girls as authentic and therefore worthy of a compassionate response. Within a digital postfeminist and consumer feminist culture, a tween girl must learn to expertly balance competing models of contemporary girlhood by being authentically themselves, which, within the logic of conventional femininity, means self-deprecating and self-ridiculing.

Pepper, a White ten-year-old, also finds the videos irksome, especially in how she reads the video subjects as specifically looking for attention from boys. Pepper says, "I think they're just trying to get more attention. And like, I think they're kind of getting, trying to get more attention, more followers, and then to be honest, I think they're just trying to get guys. And it's really kind of annoying." Similarly, Jessie, Black and age twelve, demonstrates clear distaste for the girls in the videos when she says, "Ugh, it is just girls trying to make them feel good about themselves, just so they can get boys' attention. I've rejected all the boys because I have to get my schoolwork done and bring up my grades."

When tween girls read other tween girls as attention seeking, there is significant disdain and importantly, an appreciable use of "Girl Power!" language to separate girls who are being themselves from girls who come across as fake or just showing off. Jessie takes this a step further by positioning schoolwork as more important than the conventional heteronormative tween girl goal of obtaining a boyfriend. There is clear, heightened dislike when interviewees understand girls in the videos as seeking attention from boys.

Relatedly, the tween girls in the Pretty or Ugly videos who wear makeup in their performances (Sally and Donna) are perceived as less authentic than the girl who does not wear makeup (Carlotta), which translates to more derision and the associated assumption that the girls wearing makeup are just seeking attention from boys. Tessy, a White ten-year-old, comments on this phenomenon in our conversation after watching the videos. She explains,

> Girls just want to be even prettier than they, I mean, so like if people say they're ugly, they are going to want to put on makeup. But if guys say they are pretty, they are still going to put on makeup to make them look even prettier. And if I was in one of those videos, I wouldn't put on any makeup. I would just be me.

These responses conflate wearing makeup with tween girl heteronormative performances and related outcomes of attracting the opposite sex. Girls in the videos who have more makeup on are seen as less real, and some of my interviewees see the use of makeup as a direct attempt to garner more attention from male viewers. This reaction seems explicitly age related in that they do not necessarily see makeup in and of itself as off-putting, rather seeing girls their own age engaging in practices conventionally meant for older teenagers and adult women as evidence of inauthenticity. This finding is especially interesting considering heightened recent attention in the last year around a beauty epidemic, even dubbed the "Sephora" epidemic, which traces a trend of tween girls "taking over" Sephora stores to consume beauty brands such as Drunk Elephant and Rare Beauty by Selena Gomez (Poggi 2024; Camero 2024).

Coming from a tween girl demographic, defined in part by a burgeoning interest in body and beauty work, celebrity, and pop cultural content beyond their years, this finding really surprised me—that tween girls react with disdain in seeing other tween girls wear makeup, notably while asking the pretty or ugly question on YouTube. My interviewees are critical of the girls in the videos wearing makeup, especially if they themselves articulate not being interested in or wearing makeup. The language of a "beauty epidemic" suggests that interest in makeup products is spreading and communicable. The fact that it went viral on TikTok in the early part of 2024 begs further inquiry, but I find it relatively unsurprising that tween girls' engagement with social media, brand culture, pop culture, and celebrity is translating into recognizable consumer interest in beauty products. Interest is not particularly new, but this level of broad visibility about it is.

Tween girls do not exist in a vacuum; they are influenced by the culture in which they live and must navigate the heteronormative expectations, both overt and covert, being mapped onto their bodies and associated gendered behaviors (Brumberg 1997; Thiel-Stern 2014). Girls are not supposed to come across as desperate or fake, yet they are often labeled as such when they emphasize their bodies in more sexualized ways, which, in the case of many of these videos, means wearing makeup to appear prettier or more attractive to the opposite sex.

Continued policing of the girls in the videos occurs among my interviewees as they internalize and reckon with the contradictions of protectionist discourses and "Girl Power!" ideologies in their responses to the trend. Social theorist Amy Shields Dobson offers a useful lens through which to understand these conflicting responses. She writes that "protectionist/moralist discourses have invoked fear about the damaging effects of cultural 'sexualization' on girls in particular, and have tended to associate any forms of so-called 'self-sexualization' with pathology and 'low-esteem' for girls" (2014: 99). Tween girls themselves project these notions of low esteem onto girls in the trend in convoluted and contradictory ways. The ultimate contradiction is that a girl can only demonstrate the power of being herself by performing disempowerment. By inciting "Girl Power!" rhetoric and distinguishing themselves from the girls in the Pretty or Ugly videos, my interviewees reinforce a model of digital authenticity that emphasizes girls being themselves, and any departure from that, whether it be makeup or an essence of "already knowing the answer" to the pretty or ugly question, is read as suspect or outright deceptive.

Practical Posting: Perceived Motivations for Making Pretty or Ugly Videos

Even while the girls I interviewed enact a digital authenticity values system in how they respond to the videos, there is a strong sense among them that posting a Pretty or Ugly video can be useful, even practical, especially if the video subject is experiencing bullying or teasing at school. Tween girls recognize the potential and practical motivations behind posting a Pretty or Ugly video, citing getting at the truth of the question as a meaningful reason to join the trend. From their perspectives, tween girls are motivated by gaining attention and approval (Farrell 2022; Yau and Reich 2019), but they can also see why girls want to get some kind of objective sense of honesty and truth about appearance from viewers on a public platform, especially a platform like YouTube. Girls do not want other girls to be fake or to already know that they are pretty, so performing humility and self-deprecation is an important part of tween girls recognizing other tween girls as authentic, as being themselves. How does this push for authenticity intersect with the perceived motivations of attention and affirmation? In my interpretation of girls' responses to the videos, it seems that this exposure of humility and vulnerability (e.g., getting bullied or picked on at school) balances out the quest for attention, so often met with contempt.

I meet Samantha, a funny and energetic ten-year-old White girl, at her after-school program on a bright October afternoon. We spend about thirty minutes talking about social media and how she makes YouTube videos with her sister—a humorous and playful stuffed animal puppet show series. Samantha really likes YouTube and spends most of her daily online time looking at videos or making videos to post to her channel. Our conversation eventually turns to the Pretty or Ugly trend. After showing her the sample of three videos, I ask Samantha to give her reactions.

> SAMANTHA: Well, I kind of get why they're asking that because I ask myself that sometimes. But I don't think they should be asking the world. They should just be asking themselves if they're pretty or ugly, and if they think they are ugly, then that's their opinion on whether they are or not. But they shouldn't be asking other people.
>
> KP: Why not?
>
> SAMANTHA: Well, there's like, a billion people on YouTube, so like, sometimes people are going to say mean stuff, and that will make them feel bad.

Several of my interviewees respond to the videos with protectionist discourse couched in "Girl Power!" language. My interviewee Dominique, a Black eleven-year-old, offers a response akin to Samantha's, saying,

> It's kind of hurtful for girls to do this because they don't have to care about other people's opinion. They should care about their own opinion. Because people can say stuff in the comments because they said, "Say whatever you want." [People] can say something very mean or they can say something nice. It's just a risk that you take.

Both Samantha and Dominique are concerned that the girls making the videos are going to be hurt by mean comments, so they see the public nature of the YouTube videos as potentially threatening to girls' well-being. Questions of how video subjects and tween girls in general engage with comments and responses to the digital girlhoods they create and what impact engagement has on mental health and self-esteem should be explored further. At the same time, Samantha and Dominique deliver these feelings via the use of "Girl Power!" ideology, for example, "They should just be asking themselves if they are pretty or ugly" and "They should care about their own opinion." The tension between protecting girls and empowering girls manifests in how tween girls view and scrutinize other tween girls online.

During our interview, I tell Samantha that there are a lot of videos like the three we just watched—thousands, even—and ask her what she thinks about there being so many girls asking this question on YouTube.

> SAMANTHA: I mean, I do kind of see why. Because these days people are like, being criticized a lot more than usual, I guess. And girls just want to know their truth, I guess. People are being mean to other people and teasing them and there are more ways to criticize them now.
>
> KP: Can you say more about there being more ways to criticize? What do you mean?
>
> SAMANTHA: Like, there's more than just, "You're ugly." Now, it can be like criticizing them like "They're rich and you're poor," or, uh, "Your hair is messed up and mine's all pretty," or "I go to the best stores, and you don't." That kind of thing.

Samantha recognizes that people are being teased about a lot of things, which translates to a lot of expectations: about how to look, where to consume, what products to consume, and how to maintain appearances. There are significant class connotations apparent in Samantha's acknowledgment of this issue. Girlhood success is certainly enmeshed with socioeconomic status. The ideal feminine is constructed as White, middle- to upper-class status, educated, able, and conventionally attractive and pretty (Bettie 2003; Currie, Kelly and Pomerantz 2009; Harris 2004a). Samantha relates this uptick in criticism and ways to be criticized to a rationale for posting a Pretty or Ugly video. Though she does not overtly support the trend, given her use of "Girl Power!" parlance and the protectionist approach in her initial response to the videos, she nonetheless shows understanding for why a tween girl might post a video to cushion criticism and learn the truth.

In my discussion with Brooklyn, a quiet and reserved thirteen-year-old Black girl, she similarly responds to the videos first with disapproval but then contradicts herself and suggests that she would also post one of these videos for certain reasons. After watching Sally's video, she says, "She shouldn't do that. Because for me to see that, it's like, I don't like it when people ask people if they are pretty or ugly. It's basically, it doesn't matter what other people say. If you think you're pretty, then you're pretty. It's your mind." The themes of individual empowerment and having a strong sense of self are prominent in tween girls' initial reactions to the trend, which tend to be negative. Most of my interviewees readily assert a "Girl Power!" mindset in their feelings about the videos. Most wonder why a girl would post a video like this online. However, the tension between empowerment and disempowerment tints many of their responses, and it becomes apparent that girls often offer certain disclaimers in how they situate themselves in alignment with or against the Pretty or Ugly trend. This most often has to do with whether the girl in the video is experiencing bullying or other negative treatment in physical spaces. When I ask Brooklyn if she would ever post a Pretty or Ugly video, in transparency, I expect her to say no. Instead, she says,

> I would post it if I got bullied . . . Because you would get picked on and stuff, and the bully would keep picking on you and then they'll probably convince you that you are ugly or whatever. Then you want to hear what other people say . . . [Some] people do it to see what the world thinks. So, yeah, I would do it to see what other people think.

My interviewee Noelle, also Black and thirteen years old, mirrors Brooklyn's response to the videos in terms of motivations for posting.

> NOELLE: [It's] probably because they feel insecure, and [posting on YouTube to get responses] make them feel good, and at least make them feel safe.
> KP: Feel safe?
> NOELLE: This way they can find out what people think of them, and that can really make them feel good. Then they just know.

Noelle brings up compelling ideas about safety and "just knowing," especially as these ideas suggest a decidedly static nature of whether someone is pretty or ugly, as though it is not a subjective interpretation and that girls can be safe in the knowledge of having the truth. In the preceding section on digital authenticity, my interviewee Maya indicates that she would not post a Pretty or Ugly video because she feels supported by a community of people who like her for who she is. Distrust of people in physical spaces in their ability to be objective or honest is a very prominent theme across the Pretty or Ugly videos, often qualified further by tween girls in the videos sharing their experiences of being bullied or receiving mixed messages at school, with some people telling them they are pretty and others telling them they are ugly.

My interviewees Brooklyn and Noelle bolster this connection between bullying, distrust of peer groups, and motivation for posting a video. A desire on the part of tween girls to know the truth, to feel safe, and to be affirmed in what they are becomes a catalyst for posting. The common tween girl questions, Who am I? and, What is my worth? have become remarkably conflated with another question: How do I look? While some girls in the trend present themselves as being "just curious" as to whether they are pretty or ugly, just as often, if not more so, tween girls in the trend frame the answer to the pretty or ugly question as something they "*need* to know." In this way, seeking responses and asking for comments from viewers can feel quite consequential for the girls participating in the trend.

Even though the small sample of videos I showed my interviewees does not directly employ the language of bullying, the videos made by Sally and Donna both give indication of receiving mixed messages from peers at school (Sally) or being picked on (Donna). During our discussions, I asked my interviewees why they think a tween girl might post a Pretty or Ugly video, and their responses almost all frame the motivations for posting as being a direct result of girls being targets for bullying behavior. Taylor, White and age ten, and Chrissy, Black and age thirteen, have comparable reactions to this question. Taylor suggests,

> Maybe they are being bullied or something and everybody is being like, "Oh, you're ugly, you're ugly, I don't like you," or something. And they just want to know. So, it's basically girls trying to say, "Am I pretty?" to prove them wrong.

Chrissy offers a similar response, saying,

> Well, because there's a lot of rude people at school just talking about them and calling them ugly. There's a lot of people that bully people and they think worse of theirself and it doesn't make them feel good, so they wanted to use other people's opinions.

Further examples of videos from the Pretty or Ugly trend exemplify this potential motivation of posting a video as a response to bullying behavior. Some tween girls put their bodies online in this format precisely because they are targets of bullying in offline spaces, so they seek affirmation, support, and clarity from alternative, digital communities. Given the sheer volume of these videos posted by tween girls, in becoming a trend, a virtual community was generated around tween girls asking this question online (Banet-Weiser 2014). In her work on young women, relationality, and digital culture on Tumblr, Akane Kanai writes,

Far from the narcissism often alleged in relation to young women's social media production (Tanner et al. 2013), this process of adaptation and re-interpretation was suggestive of desires to enact belonging through creating a shared space based around knowledges and feelings deemed to be "common" or even the "same" for unknown audiences (2019b:3).

A similar phenomenon of adaptation and reinterpretation of production in the Pretty or Ugly trend created shared space around a common question and concern relevant to the tween girl demographic in the United States.

Indicative of how news media, parents, and other adult authority figures have responded to the trend with sadness, outrage, and alarm is the copious concern surrounding an ongoing self-esteem crisis among tween girls, set against an ongoing emphasis on tween girls being self-empowered subjects within confidence culture (Orgad and Gill 2022). The onset of the trend came before YouTube was even a decade old; tween girls were already using YouTube in mass numbers for posting and consuming content. Today, YouTube is by far the most popular social media platform among children and teenagers (Nesi, Mann, and Robb 2023; Perez 2020; Vogels, Gelles-Watnick, and Massarat 2022). While so much of the content tween girls were and are watching on YouTube is geared toward beauty and body work, discipline and self-surveillance, and cis-hetero-femininity (makeup tutorials, beauty vlogging, fashion hauls, celebrity news, etc.)—content that readily positions tween girls as empowered subjects on the cusp of becoming adults (Banet-Weiser 2017)—I argue that how tween girls use YouTube to make Pretty or Ugly videos is set apart from other digital manifestations of tween girl confidence culture.

The vulnerability element of crowdsourcing for honest answers to the pretty or ugly question throws a major wrench into tween girls' positionality within broader discourses of gendered confidence culture, and all the while, the response to the trend falls back on simplistic dominant narratives of tween girls' body image crises. Lack of nuance clouds something compelling in the creation of these videos. Tween girls are looking in mirrors (webcams) when they make Pretty or Ugly videos, and thus they are necessarily looking at themselves in the production of these videos. Importantly, they are also making a conscious choice to post these videos as public content. The whole process—from choosing to create the video to making the video to posting the video—is crucial to consider in understanding intent and impact of the trend. There is more to explore here in relation to questions of tween girls' agency when they hit the publish button and establish themselves as a part of the Pretty or Ugly YouTube trend.

Luella makes her Pretty or Ugly video in her bedroom. She is White, twelve or thirteen years old, and wears a plain black T-shirt and no discernible makeup. She sits on her bed and glances back and forth, her eyes focused beyond the screen, not looking directly at the webcam. She brings her hand up to her face, tucks her hair behind her ear, and says quietly,

> Hi, everyone . . . [I] just wanted to do this video because I've been getting bullied a lot at school and they keep telling me that I'm ugly, not good enough, not smart enough and I want to know if that's true, because lots of people are saying that I'm ugly and it really hurts. And of course, my friends are saying you're pretty and all this type of stuff, and I'm like, no I'm not. And I just don't know who to believe.

Luella's Pretty or Ugly video script exemplifies several overarching themes from my analysis of the trend—bullying in physical space, desire for truth and honesty, distrust in friend group assessments of appearance, and confusion brought on by competing cultural models of girlhood. Luella demonstrates how the question of pretty or ugly is so often conflated with being "good enough." She expresses pain and hurt associated with being called ugly at school and indicates directly that she is making the video *because* she is being bullied. She makes the video to gain clarity and truth about her appearance, using the digital medium to garner alternative opinions and potential affirmations.

Jasmine's Pretty or Ugly video is yet another example of how a tween girl may take to social media to share her feelings about being bullied, and she notably uses her video to speak directly to the people who have been bullying her. Jasmine, who is White, approximately thirteen years old, with black framed glasses and blond-streaked hair that falls across her face, leans in close to the webcam and says,

> Okay, if you are watching this, I just have to get this out. Get it off my chest. Most of the guys in my middle school say I am a slut and a ho and a bitch and a whore. I am not any of those things. I have been bullied all my life. And say what you think about me but it's not going to hurt my feelings. And you guys, you know who you are, you guys have been calling me ugly. And it's not a fact if I'm ugly, it's your opinion if you think I'm ugly. So if you are watching this video, tell me at the bottom if you think I am ugly or pretty. And please don't write anything mean. I mean you can if you want to, but you know, I am kind of sick of everyone's crap. And I'm in eighth grade, okay? You guys act like you are in fourth. You have to start all of your drama and stuff.

Jasmine's video poignantly demonstrates the competing cultural models girls must navigate as part of their everyday lives in a postfeminist neoliberal digital landscape. Her ambivalence is obvious. She indicates that her feelings will not be hurt by what people think and asserts power and agency in her response, but she also asks the pretty or ugly question and implores people not to write mean comments. The way she talks to her viewers throughout the video ("you guys") evokes a sensibility that she is addressing people she knows, speaking to a known community. She makes a connection between people bullying her and a level of immaturity and how the people she interacts with in physical space are starting drama.

Jasmine uses the medium of a YouTube video not only to talk about how she is bullied but also to directly address those bullies, claim some power and control over how she represents herself (i.e., "I am not any of those things"), and make herself feel better (i.e., get this "off her chest"). Also notable is that her bullies are boys, targeting her using gendered and sexualized language of "slut," "bitch," and "whore." Though some scholarship suggests that the reclamation of these terms can serve as a form of resistance to gendered oppression and established norms of acceptable sexuality, especially for White women and girls (Sylwander and Gottzén 2020), this is not necessarily the reality for women and girls with historically marginalized identities, for whom this language may reify racialized violence and ableist logics.

Reclamation and resistance are possible primarily when girls and women use this language toward themselves or level it at other girls and women. All these terms, especially when exercised by boys and men, function historically and contemporarily to discipline girls and women across identity categories and threaten "ideal" femininity (Attwood 2007; Bailey et al. 2013; Jackson and Vares 2015; Kofoed and Ringrose 2012; Ringrose 2011; Willem, Araüna, and Tortajada 2019). Furthermore, contemporary confidence culture, postfeminist sensibility, and the surge of popular feminisms suggest that women can express themselves freely on social media in terms of sexual liberation and desires, yet women's bodies are far more likely to be policed and censored online than men's bodies. Discernible double standards and moralizing of women's embodied behaviors remain, especially around sex and sexualities. I address this enduring landscape further in the final chapter but suggest that continued exploration of gendered power imbalances in self-presentation on social media is necessary, though more is being done in this vein of inquiry (Farrell 2022; Mascheroni, Vincent, and Jimenez 2015; Ringrose et al. 2013). As Farrell explains, "the ideal of being postfeminism and the reality of girls' experiences are not aligned, as girls are being treated differently to boys in respect of their sexuality" (2022:26).

Annabelle is a very young, White tween girl, nine or ten years old at most. She is quiet and somber, positioning herself in her Pretty or Ugly video in such a way that much of her face and body are obscured by shadows and low light. She pleads in her video,

I want to know if I'm pretty or if you would go out with me, because everybody says that I'm ugly and I get bullied every single day. Every school I go to I get bullied, and I don't know why. And I always think it's cause of how I look and what I do . . . [I] want to know if I'm pretty. I want to know if you like me.

Annabelle is looking for answers. Through tears, she emphasizes how she is bullied at school and does not understand why. She indicates that she has gone to multiple schools, and her palpable emotion in the video suggests that she might experience social isolation from physical peer networks. She does not just ask her viewers to tell her if she is pretty; she also wants to know if they like her. Annabelle essentially equates being pretty with being good or liked and being worthy of male attention. She shares her pain and seeks affirmation about her appearance, about herself, on YouTube to mitigate impacts of the bullying she experiences in offline space.

Though I did not show my interviewees these Pretty or Ugly videos specifically, their reactions to the Pretty or Ugly videos we did watch together support the act of posting a video as a response to being bullied at school—a rational or reasonable avenue to seek out alternative modes of validation, affirmation, and clarity as a part of self- and social developmental processes. I think it is oversimplification to suggest that tween girls are *only* looking for objective truth or clarity surrounding appearance in these videos; there are obvious and significant stakes in girls being understood as pretty, as prettiness directly relates to and influences the power and aesthetic capital they have in their social worlds. They are also looking for affirmation and validation via participation in the trend, and this goal often marshals critical reactions toward them as attention seekers unless, as I outline through interviewee reactions to the trend, they suitably present themselves with humility and vulnerability.

I do not suggest that this desire for affirmation and validation necessarily or cleanly translates to crises of self-esteem and negative body image. Rather, I argue that the trend is indicative of a complex interplay between accommodation and resistance to enduring gendered protectionist discourses, dominant ideals of conventional feminine appearance, and "Girl Power!" ideology in a postfeminist/consumer feminist cultural context. In other words, the tween girls in the Pretty or Ugly trend are clearly struggling with a simultaneous desire and expectation to be seen within contemporary economies of visibility, gendered pressures associated with being pretty/attractive, and risks associated with making their bodies available to view in digitally networked publics. All the while, they want, in earnest, to self-represent in digital space as a way to navigate the frustrating and painful experiences they may be having in physical space as tween girls (Banet-Weiser 2018; boyd 2014; Farrell 2022; Shields Dobson 2015).

News media and popular media responses to the videos can hardly rationalize or critically examine why a tween girl would post a public YouTube video asking if she is pretty or ugly and subject herself to the possibility of getting trolled or cyberbullied. Many of the tween girls I interviewed feel this way, but they distinctly frame protectionist feelings within "Girl Power!" language ("She should only care what she thinks of herself"). Notably, however, tween girls also see practicality in posting as means of navigating and mitigating bullying behavior in physical spaces. Bullying then becomes not the presupposed outcome of posting a Pretty or Ugly video, as is the widely shared fear. Rather, for many tween girls, bullying is the impetus for posting one of these videos in the first place. Themes of homosocial bullying and girls' relational behavior and connections with one another on social media are explored in more depth in the next chapter.

Why Girls? Gendered Differences and the Pretty or Ugly Question

One of my longest interviews is with Noelle, an energetic and assertive thirteen-year-old Black girl. I show her the same sample of three Pretty or Ugly videos, and she has a lot to say in response. I interpret Noelle's reactions to the videos as a striking embodiment of the tension between empowerment and disempowerment discourses. Within a span of only a couple of minutes, Noelle articulates "Girl Power!" ideology, distances herself from the Pretty or Ugly trend, reasons bullying as a practical motivation for posting a Pretty or Ugly video, and finally, offers a soliloquy on gendered characteristics and what she sees as innate differences between girls and boys. We chat after watching the Pretty or Ugly video made by Donna.

> NOELLE: So, basically, what they're saying is, you want people to say you are pretty.
> KP: Why do you say that?
> NOELLE: Well, it's obvious that she wants people to tell her she is pretty. And she's also doing it to get "likes." She says that. She wants people to like the video if they think she is pretty and not like it if they don't.
> KP: Why do you think she wants to get likes?
> NOELLE: I mean, that's just like, she wants attention. She wants people to watch her videos so she can be seen.

KP: Do you think that is important for girls your age?

NOELLE: For some girls. But not for me.

KP: Why not?

NOELLE: Trust me. I get it. I mean, I have felt that from my experience. I have learned from my experience, from people calling me ugly and bullying me. I have learned that. But now I just stick up for myself and tell them I don't care what you think, that's your opinion . . . [When] I look at myself, I see a beautiful, bright girl that is sweet and kind.

KP: I think that's awesome that you feel that way about yourself . . . [So] why do you think there are so many girls asking if they are pretty or ugly on YouTube?

NOELLE: They are probably getting bullied at school, and they just want to know if they are pretty or ugly.

KP: Does that matter to girls, do you think?

NOELLE: Yes. Because the girls be the ones that are insecure and the boys, they don't be so insecure. They don't care what [other people] say. The next day they are like, "Oh okay, I don't care." But with girls it's different. Because we have more emotions, and we feel sad inside. We have a lot of different things that's going on with us and stuff. So, there are more girls than boys in [the Pretty or Ugly trend] because girls have more feelings and more emotions than boys do.

Amid contradictions manifest in cultural models of contemporary American girlhoods, tween girls must also navigate restrictive, reductive, and harmful heteronormative social forces that reify belief in a natural gender binary: the idea that there are certain traits or characteristics inborn to males and others to females (Butler 1990; Schilt and Westbrook 2009; West and Zimmerman 1987). Indeed, Noelle is not alone in her feelings. Tween girls articulate significant differences between boys and girls in how they use social media. At the root of these differences are elements of widely recognized and normalized socially constructed gendered scripts; girls are coded as more sensitive, more immature, needing more attention and assurance about how they look, while boys simply do not care. These beliefs permeate social structures and interactions between and among girls. Tween girls may be lambasting each other for overtly seeking attention from males (viewed as an undesirable quality and as inauthentic), but at the same time, they have been conditioned to compete with one another for male attention. This conditioning is not so easily cast aside.

The "Girl Power!" cultural model being sold to tween girls complexly intersects with continued insistence on compulsory heterosexuality and adherence to heteronormative behaviors and hegemonic gender roles. While academic research in girlhood studies, cultural studies, media studies, and other areas of inquiry is gaining ground on queering girlhoods, there is still a long way to go (Brickman 2019; Gonick 2006). Persistent contradictions in dominant narratives of girlhood result in toxic and backbiting behavior among tween girls, often undercutting rather than supporting one another (Mikel Brown 2003; Currie, Kelly, and Pomerantz 2007; Hadley 2003; Hadley 2004; Mcqueeney and Girgenti-Malone 2018; Simmons 2002). The Pretty or Ugly videos showcase that tween girls understand their worth as being attached (in no small part) to appearance and ability to attract the opposite sex. A tween girl's ability to attract the opposite sex is directly tied to her ability to embody and perform ideal femininity, which requires a skillful balance of concurrently performing empowerment and disempowerment.

During our discussions of the Pretty or Ugly videos, I asked my interviewees why there might be so many of these videos, but more than this, why tween girls specifically might be asking the pretty or ugly question on YouTube. Ariel, White and age ten, offers, "Boys don't really care. Usually, ladies want the man. So, men don't really care about whether they are like, ugly, or like, handsome." Ariel's answer suggests a learned knowledge of how gender roles and scripts work when it comes to caring about appearance, and it is directly related to cis-hetero attraction between men and women. She positions women in the role of seeking or desiring the man, so women take more care in their appearance because it allows them to attract male attention. Conversely, according to Ariel, boys do not care about what they look like because men do not care about what they look like.

I do not speak with tween boys in this study, so I will not project or purport to know how they feel about pressure and care surrounding appearance—even then, their answers would likely be delineated by a variety of factors surrounding different identities and embodiments. I hesitate to even situate a *tween* prefix in front of *boys* because the term is so heavily gendered feminine. Tween boys, to the extent that this demographic has been explored in academic inquiry, have also been framed as a consumer category, especially in relation to interests such as gaming, e-sports, and athletics (Cook and Kaiser 2004; Searle and Kafai 2012).

I consistently find that tween girls *perceive* boys their age as not caring about appearances. Tween girls caring about appearances is a recognized and accepted (though often lambasted and lamented) gendered script. Boys, on the other hand, may be coded as feminine if they come across as caring too much about appearance, which throws their proximity to hegemonic masculinity, and thus embodied privilege, into question. If they do emphasize care in appearance, it needs to be performed in conventionally masculine ways, such as building strength and cutting a more powerful and dominating image (Bordo 2000; Callen 2018; Connell and Messerschmidt 2005). The connection my interviewee Ariel makes between young people enacting gender roles that are projections of what they will experience as adults reinforces how these characteristics are learned and understood in the context of social media participation.

I ask Brooklyn the same question about why tween girls specifically are asking if they are pretty or ugly, and she has a quick response.

> BROOKLYN: I just don't think boys really care if they are ugly or not.
> KP: Do you think it is more important for girls?
> BROOKLYN: Uh, yes. (Rolls her eyes.)

I chuckle at her sardonic reaction, not least because I relate to her sentiment while reflecting on my own experiences as a tween girl navigating gender dynamics pertinent to expression, appearance, and performance. She conveys that the answer to my question is so obvious that the question did not even need to be asked.

> KP: Can you say more about why you think that?
> BROOKLYN: Well, like on social media, boys just use it to like, text and stuff, or post stuff about them doing basketball. It's all sports and stuff. But then girls post beauty stuff and like, "I just got my hair done." All this stuff. It's more about what they look like. They care more about that stuff.

Phenomena such as the Pretty or Ugly YouTube trend are normalized via conventional cultural understandings, dominant narratives, and central findings in the tradition of girlhood studies of girls' loss of self-esteem in the tween years, as well as societal emphasis on girls' appearances being attached to their overall value and worth (Brown and Gilligan 1992; Brumberg 1997; Orenstein 1994; Pipher 1994). These knowledges elucidate the mixed and contradictory popular and news media responses to the trend as both evidence of girls in crisis and normal adolescent female behavior. Because girls are seen differently from boys, see themselves as different from boys, and have different societal expectations attached to their bodies and behaviors, it follows that their use of social media, as an extension and reflection of their physical social world (boyd 2014; Palfrey and Gasser 2016), would also be markedly gendered, especially related to the politics of appearance.

Tania, a soft-spoken eleven-year-old Latina girl, emphasizes the importance of appearance for girls after watching the sample of Pretty or Ugly videos. She says,

I don't think dudes really care. I don't think they think it is such a big thing. They wouldn't post this stuff and share it to everybody. It's a bigger deal for [girls]. If the dudes asked, they would probably be a little embarrassed. The girls, they're just really confident, confident they wouldn't care what people say.

Tania's final statement comes across as a contradiction, but I think it necessarily speaks to the gender codes that structure a politics of caring about appearance. Tania indicates that boys might be embarrassed to ask the pretty or ugly question, which suggests that it is less acceptable for them to care in the first place and that they might be stigmatized for asking. They likely also would not use the language of *pretty* if they were to ask, as it has deep gendered connotations attached to girlhood and young womanhood. The idea of a boy being embarrassed to seek validation about appearance on a public platform resonates with constructions of hegemonic gender norms in American culture (Connell 1987; Connell and Messerschmidt 2005; West and Zimmerman 1987). Boys may feel insecure about their appearances, but that insecurity is perhaps less accepted, and certainly less expected, when compared with girls during adolescence.

Conversely, a tween girl can confidently ask the pretty or ugly question on a public digital platform, but her social position much more fervently obliges her to ask the question in the first place. Tania's response implies the high stakes that tween girls place in seeking validation and affirmation about their appearances, especially when it comes to the moral values system attached to being pretty or ugly and performing and achieving girlhood in successful ways (Currie, Kelly, and Pomerantz 2009; Harris 2004b). She positions it as being a "bigger deal" for girls.

My interview with Dominique reflects similar gendered differences in her response to the Pretty or Ugly trend. I ask Dominique what she thinks about tween girls asking the pretty or ugly question on YouTube. She lets out a quiet laugh.

DOMINIQUE: It's girls asking because, well, because boys don't care.
KP: Why don't they care?
DOMINIQUE: Because they're boys. They can come on however they want. They just really don't care. Like they don't care what other people think. They're like "Oh, it doesn't even matter." You can say whatever you want. Like I have a friend and he's like "Okay, let them talk and it doesn't even matter. Let them say what they want about me, I don't care." Because literally people talk about him a lot and he's just like "Okay, I don't care. It's not that big a

deal." And every day he still comes happy. Even though people are talking about him behind his back . . . [We] always be talking on the bus. We be laughing. We be cranking and laughing and he's always happy even though people always talk about him behind his back.

KP: Is it different for girls?

DOMINIQUE: Yeah, girls just care more about what people think. And as we get older, I think the older girls really, really care about what boys think.

KP: You think it's about boys?

DOMINIQUE: (laughs) Like they really, really care what boys think about them. And boys don't even care. They barely care. They're just like, "Do it, you're not bringing me down." But for some reason, it always brings girls down.

Dominique's response recalls what Noelle expresses about girls being more sensitive and insecure, and it speaks to some of the crucial themes that emerge within this research: how tween girls must strategically navigate strict expectations of body, beauty, and sexuality while demonstrating and embodying confidence, the compulsion for tween girls to seek attention from boys based on hegemonic cis-het gender norms and to compete for attention, and how tween girls identify with and engage with one another related to these things, often through gendered bullying behavior. This confluence is then reified within popular culture representations of teenage girls, which champion narratives of teenage girls relating to one another in toxic, nefarious, and aggressive ways (Mcqueeney and Girgenti-Malone 2018).

A sense of tween girls feeling isolated from one another comes to the fore within interviews, especially within this framework of gendered differences among boys and girls. Michelle demonstrates this feeling in her thought-provoking response to my question about why girls specifically are posting the videos.

MICHELLE: Because guys don't really care what anybody thinks of them.

KP: Why do you think that is?

MICHELLE: Because they have each other.

KP: Can you tell me what you mean?

MICHELLE: So, this actually leads to a good story. These two, well, there was one guy in my class, and a girl who was saying "You're ugly" to him and all this and this other guy walked up to the girl and said, "He's not ugly, he's my bro" or something, and like they have a bro code or whatever and they stick to it.

KP: Oh, I see. Do you think that is different for girls?

MICHELLE: Yeah.

KP: How so?

MICHELLE: Well, like, girls bully girls. And a girl might be bullying a boy, but I don't think the boy really cares, because it's a girl. Like, that doesn't matter as much because it's a girl.

Implicit in Michelle's explanation of how boys support one another and how girls bully one another is a gender hierarchy that positions boys as somehow more impervious to bullying behavior, especially if carried out by a girl against a boy, which reproduces gendered power dynamics that devalue femininity. According to Michelle, bullying matters more to boys if another boy is doing it. Michelle's statement renders girls powerless against boys in these circumstances and against the "bro code" boys have with each other.

Earlier in this chapter, bullying is teased out as a motivation for why a tween girl might post a Pretty or Ugly video. I see the logic and rationale behind this reasoning in how my interviewees react in similar ways to the question of the "why" behind the videos. What I am more surprised to find is how deeply gendered that "why" is, and how it results from complex and nuanced gendered expectations, politics of appearance, relational behaviors between boys and girls as well as girls and girls, and importantly, how girls are conditioned to respond differently than boys to what people think of them, especially when it comes to seeking attention and approval about appearance.

Conclusions: Conditioning Tween Girls

Well-trodden gendered scripts such as girls being more emotional and sensitive are prominent in how the girls I interviewed reflect on how and why girls use social media differently than boys. However, the tween girls I talked with are also quick to employ "Girl Power!" ideology in their responses to the Pretty or Ugly trend, shoring up a spirit and attitude of internal worth, self-empowerment, and confidence. The contradictions that underscore contemporary American girlhoods are evident in the Pretty or Ugly videos as well as the interview reactions to them. The Pretty or Ugly YouTube trend is a digital manifestation of clear tensions between empowerment and disempowerment in how tween girls perform their bodies and ask the pretty or ugly question. Interviewees' responses to the videos reveal these tensions as enacting a digital authenticity values system. Currie, Kelly, and Pomerantz write,

Girlhood as a culturally constructed "way of being" is regulated by conventions that girls must be pretty but not "self-absorbed" about their appearance; they must be attractive to boys but not seen to be too sexually "forward"; they must be noticed and liked by the "right people" but not be a social climber; independent but not a "loner"; and so on (2007:24).

These competing ideas are readily apparent in how tween girls respond to the videos and police the girls taking part in the trend.

Through all the contradiction, tween girls articulate a perhaps obvious but nevertheless affecting overarching motivation for why they participate on social media and what they like about it: they just want to feel connected to each other, and they do not want to miss out on what their friends are doing (Barry et al. 2017; Underwood and Ehrenreich 2017). Taking into consideration the gendered politics of visibility on social media and the digital authenticity values system explored in this chapter, the next chapter further investigates themes of bullying and friend connections prominent across my interview findings. Tween girls are conditioned to relate to one another in complex, often pernicious and harmful ways. Social media participation among tween girls facilitates a compelling spectrum of relational behavior, from girl-to-girl bullying to manufactured "drama" to homosocial support and affirmation. This behavioral spectrum is reflected in how tween girls characterize the depth and breadth of their experiences on social media and its importance to them—the "how" and "why" behind their prolific use of these platforms.

5

COMPLEX CONNECTIONS

Bullying, "Drama," and Friendship

"Girls depend on close, intimate friendships to get them
through life . . . [but] girls can be excruciatingly tough on
other girls. They can talk behind each other's backs, tease
and torture one another, police each other's clothing and
body size . . . and can promote a strict conformity to the
norms and rules of idealized femininity, threaten rejection
and exclusion, and reinforce gender and racial stereotypes."
—MIKEL BROWN 2003:109

"But this was girl world . . . [and] in girl world, all the
fighting had to be sneaky."
—*MEAN GIRLS* (2004)

R ecent years have seen heightened concern about young people and the
matter of safety on social media, and amended moral panics on the
part of adult stakeholders have reified a presiding public discourse of
social media as harmful to adolescents (Barry et al. 2017; Ging and O'Higgins
Norman 2016; Keles, McCrae, and Grealish 2020; Marciano et al. 2022). In
2023, U.S. Surgeon General Dr. Vivek Murthy issued an advisory surrounding the effects of social media on youth mental health (Office of the Surgeon
General 2023). Conceptualizing harm is complex and varied, ranging from
increased risk of mental health symptoms such as depression and anxiety to
issues with sleep, addiction to devices, feelings of isolation, and the potential
for cyberbullying. In this chapter, I focus on public perception of cyberbullying and whether perceptions of online aggression align with or diverge
from how tween girls themselves feel about bullying behavior online, as well
as their homosocial experiences with other girls online more broadly.

Both my YouTube textual analysis and my interviews with tween girls
revealed gendered (cyber)bullying as a prominent theme. Bullying was often
cited as a reason why a girl may post a Pretty or Ugly video, and at multiple
points during interviews, participants brought up the matter of girls bully-

ing girls, both online and offline. Tween girls have complicated feelings about social media; they see it as a place where bullying can and does occur, as well as a place that creates "drama." However, they also characterize social media as a site of respite from bullying (especially bullying in physical settings such as school) and negative gendered relational behavior, an important tool for maintaining strong connections with friends, and a means of seeking out and offering homosocial support and affirmation.

A central reason tween girls use social media is to remain in nearly constant connection with friends and peer groups—predominantly groups they know in physical spaces (Farrell 2022; Kennedy and Lynch 2016; Lenhart et al. 2015; Malvini Redden and Way 2017). The blurring of physical and digital worlds is more prominent than ever, as tween girls emphasize and engage in continual communication with one another via interactions on social media (boyd 2014; Buckingham 2013b; Palfrey and Gasser 2016). While these interactions are unequivocally recognized as important and a big part of how tween girls communicate with each other today, girls do not see them all as positive. Rather, tween girls may experience and enact a complex spectrum of relational behavior with one another that ranges from bullying to manufactured drama to homosocial affirmation and support, with social media being a medium for the production and mediation of all these things. My findings demonstrate that tween girls accentuate the role that connection with friends on social media plays in trumping negative aspects, mitigating gendered bullying behavior, and cultivating homosocial support.

Competing cultural models of girlhood manifest in this dynamic relational behavioral spectrum among tween girls. These models intersect with the dominant "mean girl" cultural paradigm that effectively naturalizes bullying among girls and assumes girls relate to and engage with one another in primarily toxic and virulent ways (Bailey and Steeves 2015; García-Gómez 2011; Hadley 2004; Hey 1997; Ringrose 2006; Simmons 2002). In the 2004 film *Mean Girls* (which has seen a contemporary resurgence in popularity, with a 2024 version of the film that is notably queerer in its imagining and design), girls undercut one another, scheme, behave passive aggressively, and generally treat each other duplicitously, all while seemingly acting as the best of friends ("Love ya!"). As the protagonist Cady Heron intimates, "[In] girl world, all the fighting had to be sneaky." The work of psychologist and educator Lyn Mikel Brown takes this culture of meanness to task in her 2003 book *Girlfighting: Betrayal and Rejection among Girls*, arguing that a "girls will be girls" explanation of this behavior is negligent; rather, a sexist society that cultivates competition among girls for male attention is a crucial culprit.

I examine how American society perceives the matter of bullying and cyberbullying among youth in specifically gendered ways and investigate how these perceptions converge with or diverge from how my interviewees articulate perceptions and experiences of girl versus girl bullying, both online and offline. I also consider how girls view social media as a catalyst for starting gendered drama (Marwick and boyd 2014; Remillard and Lamb 2005; Wiseman 2003) and how they navigate and manage drama in online spaces. Finally, I explore how tween girls highlight connections with friends as a primary motivation for being on social media, emphasizing the importance of homosocial support and affirmation in their online communities. While tween girls characterize social media as a site where bullying can and does occur, they also view social media as a crucial tool for maintaining continual connection with friends, especially in terms of seeking and offering homosocial support and affirmation.

Classic "Frenemies": Forging Toxic Girlhood Culture

American tween girlhoods are a series of contradictions and entanglements between empowerment and disempowerment girls grapple with across social arenas and institutions including school, media, peers, and the Internet. These entanglements are necessarily affixed to how tween girls relate to one another in their social worlds. Internalization of protectionist discourses and the innocence model may manifest in girls policing one another toward respectable girlhood femininities (especially surrounding sexuality, sexual expression, attention seeking, and associated behaviors), which are profoundly interwoven with White centered, cis-heteronormative, ableist, and classist notions of ideal girlhood (Bailey et al. 2013; Marwick and boyd 2014; Ringrose and Harvey 2015; Sylwander and Gottzén 2020). Meanwhile, the "Girl Power!" model encourages girls (via consumptive practice) to just "be themselves," fostering a digital values system that Others girls for coming across as fake, self-absorbed, or inauthentic.

Paradoxically, the "Girl Power!" model is defined by postfeminist neoliberal sensibilities of individualism, personal responsibility, and competition, which can result in heightened comparative practices between and among tween girls (Farrell 2022; Mascheroni and Ólafsson 2014; Mascheroni, Vincent, and Jimenez 2015; Gill and Orgad 2017; Ringrose et al. 2013). Engaging in processes of Othering, girls differentiate themselves from one another and establish in-groups and out-groups based on certain values and behaviors (García-Gómez 2018). Tween girls are encouraged to improve and empower themselves via body and beauty work and, in a heteronormative social structure, compare themselves to one another in the competitive pursuit of male sexual attention.

Tween girls must learn to navigate these entanglements as they are called to both protect themselves and make themselves visible in suitably feminine ways. Within the framework of the competing cultural models of "Girl

Power!" and innocent girls who need protection, tween girls must be up for a good time and appropriately modest or prudish. They must be pretty but not know it or outwardly advertise it. They must make themselves seen but in socially acceptable and respectable ways that align with ideal femininity (e.g., appear sexy but not slutty) (Miller 2016; Mishna et al. 2020; Payne 2010; Tanenbaum 2015). How girls attempt to meet the demands of these paradoxes, and interact with one another in the process, manifests in a complex spectrum of relational behavior that ranges from covert and overt girl-to-girl bullying to relational drama to friendships characterized by homosocial affirmation and support.

American society tends to view adolescent girlhood as a time marked by inherent toxicity between and among girls. Popular culture is stacked with examples of girls bullying girls, tween and teen girl drama, and girls being vicious and aggressive toward one another in blatant and arcane ways (e.g., *Mean Girls*, 2004; *The DUFF*, 2015; *To All the Boys I've Loved Before*, 2018; *Booksmart*, 2019). From popular films to reality television shows, the "mean girl" paradigm reigns as the titillating narrative that enthralls young people regardless of gender, serving as the script by which society expects girls to interact with each other (Mikel Brown 2003; Oppliger 2013; Ryalls 2012).

The difference between how boys bully one another and how girls bully one another is well established in academic literature, though more investigation into how bullying behavior maps onto social media use in gendered ways is necessary. Certainly, there needs to be increased inquiry and critique surrounding the boy/girl gender binary and the harm it perpetrates in reproducing patriarchal and heteronormative gendered scripts that render girls, gender diverse, and LGBTQIA+ youth more vulnerable to bullying victimization both online and offline (Birkett and Espelage 2015; Hlavka 2014; Nilan et al. 2015; Pascoe 2013). It is socially and culturally recognized that gender identity and expression inform how bullying and cyberbullying are carried out and experienced, with boys positioned as more likely to externalize aggression and engage in physical forms of bullying (Khan et al. 2020; Mishna et al. 2020; Viljoen et al. 2005) and girls more likely to bully via relational means (Khan et al. 2020; Mishna et al. 2020; Raskauskas and Stoltz 2007; Snell and Englander 2010; Viljoen, O'Neill, and Sidhu 2005). Mishna et al. succinctly note,

> Gendered and sexualized bullying is remarkably prevalent (Bailey and Steeves 2015; Coker, Austin, and Schuster 2010; Poteat, Mereish, Di-Giovanni, and Koenig 2011). Girls disproportionately experience gendered and sexualized bullying (Faucher, Cassidy, and Jackson 2015; Guerra, Williams, and Sadek 2011), boys commonly experience

homophobic bullying and bullying linked to masculine norms (Chiodo et al. 2009; McMaster, Connolly, Pepler, and Craig 2002), and gender and sexual minority youth frequently experience sexual harassment and verbal abuse related to their gender and/or sexuality (D'Augelli, Pilkington, and Hershberger 2002; Telljohann and Price 1993) (2020:407).

Girls, especially tween and teenage girls, have been socially constructed as all at once innately caring, nurturing, "sugar and spice and everything nice," and naturally mean or toxic to other girls. Citing the work of Emma Renold (2002, 2006) and Jessica Ringrose (2006), Ging and O'Higgins Norman suggest that "female aggression is understood, paradoxically, as the expression of that which is repressed within girls' 'innately' caring and nurturing personalities" (2016:808). Further, as Renolds's work helps illuminate, entrenched gendered and sexualized cultural discourses are how young people both create and traverse cis-het normative hierarchies and exchanges of power. The relational aggression girls may demonstrate toward one another is often discursively situated as an intrinsic symptom of being a girl rather than a product of the deep-seated cis-het normativity that structures girls' worlds (Ging and O'Higgins Norman 2016; Letendre 2007).

Girlhood studies scholarship largely agrees that female adolescence is a time in which girls question who they are, experience issues with low self-esteem, increasingly compare themselves to each other and adult women regarding appearance and presumed attractiveness to the male sex, and, because of these things, behave toward one another with heightened aggression. This aggression is expressed in culturally acceptable ways associated with girlhood such as gossip, insults, rumor spreading, withholding friendship, and character sabotage (Currie, Kelly, and Pomerantz 2007; Hadley 2003; Mikel Brown 2003; Simmons 2002; Simmons 2018), all of which reprint seamlessly onto social media platforms. Not unlike "boys will be boys" ideology, toxic girlhood and girls' bullying behavior are naturalized in American culture as a rite of passage:

> The rite-of-passage theory suggests several disturbing assumptions about girls. First, it implies that there is nothing we can do to prevent girls from behaving in these ways because it's in their developmental tea leaves to do it. . . . [Bullying] as a rite of passage also suggests that it is necessary and even positive that girls learn how to relate with each other in these ways. Rites of passage, after all, are rituals that mark the transformation of an individual from one status to another. So the rite of passage means that girls are becoming acquainted with

what is in store for them later as adults. Because adult women behave in this way, it means it's acceptable and must be prepared for (Simmons 2002:33).

Youth and gender development researcher Martha Hadley argues that adult response to girls' relational aggression generally manifests in one of two reactions: 1) So, what's new? or 2) How is this possible?! She writes that "the tension between these two reactions—familiarity and dismissive disdain versus disbelief and shock—is at the crux of the muddle surrounding aggression and girls" (2003:368). And, as Simmons (2002) points out in the rite-of-passage framework, common gendered bullying practices are recognizable in behaviors among adult women, including gossip, passive aggressiveness, the "silent treatment," and compulsion toward bodily comparison, fat talk (Nichter 2000), denigration, and normative discontent (Rodin, Silberstein, and Streigel-Moore 1984). Bullying and relational aggression, then, are not discrete or natural passing phases of adolescent life but rather highly gendered cultural norms that permeate multiple life stages for women and girls. For tween girls, this permeation is particularly salient, as they are navigating the liminal space between childhood and adulthood. Ging and O'Higgins Norman argue that "we cannot divorce girls' relationships or sense of self from a wider post-feminist culture, which continues to stereotype women as narcissistic, submissive, and emotionally complex and men as aggressive and emotionally straightforward" (2016:808).

Bullying among tween and teen girls most often centers on conditions such as sex (how much someone is having, whether too much or not enough), body image and appearance, and being perceived as inauthentic or fake (Miller 2016; Mishna et al. 2020; Payne 2010; Simmons 2018; Tanenbaum 2015). The vitriol and contempt that distinguish toxic girl culture in the United States and naturalize gendered bullying are rooted in deeply contradictory gendered expectations born out of a postfeminist, neoliberal, consumer-driven social structure and enduring cis-heteronormativity that positions girls in competition with one another for male attention and approval.

Defining Cyberbullying: The Problem with Gender

Bullying among youth has long been viewed as a normal part of growing up, one that may not merit much attention (Limber and Small 2003). Only within the past three decades or so has bullying become a national conversation, with more adult-centered emphasis on curtailing, preventing, and intervening in "school yard" bullying (Campbell 2005). In recent years, more societal consideration has been paid to cyberbullying, which, like traditional or conventional bullying, has multiple and sometimes contrasting definitions. Palfrey and Gasser define cyberbullying as "the intentional use of any digital medium, including text-messaging, email, and phone calls, to harm others" (2016:100). Hinduja and Patchin of the Cyberbullying Research Center define it as "willful and repeated harm inflicted through the use of computers, cell phones, and other electronic devices" (2015:11). Both define cyberbullying by intention or will to harm, but one definition suggests that the harm must be repeated or ongoing, while the other does not. For the purposes of this research, when analyzing how my interviewees think and talk about (cyber)bullying, I use Hinduja and Patchin's (2015) definition because it aligns with how the tween girls I spoke with gave meaning to bullying behaviors as persistent or ongoing.

As cyberbullying has gotten more headline attention over the last decade, a significant amount of academic and journalistic research has been conducted, but this emerging body of knowledge still has abiding gaps in understanding, mixed results, and discrepancies in research findings (Chang 2021; Ging and O'Higgins Norman 2016; Khan et al. 2020; Mishna et al. 2020; Wade and Beran 2011). There is no clear picture of how prevalent cyberbullying is, in part because research studies routinely define the matter in different ways (Sheanoda, Bussey, and Jones 2024). Cyberbullying research and findings are afflicted with inconsistencies; cyberbullying runs the perpetual risk of being either over- or underexaggerated in the public imagination, especially in terms of prevalence and overall potential impact on young people.

A 2016 national survey conducted by the Cyberbullying Research Center found that among a sample of 5,700 middle and high schoolers in the United States, approximately 34 percent indicated having been cyberbullied during their lifetime (Patchin and Hinduja 2016). A 2018 Pew Research report surveying 743 thirteen- to seventeen-year-olds indicates 59 percent of respondents have experienced cyberbullying, the most common reported forms being name calling and rumor spreading (Anderson 2018). Yet another recent report from the National Center for Education Statistics presents findings from a nationwide survey of twelve- to eighteen-year-olds indicating that 15 percent of those surveyed have experienced cyberbullying either online or via text messaging (Seldin and Yanez 2019). Some studies and reports treat cyberbullying as a separate entity from more traditional forms of bullying (Lenhart 2007; Waasdorp and Bradshaw 2015). Others conflate cyberbullying with traditional bullying and define them in similar terms, electing not to separate them in survey questions (Seldin and Yanez 2019). Still others conflate definitions of bullying and harassment, and there is ongoing debate as to whether definitions of bullying require a component of differential power between victim and perpetrator (Kowalski, Limber, and McCord 2019;

Smith et al. 2008; Ybarra 2012). Some report solely on respondent behavior and impacts of bullying, while others consider the specific mediums and platforms used to enact cyberbullying behavior (e.g., text messaging with cell phones versus social media).

There also remains a lack of qualitative research on cyberbullying, the majority of studies using quantitative methods and aggregate data from large-scale surveys (Snell and Englander 2010; Vandebosch and Van Cleemput 2008); there has been more attention paid to qualitative research design for studies on cyberbullying in recent years (Balt et al. 2023; Ranney et al. 2020; Sheanoda, Bussey, and Jones 2024). Operationalizing cyberbullying remains a persistent problem in the literature. Discrepancies matter when trying to understand the overall picture of youth bullying and cyberbullying behavior in terms of prevalence, impact, and potential intervention and prevention. Often, public response and policy response to bullying and cyberbullying are gender blind and do not address central social conditions that influence how bullying behavior is enacted and experienced (Marr and Duell 2020; Ringrose and Renold 2010). Crucial to note is that what researchers and adult authorities consider cyberbullying might not be what survey respondents consider cyberbullying. And, as I explore further here, tween girls themselves perceive cyberbullying and traditional bullying in multivalent and incongruent ways (boyd 2010; Ging and O'Higgins Norman 2016; Nilan et al. 2015; Ranney et al. 2020).

The line between cyberbullying and bullying in physical space is often blurred. Cyberbullying tends to overlap with more traditional or conventional modes of bullying (Waasdorp and Bradshaw 2015), and individuals who experience bullying at school are more likely to experience cyberbullying, often by the same perpetrators (Khan et al. 2020; Olweus and Limber 2018). As is the case with traditional bullying in physical spaces, cyberbullying most often occurs between friends and acquaintances. The highest likelihood of cyberbullying perpetration comes from close, personal connections: people who know each other and have relationships offline (Felmlee and Faris 2016). In the case of tween girls, bullying one another online largely happens among girls who know each other in physical peer networks.

Some studies suggest tween girls experience cyberbullying, both as victims and perpetrators, at higher rates than boys in the same age demographic (Felmlee and Faris 2016; Snell and Englander 2010; Thompson 2018). Other findings remain inconclusive surrounding how gender mediates cyberbullying behaviors and impacts (Ang and Goh 2010; Beckman, Hagquist, and Hellström 2013; Chang 2021). The data on whether gender is a mediating factor in how young people experience cyberbullying (whether as perpetrator, victim, or bystander) is messy and inconclusive, even when controlling for social media and Internet behavior.

Findings that show girls experiencing higher engagement with cyberbullying as both perpetrators and victims may be due in part to how cyberbullying often takes forms that match societal expectations and conditions of tween girls' bullying behavior; that is, online experiences reflect offline conditions of life (Nilan et al. 2015; Waasdorp and Bradshaw 2015). Girls are less likely to enact physical violence on one another and instead bully through language and various social strategies such as rumor spreading, gossip, purposeful exclusion, name calling, and passive aggressive comments. Digital platforms are uniquely suited for these types of behavior to translate from offline to online space. Additionally, as Mishna et al. write in their work on gender and cyberbullying, "gendered and sexualized bullying and cyberbullying have been defined variably, leading to a constellation of terms such as harassment, aggression, violence, and bullying to describe similar behaviors and experiences" (2020:404). Ranney et al. (2020) find that young people often reject the term *cyberbullying* as they associate it with suicidality and severe depression, instead favoring language such as *online conflict*, which they connect with a broader spectrum of peer violence and negative relational behavior, reflecting my own findings in how tween girls articulate different points on this spectrum.

The definition of these terms is necessarily political and shapes how we perceive and respond to behaviors. Ging and O'Higgins Norman suggest,

> Problems relating to the definition of cyberbullying arise not only from the lack of a comprehensive published instrument to measure cyberbullying (Wade and Beran 2011) but also from the fact that gender normativity imposes different standards on boys and girls regarding what constitutes acceptable—or even desirable—levels of aggression (2016:809).

How might incongruencies converge with or diverge from how tween girls perceive and experience girl-to-girl bullying behaviors?

Tween Girls' Perceptions of (Cyber)Bullying

Tween girls are socially conditioned to relate to one another in ways that naturalize and normalize toxic girlhood culture, and my research demonstrates that tween girls recognize, and sometimes experience, bullying by other tween girls offline and online. They understand and seem to accept that, just as in physical space, bullying can and does occur on social media.

Brooklyn, a thirteen-year-old Black girl, tells me during our conversation that she herself has not been bullied, but she has seen bullying happen at her school and at basketball practice. She says, "I've seen some people yelling at or picking on other people and stuff. And I'm just thinking, like, 'Why do they let that person run over them?' Why can't they just tell them to stop?" Brooklyn interprets putting a stop to bullying behavior in simple terms. I am a little surprised by Brooklyn's response because on first meeting her, she is quiet and reserved; now she speaks with the sort of self-assuredness that suggests she would respond with strength in such a situation, though she tells me she has not been the victim of bullying herself. She clearly advocates for people standing up for themselves in the face of being bullied. I am curious whether she sees cyberbullying in the same way.

> KP: Is bullying face-to-face like that different from how bullying happens online?
> BROOKLYN: Yeah. Bullying online, they can like, well, the bully can just keep calling you ugly and start some drama. Pretty much they're going to run over you online.
> KP: So, it can keep going online? Like, can bullying keep happening?
> BROOKLYN: Yeah. I think when it's happening like, right here, face-to-face, you can stop it easier.
> KP: Can you say more about that?
> BROOKLYN: Well, like you can just get in someone's face and tell them to stop. But you can't really do that online.

Twice during our discussion of bullying, Brooklyn uses the language of someone running someone over or being run over. There is a strong presence of differential power in how she talks about bullying (Smith et al. 2008; Ybarra 2012). Additionally, Khan et al. remark that "the online realm is perceived as anonymous and invisible, and it offers a lack of personal boundaries. Punishment, repercussions, and consequences of these actions are also thought of as slim in the virtual world" (2020:1). Brooklyn perceives the nature of online space as making it easier for bullies to exercise power and continue bullying behavior versus a face-to-face bullying interaction, where a victim might stand up to their bully in a more direct or assertive way.

Jazz, Black and ten years old, has an entirely different take on offline versus online bullying. About halfway through our interview, the topic turns to bullying. I ask her if she thinks bullying at school is different from bullying online. She responds,

> Bullying at school, I think that's more effective because it's happening in real life. Online, it's, I think it's less effective because you don't know who it is and then you would be like, "No way. I'm just going to make sure that this person doesn't text me anymore." Like, stay off your phone for a couple of days. Maybe they will stop texting you or whoever it is. When you're on social media, you can stop it, like,

by deleting it or something. But at school, you can't, unless the person, you know, the person agrees to stop it. But you could stop it really easy on social media . . . [I] think bullying at school is worse than bullying on social media.

Jazz and Brooklyn have seemingly diametrically opposed ideas of whether offline or online bullying is worse. While Brooklyn thinks face-to-face bullying can be more readily stopped, Jazz declares the opposite, suggesting that a victim of bullying on social media could simply delete the bullying content. In both cases, the girls see stopping the bullying behavior or responding to it in straightforward terms ("get in their face" or "delete it"), but the context of online versus offline colors their perceptions of bullying in markedly different ways.

Meanwhile, my interviewee Starr does not consider traditional bullying and cyberbullying to be notably different. Starr, a Black twelve-year-old, talks about bullying specifically among girls with noticeable exasperation. She audibly sighs before speaking.

STARR: So, if you have social media, you can get cyberbullied. But you can also get bullied in person. It makes no sense to me because they are both bullying, so either way you're going to get bullied basically. [It's] hurtful either way it goes.

KP: So, you don't see much difference between them?

STARR: No, it's like, not that different. It's still hurtful. Like, we watched a video of it happening, like, getting bullied online.

KP: Who is "we"? What was the video about?

STARR: My friends. We watched this video called "Cyberbully." And you could see how her face changes when people send her mean comments and stuff. And she never wanted to tell her mom or anything because she was scared. But like, I still don't think they are that different. You can still get bullied at school too.

KP: It was a girl being bullied? In the video?

STARR: Yeah, it's usually a girl.

Returning for a moment to my interviews with Jazz and Brooklyn, I am compelled by how, like Starr, they both emphasize the intragender nature of bullying behavior, as well as how girls are often represented as primary victims of bullying (Ging and O'Higgins Norman 2016; Mishna et al. 2020). I ask Brooklyn, "When you see bullying happening on social media or at practice, do you see girls bully each other? Or boys bullying girls? Or . . . ?" She matter-of-factly responds, "Oh, it's girls bullying girls. I think it is mainly what girls do."

Jazz reinforces Brooklyn's statement when she talks about the bullying she has seen at school and in movies.

JAZZ: Girls in particular are the ones getting bullied.
KP: Why do you think it is girls in particular getting bullied?
JAZZ: Well, if I've seen boys getting bullied it's for very different reasons than girls.
KP: What do you mean?
JAZZ: Like, in most movies you see a girl being bullied and then somebody trying to help her, but, and she ends up dying because she's getting bullied. That's when you know you have to stay away from those type of situations . . . [You] got to make sure that you safe and you all right. You can't just end your life.

While Brooklyn, Jazz, and Starr all have notably distinct perspectives on differences between cyberbullying and face-to-face bullying, and whether one kind of bullying is worse or more negatively impactful than another, all three of them emphasize a shared perspective on how girls are bullying girls. Furthermore, Jazz and Starr's responses imply that their perceptions and knowledge of cyberbullying specifically are gendered. Girls are the victims of bullying behavior in the cyberbullying films they have seen. Starr associates fear with cyberbullying, suggesting that the girl she saw in the video was afraid of what was happening to her, and fear precluded the girl from reaching out to a parental figure for help and support. Jazz instead draws focus to death as a possible outcome of being bullied, which speaks to how public media and news media often represent (cyber)bullying as dangerous and potentially deadly (Hinduja and Patchin 2018; Nilan et al. 2015).

I ask my interviewee Noelle, Black and age thirteen, if she can tell me about her thoughts on cyberbullying. She says,

It is when people bully you on a website, and they talk about you and give you threats, and they message you and be texting you on Facebook and Instagram and stuff and Snapchat, and they give you threats, and sometimes [the person] commits suicide . . . [And] it can also lead to school, and they end up being in a fight, and that person feels insecure, and they push over to the point where they are ready to kill themselves most of the time. I have seen a cyberbullying movie.

In Noelle's definition, the impacts of being cyberbullied translate from digital to physical space, carrying over to the school environment and again possibly resulting in death. The fact that multiple girls reference videos they have seen on the matter indicates that media representation plays an important role in how tween girls perceive bullying behavior and impacts as they intersect with gender.

Suicide is prominent in these representations, especially in recent productions such as the highly popular television show *13 Reasons Why* (2017), which focuses on sixteen-year-old high school student Hannah Baker committing suicide in response to a series of traumatic incidences including salacious rumors about her sexual behavior, stalking, and a violent sexual assault. Other recent films such as *Odd Girl Out* (2004), *Cyberbully* (2011), *Girl Fight* (2011), and *A Girl Like Her* (2015) further showcase narratives of tween and teen girls as the primary perpetrators and victims of offline and online bullying behavior.

The news media proliferates stories of cyberbullying and trumpets the issue, particularly if the cyberbullying case in question results in suicide. News reports of these stories do not necessarily encapsulate the complex realities of how bullying behavior interacts with suicidal ideation and intention, and this interaction is still being teased out in academic literature. Cases of suicide caused solely by cyberbullying are rare, with cases of bullying-related suicide most often involving multiple forms of bullying and mixtures of offline and online aggression as well as high incidence of preexisting mental health conditions such as anxiety and depression (Brailovskaia, Teismann, and Margraf 2018; LeBlanc 2012). The relationships between bullying and suicidal ideation, intention, attempt, and completion are complex and often mediated by an accumulation of existing factors such as depression, abuse, low self-esteem, isolation, poor school performance, and anxiety (Dorol-Beauroy-Eustache and Mishara 2021; Elgin 2014). In a recent Common Sense Media report on girls and social media, findings show that

> Girls with depressive symptoms were more likely to come across both harmful suicide-related content and helpful mental health content, compared to girls with no depressive symptoms. Girls with moderate to severe depressive symptoms were nearly three times as likely as girls without depressive symptoms to come across harmful suicide-related content across platforms at least monthly. . . . [Yet] girls with moderate to severe depressive symptoms were also roughly one and a half times as likely as girls without depressive symptoms to say they come across helpful mental health resources and content across platforms at least monthly (Nesi, Mann, and Robb 2023:10).

Positive mental health has been shown to mitigate negative potential impacts of cyberbullying victimization (Brailovskaia, Teismann, and Margraf 2018; Nesi, Mann, and Robb 2023), and a variety of support measures can help to shield young people from the harmful impacts of (cyber)bullying.

The matter of youth and suicidal ideation, attempt, and completion must be taken extremely seriously. An influx of research in recent years has brought further attention to the issue, with a new term, *cyberbullicide*, coined by Sameer Hinduja and Justin Patchin of the Cyberbullying Research Center. The term notes suicides "directly or indirectly influenced by online aggression or cyberbullying" (Schonfeld et al. 2023). The COVID-19 pandemic has brought further attention to the question of young people and mental well-being (CDC 2022; Marciano et al. 2022; Tanner and Wang 2023). Interventions, support, and resources must be channeled to demographics of young people who are most likely to experience social isolation, targeting, victimization, and discrimination and who have less access to crucial resources such as mental health care. Research has yet to bear out the weight and relationship of social media as a direct cause of suicidal ideation, intention, attempt, and completion (Bauman, Toomey, and Walker 2013; Hinduja and Patchin 2010; Kim and Leventhal 2008; Klomek, Sourander, and Gould 2010; LeBlanc 2012; Van Geel, Vedder, and Tanilon 2014), in particular as it relates to gender. In a systematic review of the literature on cyberbullying and suicidal and self-harm behaviors, Dorol-Beauroy-Eustache and Mishara report,

> Gender or sex was also investigated, but studies did not have consistent findings using different methodologies. Studies generally simply compared girls and boys. Some studies found no significant interaction with gender or sex (Arango et al. 2016; Bonanno and Hymel 2013; Fredrick and Demaray 2018; Lucas-Molina et al. 2018), whereas others found significant differences, often showing greater incidence in girls (victims and perpetrators) (Kim et al. 2019a, Kim et al. 2019b; Sampasa-Kanyinga et al. 2018; Strohacker et al. 2019; Wang et al. 2018; Williams et al. 2017; Zaborskis et al. 2019). All studies reported low to moderate effect sizes (2021:5).

Considering cyberbullying as a sole or direct cause of youth suicide is a crucial question, and further inquiry is necessary to critically conceptualize this relationship. Accounting for many variables is prudent, as arguing direct causation can cloud the complexity of how sociopolitical realities and identities influence how young people experience their digital worlds and strip back the positives of social media participation regarding self-presentation, agency, community building, and connection (Austin et al. 2020; Berger et al. 2022; boyd 2014; Erigha and Crooks-Allen 2020; Farrell 2022; Nesi, Mann, and Robb 2023; Kelly 2018). Evidence suggests that there is an increased possibility of suicidal ideation and intention when there are multiple and co-existing risk factors (Alavi et al. 2015; Elgin 2014). How cyberbullying cases are reported, in company with popular culture representations of the issue, can make it seem as though most teens and tweens experience cyberbullying as symptomatic of just being on social media (Briggs 2012; Ybarra 2012) and that girls are most at risk of its harmful impacts. More research is necessary to understand if and how gender differences result in higher risk and likelihood of suicidal ideation, intention, attempt, and completion in relation to cyberbullying.

The whole notion of cyberbullying, as both lexicon and area of inquiry, is still tremendously new, and thus it is difficult to draw any definitive conclusions on the impacts of cyberbullying. That said, because some existing literature on cyberbullying does suggest that tween and teen girls are at heightened risk of cyberbullying as both victims and perpetrators (Dorol-Beauroy-Eustache and Mishara 2021; Felmlee and Faris 2016; Mishna et al. 2020; Snell and Englander 2010), more needs to be done in terms of tailoring cyberbullying responses and interventions to the uniquely gendered ways tween girls relate to one another. I emphasize once again that dissonant definitions of cyberbullying may obscure the scope and prevalence of the issue and create more cause for alarm among parents and adult authorities than is perhaps productive, especially because girls themselves may not define or characterize (cyber)bullying in the same terms as academics, health professionals, and educators. Exchanges of drama among tween girls online can look remarkably like hallmarks of gendered bullying (gossip, rumors, exclusion, etc.) in the eyes of parents and concerned adults, but tween girls themselves do not see such exchanges that way. They frame drama as a highly routine part of their normal social media practices—but the tween girls I talked with are definitely "over" the drama.

Relational "Drama"

Bullying and drama are sometimes understood by adult authorities as being one and the same (boyd 2014; Mishna et al. 2020), but tween girls generally view them as distinct from one another. Bullying is roundly viewed as something uniquely harmful and persistent that can have very real and damaging impacts on its victims, including death. According to the tween girls I spoke with, bullying is not something that happens to everyone, but girls learn about it, see it happening in media and in their lives, and articulate specific outcomes of bullying that render it different from relational drama. Conversely, drama is framed by tween girls as a highly normative—albeit annoying and sometimes frustrating—part of everyday existence. Tween girls lament social media as a vehicle for creating and heightening drama in their lives.

As part of the dominant "mean girl" narrative, American society associates drama with tween and teen girls (boyd 2014; Marwick and boyd 2014). boyd defines *drama* "as various forms of interpersonal conflict that ranges from insignificant joking around to serious jealousy-driven relational aggression" (2014:137). Drama on social media is performance in that it takes place in front of some kind of audience, whether on a public platform or within a private group of friends. Both offline and online drama among girls may reproduce gendered norms and reinforce gender scripts of heteronormative girlhood, particularly surrounding seeking male attention and ascribing to certain standards of feminine appearance (Marwick and boyd 2014).

While drama often includes elements of what adults might see as gendered bullying behavior, such as gossip and rumor spreading, girls themselves see drama as set apart from bullying. This is not to suggest that experiences wrought by drama between and among girl peer groups are somehow devoid of harm but rather to emphasize that tween girls themselves make discursive distinctions between bullying and drama and how these things are felt in their lives. There may be some social desirability bias happening in girls' responses, as some research (and my own experience as a tween girl) demonstrates that tween girls may be drawn to drama as they test boundaries in their relationships, navigate friendships, and continue to self- and socially develop (Ging and O'Higgins Norman 2016; Hey 1997; Letendre 2007; Nilan et al. 2015; Shields Dobson 2011). It was interesting to find that the girls I interviewed actively express disdain for drama on social media while simultaneously viewing it as a normal part of how they relate to one another—a part they would ostensibly prefer to do without.

Dani, thirteen years old and Black, almost exclusively uses her social media accounts to interact with friends and family rather than post public content. She strongly dislikes the drama she sees on social media and explains how when drama happens among her friends online, she takes control of the content on her Facebook feed and deletes or blocks it.

> DANI: If it gets, like, that serious with this drama, I just delete it off my Facebook. Even if it's not me, even if I'm not involved in the drama, like if I just see it and it's just like, ugh, then I just block it off my Facebook because I don't like to see it.
> KP: So, drama is a bad part of being on Facebook?
> DANI: (laughs) Some people just don't know how to use social media correctly.
> KP: Can you tell me what you mean?
> DANI: Like, they use it in a negative way, you know? Like to start drama. Or they advertise drama when they shouldn't be like that. They should just talk to people or share what's going on in their lives.

Chrissy, also thirteen years old and Black, similarly points out how Facebook is a platform for drama.

CHRISSY: I'm so over the drama. Facebook is just too much drama, so I just stay on Snapchat basically, so I can just talk to my friends.

KP: Snapchat doesn't have as much drama?

CHRISSY: No, because like, you just send snaps to your friends, and they send them to you. It's more chill. I have more of my close friends on Snapchat.

KP: Does Facebook feel different? Like, in terms of talking and connecting with friends?

CHRISSY: It's just like, bigger. You see more of what people got going on. I like knowing what's going on, but I don't like the drama. I don't really like it too much, so I just stay off Facebook for the most part.

In addition to Dani and Chrissy, other girls suggest that social media can contribute to the escalation of drama among friends and peer groups. The social nature of the platforms creates more mechanisms for people to see drama-related content and potentially incites participation. When this happens, girls may remove themselves, emotionally and literally, from the platform in question or remove the content to disengage and indicate their desire to not get involved.

Drama comes up again in my interview with Jessie, a funny and animated Black twelve-year-old. When we talk about how people her age use social media, Jessie launches into a tirade about relationships, gender roles, and drama. She explains,

Oh my god, so, like, it seems like out of all the relationships in my school, they all just start drama. That's why I'm like, no I don't want to have a boyfriend, it's going to start drama. And I don't want to be in no drama. [Boys] at my age, they're really dumb. Like seriously. Like the girls will have all this drama with each other online about, "You stole my boyfriend, and I don't like you because you're ugly" and all this stuff, and I just think it's stupid. Nobody should be arguing over that. Nobody should have a boyfriend at this age because you still have a long ways to go in school and you should be getting your grades up instead of talking about having boyfriends and girlfriends. And that's just how I feel. I just had to let it out.

Jessie seems authentically irritated at how other girls behave and sets herself apart from them. The gendered nature of drama is evident in how she expresses her negative feelings about these interactions and performances. Girl-specific drama is related to stolen boyfriends and physical appearance, reinforcing a heteronormative script of tween girl concerns. Jessie indicates that she sees drama playing out among relationships at her school but that girls are engaging in relational drama in online space as well.

Jessie adopts a second-person point of view at the end of her rant, suggesting that girls her age should be focused on doing well in school rather than on what she sees as petty or frivolous concerns with boyfriends and looking a certain way. There is a "Girl Power!" ethos at play here. Jessie emphasizes doing well in school and effectively distances herself from girls who occupy themselves with things like boyfriends and physical appearance. Likewise, my interviewees respond to the Pretty or Ugly trend by setting themselves apart from producing that kind of appearance-related content on YouTube. They recognize attention seeking as a motivation behind why some tween girls post Pretty or Ugly videos and largely disassociate with such online behavior. Referencing a 2014 study by Brandes and Levin, Ging and O'Higgins Norman reflect on research findings with teenage girls on friendships and what it means to be a "good girlfriend," including, "knowing whom to friend, avoiding danger and conflict, showing support, and not posting too many trivial or attention-seeking statuses or selfies. There was consensus that if a girl posted sexual or self-indulgent photos of herself, she was asking for criticism" (2016:807). More needs to be explored about how tween girl relational drama as a gendered performance on social media (Butler 1990; Marwick and boyd 2014) intersects with social and cultural expectations that tween girls make themselves visible online.

There is a compelling connection between my interviewees' disdain for drama on social media and the digital authenticity values system they often leveled against the girls in the Pretty or Ugly videos. The feeling I got from my interviewees is that drama among friends and peers on social media is generally viewed as shallow, superficial, and attention seeking—not unlike how many of them describe the content of Pretty or Ugly videos. There is a clear value difference in how tween girls characterize posting publicly on social media about personal passions and interests, such as dance and art, and posting more gender laden and loaded content, such as dating and appearance, that could catalyze drama.

None of the girls I interviewed articulated an appreciation for or desire to be involved in drama. The girls position themselves as "above" the drama they see happening around them (again, at least in terms of what they shared with me). They see it as an expressly negative and unappealing aspect of participation on social media, but one set apart from bullying in the sense that it is less harmful and more routine, something that "comes with the territory" that they have come to expect as part of being active online. They find ways to remove themselves from drama by staying off certain platforms and by blocking or deleting drama-related content from their social media feeds. So while tween girls do define social media in part by the possibility of witnessing and experiencing social conflict either through (cyber)bullying or relational drama, neither of these aspects are enough to annul their desire to stay connected online. Indeed, the girls regularly verbalized connection with friends as their primary motivation for signing on.

Staying Connected: Friendship, Homosocial Support, and Affirmation

Returning once again to my interview with Jessie, I am compelled by how she levels a diatribe against girlhood drama on social media but a few moments later shares a story about posting her own appearance-related content, not publicly on YouTube but on Snapchat. She explains why one day she decided to post her own version of a Pretty or Ugly video to a small circle of friends on Snapchat:

> So on Snapchat I asked [my friends], Am I pretty or ugly? It made me feel good because most people said pretty, but I think I'm ugly. I don't know why I did it. I really don't. I just did it for the moment. I mostly have my friends on Snapchat, and I know they can tell the truth to me. [Because] at that time I was kind of in a dark place. And like, I don't know, I just had an emotional breakdown. Like sometimes I just cry and I don't know why. I think it might be about schoolwork, drama, because there's lots of things going on. But yeah, that's why. I just thought about it, and was like, well, maybe my friends can make me feel better, and they did.

Girlhood studies scholars widely acknowledge the gravity of connection, friendship, and support among tween girls during crucial developmental years (Hadley 2003; Hinkelman 2017; Mikel Brown 2003; Simmons 2002), and maintenance of friendships online relates to bolstering girls' self-esteem (Brandes and Levin 2014; Letendre 2007; Shields Dobson 2011; Wade 2019b). Even while recognizing gendered bullying behavior and relational drama as unfavorable aspects of social media participation, tween girls characterize social media as a place where they seek respite from bullying and drama, support and affirm one another, maintain strong connections to existing friends, and in some cases, make new friends.

Jessie frames her Pretty or Ugly snap as a spur of the moment decision but sees it as a mechanism for seeking social support from a group of friends on social media. She talks about the drama in her life, the stress associated with school, and how she turns to friends in moments when she is feeling downtrodden. Unlike how girls in the Pretty or Ugly YouTube trend position their friends in physical networks as untrustworthy in offering objective assessments of appearance, Jessie tells me she can trust her friends to tell her the truth. She explains to me how her friends always "like" each other's content on social media as a "way to support one another."

My conversation with Kendra stays with me long after our interview ends. I meet Kendra, Black and age thirteen, at her after-school program. It takes her a while to warm up in our conversation. She gets perceptibly closed off during our interview, and it is clear that she is uncomfortable talking about her experiences at school. Kendra tells me that every day at school, people call her ugly. She shifts around in her chair and looks down at her feet. When I prompt her to say more if she is willing, she gets quiet and indicates that she would rather not. She clearly experiences pain and discomfort connected to the politics of appearance and the social and cultural value associated with being a pretty girl. Importantly, Kendra indicates to me that her experiences of being bullied occur in the school environment, not on social media.

Kendra uses several social media platforms daily (Snapchat in particular) and articulates that her favorite thing about being online is being constantly connected to her friends. She tells me, "I can just be myself. I can send pictures and videos to my friends. We can just talk and be good. It just makes me feel good." Rather than experiencing social media as a medium of bullying, Kendra finds solace through participation in online space. Tween girls use social media to seek out connection and support one another—a crucial counterpoint to the "mean girls" narrative that dominates popular culture representations and public perceptions of tween girl relationships.

Throughout the interview process, girls often talked about or showed me how they interact with their friends on social media. Many literally pulled out their phones and showed me Snapchats, images, and short videos they sent to their friends. Some of the content was completely unintelligible to me, and when I asked about ask what it means, I got smiles and coy responses, suggesting that some girls create almost secret languages with friends on social media using emoji, images, hashtags, and special words to ensure group privacy and foster deeper connections (Thompson 2018). The content I did understand ranged from mundane, everyday exchanges to silly expressive content, gentle ribbing, and inside jokes to obvious affection, affirmation, and support.

Noelle, the thirteen-year-old Black girl who loves nail art, tells me that she, along with two of her friends who share her passion, exchange pictures nearly every day, showcasing their own nail art or expert nail art to one another for inspiration. She shows me a series of photos that she and her two friends shared in a Snapchat group.

KP: Is that something you like about social media? Being able to share pictures like this?

NOELLE: I love nails, like doing my nails in different ways. When I
send pictures of my nail art to [my friends], they support me, or
like, tell me what I need to do better. I do it for them too.
KP: What else do you do with friends on social media?
NOELLE: I can talk to my friends and ask them for advice, like whenever I need help and stuff. Maybe we can connect to hang out and
study and do stuff like that. And other than that, we just be talking to each other all the time. I'll be on Snapchat and just be on
my phone, chillin' with my friends.

Noelle uses social media to contact friends to study or spend time together,
but she also describes Snapchat almost as its own tangible space, as though
it is not entirely unlike being with her friends at school or the mall.

Snapchat operates in such a way that users can send and watch content
in real time (Common Sense Media 2024). If tween girls are on Snapchat with
a circle of friends at the same time, they can send short burst images and video
content to each other quickly enough for it to feel like a regular conversation
and continual flow of information. Noelle is not the only interviewee who
implies a fluidity between the physical and the digital—or the importance
of using social media to facilitate spending time with friends in physical space.
Toward the end of our interview, I ask Black twelve-year-old Starr to tell me
how she would feel if she did not have social media anymore. She responds,

Like if I didn't have social media, I don't know what I would do. Like,
you can't give someone something and then get too attached to it and
then take it from them. I think the best thing that's happened to me is
social media. Because before social media, I was always in the house
not doing anything. Now, I'm able to get out of the house on my own
and see friends, make plans, and we hang out and stuff like that.

Some of this feeling may be a function of Starr's age as she gets older and spends
more time independently with friends and peers with less adult supervision,
but the ability to contact friends to see them in physical space registers as an
important function of social media. Tween girls also suggest that they want
interactions to continue beyond the boundaries of the physical. As Sinead,
a ten-year-old Black girl, explains,

I think it's important for us to be on social media, because, like, what
if you're not able to see your friends? Then you can just talk to them
on social media and interact. Sometimes I feel like I need that, like,
just interacting with my friends and stuff. Social media is basically
like that, instead of talking in a person's face.

Like Sinead, other girls indicate a sense of concern that they would feel disconnected or isolated if they no longer were able to use social media to communicate with friends. Brooklyn, Black and thirteen years old, expresses,

> I honestly don't really know what I would do if I didn't have social media. Because I like to talk to my friends when I am not with them . . . [If] I didn't have social media, like, well, you wouldn't be able to communicate with your friends outside of school if you only see them in school and stuff.

Tween girls place significant emphasis on being able to stay in contact with one another outside of school and on knowing that they can reach out to one another if they need (Anderson and Jiang 2018a; Bulger et al. 2021; Vogels, Gelles-Watnick, and Massarat 2022; Wade 2019b).

Tania, a Latina eleven-year-old, tells me, "It's really important to me to be able to stay in contact with my friends. Like, it's literally the only reason I have [social media], is so I can talk to my friends." Research corroborates how young people think about social media as a critical platform for staying in touch with friends (boyd 2014; Lenhart et al. 2015; Thompson 2018). Not only do they use it to stay in regular contact with friends, but the user-generated nature of social media and the possibilities of self-representation online also help tween girls engage with one another's content in meaningful ways, allowing them to know more about what is going on in each other's lives and understand how each other are feeling.

Tween girls commonly reference using social media to prevent feelings of isolation and emphasize belonging. Though I did not address race in a critical way in my interview guide or explicitly bring up racial identity during the interview process, the majority of my interviewee participants identify as girls of color (thirteen Black girls and three Latina girls) and place clear significance on friend relationships and community in digital space (Barner 2016; Brown 2013; Erigha and Crooks-Allen 2020; Kelly 2018; Wade 2019b). The dynamics of Black girls' friendship communities on social media is an area ripe for continued sociological inquiry toward disrupting hegemonic constructions and limiting tropes that position Black girls as deviant or delinquent (Morris 2015; Wade 2019b). Both Jazz (Black and age ten) and Michelle (Black and age eleven) offer thought-provoking perspectives on why social media is important to them for feeling connected and supported. Jazz tells me,

> If I didn't have social media, I would feel left out, like I couldn't talk to my friends or nothing. I would feel lonely because I just couldn't do anything . . . [I] think that would get so many people frustrated

if [social media] just didn't exist. The world would be foggy, lonely. What's the word? Where it's so weird and dark and nothing's up there? I think it's called a desert? Yeah, like a desert.

Relatedly, Michelle explains how social media helped her adapt after a big transition in her life:

When we moved this summer, it was kind of a big move, and I didn't know anybody at my new school. And then I started to meet people and I started to have friends, and social media just came with it. And the people I knew last year, I didn't know what they were up to, and I got my new friends' social media, so now I can just snap everyone and do all of this on social media . . . [social] media helped me make friends, and my friends helped show me about social media.

Social theorist Barrie Thorne, in her work *Gender Play*, positions children as agential social actors, suggesting, "Children's interactions are not preparation for life; they are life itself" (1993:3). Social media participation, for American tween girls, is the stuff of life in contemporary society, and they use it to feel more connected to one another. There can be safety in how tween girls create homosocial spaces in the digital realm—where girls can be real, silly, sad, or struggling (Nesi, Mann, and Robb 2023; Tanner and Wang 2023). They can share experiences, publicly or privately, with friends and/or other tween girls via the digital girlhoods they produce and participate in. Social media can literally function as a safe space for girls, and tween girls consistently use their friend communities on social media to bolster and offer homosocial connection, support, and affirmation. Bullying at school or in other physical spaces may be an impetus for increased social media participation among girls, which can be a very positive thing. For some girls, connection on social media can make all the difference.

Conclusions: The Importance of Social Media in Maintaining Friendships

The spectrum of tween girls' relational behavior—from intragender bullying to relational drama to friendship, homosocial affirmation, and support—occurs across social media with nuance. Bullying remains a serious social issue that must be addressed with care as well as consideration of how youth define and characterize bullying experiences. Research is this area needs to continually center experiences and voices of young people, who may define bullying behavior and relational aggression in ways set apart from the adults who care about them. Without consistent definitions and measures of (cyber)bullying across inquiries, it is highly difficult to ascertain broader impacts and implications for American tween girls within different identity categories. Questions of gender and sociocultural conditioning of young people within a cis-hetero patriarchal system must be considered as we address (cyber)bullying as an ongoing social problem. As Ging and O'Higgins Norman argue,

> Understanding how girls (and boys) do friendship, conflict, and conflict resolution off- and online must therefore go beyond gender-blind anti-bullying policies and internet safety programmes, many of which reinforce the notion of female victim culpability (Shields Dobson and Ringrose 2016), to take into account the wider social and cultural contexts in which young people operate (Martha Hadley 2003) (2016:818).

Tween girls demonstrate that despite the possibility of having negative social experiences online, social media is unequivocally important in their lives, and they largely use it to stay connected with friends and find support within existing peer networks. Young people, especially those in the tween and teen categories, are likely to spend more time interacting with their friends than with their parents (Davis 2010; Palfrey and Gasser 2016), and they are doing a significant portion of this interacting in digital space. While realities of increased time online among youth may heighten feelings of concern among adults, my findings show that it is important for tween girls to make themselves visible on social media and interact with other girls in digital spaces, in no small part to maintain friendships, connections, and support one another.

6

Playing It Safe

Parents, Privacy, and "Appropriate Behavior"

"The way the media treats women on the edge of adulthood sets a standard for limiting their political and social power for the rest of their lives."

—Goetzman 2014:1

In May 2019, a New Jersey online newspaper reported a story about a twenty-three-year-old man who attempted to lure a twelve-year-old girl into a sexual encounter using social media with the headline "Family Catches Online Predator Trying to Lure 12-Year-Old N.J. Girl for Sex through Social Media, Prosecutor Says" (Attrino 2019). Using an undisclosed chatting application, the man contacted the girl, initiated sexually explicit dialogue, and suggested they meet in person. The family of the girl found out about the online communication and intervened, reporting the man to local authorities. Detectives from the county cybercrime unit traveled to Delaware armed with a search warrant and proceeded to arrest the man on counts of luring, attempted aggravated sexual assault, and attempted endangering the welfare of a child. In the article, the girl's role and perspective are not mentioned at all; we are given no sense of how she interacted with this person, whether she responded to advances, and how they made her feel. Although understandable that the article seeks to protect the privacy of a minor, the total lack of her presence in the story situates her without voice and the reader without context. The article is peppered with inserted clickbait links to other websites such as "Predators use these 19 apps to lure minors. This is what parents need to know."

A quick Internet search on safety tips for parents with kids and teens on social media reveals countless websites and blog posts about the subject, most of which emphasize a tone of concern or outright fear: "A Complete

Guide to Potentially Dangerous Apps All Parents Should Be Aware Of" (Rohm Nulsen 2023), "What Do Parents Need to Know about Teens and Sexting" (Ehrenreich 2020), "The Facts about Online Predators Every Parent Should Know" (Elgersma 2017), "11 Parental Control and Monitoring Apps We Recommend in 2023" (Modglin and McCormick 2024). These websites are geared toward parents gaining knowledge about how to mediate and potentially intervene in what their children are doing online. The headlines clearly capitalize on adult fears with language like *dangerous*, *predators*, and *need to know*.

What kind of information leads to and reproduces gendered moral panic about tween girls on social media? And how is that information being framed (Cohen 1972; Driscoll and Gregg 2008; Thiel-Stern 2014)? I contextualize the risks tween girls face online and investigate how popular and public media often capitalize on adult concerns by reiterating inflammatory narratives of the ways girls are perceived to be at risk in digital space, including fears brought to the fore by the Pretty or Ugly YouTube trend. Tween girls internalize parental concerns, and they emphasize the role parents play in establishing rules and determining what is appropriate and inappropriate online content. They also articulate how the age of a girl matters in characterizing and enacting safety on social media.

Tween girls demonstrated their digital knowledge to me in how they make accounts public versus private, how they follow someone or let someone follow them, and how they block someone from seeing their content. Incorporating what they learn from parents, peers, and through their own use, tween girls develop strategies of assessing risk and potential harm and learn to keenly balance the importance and desire to participate on social media and maintain visibility and self-presentation with keeping themselves safe in digital spaces.

In 1999, sociologist Barry Glassner published *The Culture of Fear*. In it, Glassner argues that it is not the actual level of risk and danger that has increased in the lives of Americans in recent decades but rather the perception of risk and danger. Glassner points out the strategic functions of social institutions and organizations that profit from the cultivation of fear in American society, using fear to regulate and control everyday social practices. Crucially, fear is not necessarily related to a direct level or possibility of a specific risk or threat; it is a product of perception and how the media shapes public perceptions of critical social and cultural issues (Glassner 1999). The overarching connotation from the web search on keeping children safe online is that parents fear (or should fear) their children putting themselves at risk of victimization by online predators. However, my findings show that tween girls largely use social media to connect with friends and engage their interests (Farrell 2022; Metcalfe and Llewellyn 2020; Ringrose et al. 2013). Parents play a significant role in helping tween girls learn not only to use and navigate these platforms but also to approach them with a level of fear and caution.

All twenty-six of my interviewees articulated having some form of parental involvement in their social media use, whether having discussions with parents about social media or parents looking over the content girls intend to post. More than this, I found that girls rely heavily on their parents and other adult figures they trust in mediating and navigating social media use and participation, particularly in a younger tween age bracket of ten or eleven years old. The girls in my study both outwardly articulate the paramount position of parents in managing social media participation and demonstrate an internalization of adult-centered fears and concerns about girls' visibility on social media.

The Goetzman (2014) quote that opens this chapter brings to the fore the harm that media does in impacting girls' social and political power when they are painted in stark terms and positioned solely as vulnerable subjects. Societally speaking, we cannot and should not paint online space as inherently bad, perilous, or hazardous for tween girls. Nor can or should we proclaim it as inherently good, safe, secure, and democratizing. Gendered power dynamics inform all our social structures, institutions, and relationships, including social media, which necessarily colors how adult stakeholders feel about girls participating on these platforms. That said, most American tween girls are now living their lives in a fluid exchange between offline and online interactions and experiences (Anderson 2018; Common Sense Media 2018; Vogels, Gelles-Watnick, and Massarat 2022), and that reality is unlikely to change. Social media participation and visibility have become normal parts of their daily lives. As today's tween girls grow up on social media, they learn how to balance the importance of online visibility (Banet-Weiser 2014; Harris 2004b; Shields Dobson 2015; Zaslow 2009) with understanding risks and internalizing fears associated with that visibility. Some of this balance they learn by themselves, some from their peers, and a noteworthy amount from their parents.

Contextualizing Risk: What Are the Fears?

Cassell and Cramer write in their 2008 article "High Tech or High Risk: Moral Panics about Girls Online,"

> There has been a recurring moral panic throughout history, not just over real threats of technological danger, but over the compromised virtue of young girls, parental loss of control in the face of a seductive machine, and the debate over whether women can ever be high-tech without being in jeopardy (2).

In recent years, networks have broadcast several news media and popular media stories of children, almost always girls, some as young as nine or ten, being sought out by Internet predators (Borrelli 2018; Nicolaou 2020; Russell 2019). Private information is collected and shared, and strange men target and solicit girls for online sex or explicit images and videos of their bodies. Stories warn against girls sharing too much information and suggest that the best defense for avoiding unwanted online attention is to not make oneself vulnerable in the first place, often trumpeting the tagline "What happens on the Internet, stays on the Internet." Parents of young girls, and young girls themselves, appear to be the most common intended audiences for these provocative stories, websites, and online organizations.

The story of the girl in New Jersey needs to be taken seriously. No child should ever be the victim of any form of violence, period. The way such stories are reported, however, can work to reproduce gendered moral panic that renders the perceived threat of online predators ultimately more substantial than is perhaps necessary or useful. When news media and online news outlets report about an online predator, whether at a local or national level, the story may proliferate, get shared on various sites and platforms, and become widely available to audiences via the information-passing nature of the Internet. Incendiary headlines become clickbait influencing more clicks and shares, and as the story becomes more popular, it plays more heavily on societal fears and perceptions. People are left feeling like these incidents are common. But the hyperbolized spin of these kinds of stories distracts from a crucial reality of child abuse and violence, whether sexual or otherwise; most of these occurrences are not taking place online but in private spaces such as homes, and they are most often perpetrated by a person a child knows and trusts (boyd 2014; Wolak, Finkelhor, and Mitchell 2008).

A study conducted by the Crimes against Children Research Center at the University of New Hampshire finds that reports of unwanted sexual solicitation online declined well over 50 percent between 2000 and 2010. This study analyzes findings from the 2010 Youth Internet Safety Study (YISS), which indicate that 9 percent of young people (ages ten to seventeen) had received unwanted sexual solicitation; importantly, these solicitations more often than not came from fellow youth, not adult strangers (Jones, Mitchell, and Finkelhor 2012). However, the image of the creepy adult man stalking young girls and asking for sexually explicit content on the Internet is powerful, and the possibility of sexual predation is regularly cited as a prominent concern adults have about tween girls online. There has been some indication that sexual predation increased during the COVID-19 pandemic; this needs to be addressed in earnest (Jakes 2021; O'Donnell 2021), yet the research is cloudy and indefinite. It is difficult to parse whether this increase is statistically significant given the overall increase of Internet use that occurred during the first year of the COVID pandemic.

Communications scholar Amy Hasinoff poignantly suggests that "girls' online media production and forms of digital authorship are seen as dangerous and irresponsible if they merely self-identify as young and female" (2013: 452). From a social constructionist lens that inscribes meanings to a gender binary, the discursive framing of being young and female online as inherently risky in the American adult social imaginary precludes any possibility of tween girls experiencing gender equity and empowerment in digital space. Tween girls across identity categories can be and are agential online and in their social media use (Barner 2016; Erigha and Crooks-Allen 2020; Farrell 2022; Preston-Sidler 2015; Shields Dobson 2015; Wade 2019a), and to suggest that girls are in danger by virtue of assigned sex category and age alone is to critically flatten the empowering and liberatory possibilities of digital space.

In addition to sexual predators, adults fear that strangers may gain and use private information against young girls. They worry about tween girls posting sexualized content and this content living on the Internet forever with the potential to damage or negatively impact girls' reputations and possibilities for future careers, relationships, opportunities, and so on (Albury and Crawford 2012; Ramirez et al. 2022; Sales 2016; Salter 2016). There is also a concern among older generations that young people today are addicted to social media and unable to connect in other more "meaningful" ways (boyd 2014). Furthermore, recent years have seen an uptick in inquiry into moral panic surrounding teen sexting, which is defined as sending sexually explicit photographs or messages via mobile phone (Best and Bogle 2014; Hasinoff 2013; Klettke, Hallford, and Mellor 2014; Lippman and Campbell 2014; Salter 2016). Because sexting occurs most often through private messaging and not via social media applications, it is not within the scope of my study, but it certainly demands further sociological inquiry as a recognized cultural phenomenon, prominent practice of tween and teen digital communication, and catalyst for contemporary gendered moral panics.

Some view tween girls as narcissists, obsessed with looking at themselves and taking selfies to post and publicize on social media (Boursier, Gioia, and Griffiths 2020; Dvorak 2013; Saeed 2017).

There also appears to have been a shift away from predominantly verbal interchange online to a visual and audio exchange online, which has been facilitated by technological advancements. Mobile devices now have state of the art cameras that are designed to take professional-quality photos and videos. Additionally, the nature of social media applications like Snapchat and Instagram provides the tools for image capture, manipulation, and display. This has led to a notion of the "female selfie"; that is, pictures of the self, which have been described at an individual level as a form of narcissism, with concerns being raised around the effects on self-esteem (Butkowski et al. 2020; Dobson 2012; Twenge 2010) (Farrell 2022:8).

Cyberbullying has emerged as a chief concern, as well as social media use among youth as a public health issue. These arguments frame social media as responsible for increases in depression and anxiety among American youth—and among girls in particular (Attia 2023; Keles, McCrae, and Grealish 2020; Kelly et al. 2018; Salomon 2017; Seabrook, Kern, and Rickard 2016; Twenge 2023; Vidal et al. 2020; Valkenburg, Meier, and Beyens 2022). This picture is more complex than it first appears. As mentioned in the previous chapter, cyberbullying is frequently defined in various ways, and its logics and legibility often differ between adults and youth. Much of the research on social media as correlated with depression and anxiety in adolescents is systematic review, cross-sectional methodology, and there remains a general dearth of qualitative inquiry and longitudinal study design to provide a fuller conception of the impacts and influence of social media on adolescents across and within identity categories. It is imperative that we address social media use with nuance and that tween girls are an active part of that conversation.

The Pretty or Ugly YouTube trend and responses to it showcase how a variety of adult-centered fears are brought to the fore as girls make their bodies available on a public digital platform. In 2012 and 2013, as the trend was growing and being picked up by the news media, reaction and commentary from adult journalists, health professionals, and a handful of academics emphasized how girls are already vulnerable in digital space and how the trend was only exacerbating the issue (Nurka 2014; Italie 2012). Importantly, the tween girls making videos as part of the trend were blamed for making themselves targets for not only predators and trolls but also public scrutiny and derision. The trend was largely considered evidence of a gendered crisis of self-esteem (Banet-Weiser 2014; Nurka 2014; Orenstein 1994).

These alarmist reactions are underscored by gendered narratives of girls as more vulnerable to criticism and more likely to seek and need approval from external sources. Some news stories labeled the trend "dangerous" and "disturbing" (Maldonado 2013; Quenqua 2014) while others called it "sad" or "heartbreaking" (Kennedy 2013; Waldman 2013). Emma Gray of *Huff-Post* wrote of the trend, "Given how fragile kids are at this stage, not to mention privacy concerns and the potential longevity of Internet exposure, bloggers have responded to these videos by urging YouTube to shut them down"

(2012:para. 7). The tween girls making Pretty or Ugly videos were labeled either profoundly insecure or overly confident and attention seeking and widely policed in the media and on social media itself. Many people took to YouTube filming videos in response to the trend to offer girls feedback—in other words, to demand "Where are the parents?" and paternalistically declare "You're too young to be on YouTube," challenging why the idea of asking the pretty or ugly question on YouTube would ever enter a girl's mind. Overall media response to the trend reinforces how tween girls are viewed in the collective American imagination in dualistic terms. They are either portrayed as innocent, naive, and vulnerable to predators or as risky, irresponsible, and reckless if they are thought to be creating and sharing any kind of content that could be interpreted as provocative or sexual (Draper 2012; Hasinoff 2015; Thiel-Stern 2009).

Much of the cultural narrative of girls in danger online comes from White middle-class media and a history of sexual hysteria surrounding girls' bodies (Brumberg 1997; Cassell and Cramer 2008; Driscoll 2002; Hasinoff 2015; Thiel-Stern 2014). The need to protect White, middle-class girls is an enduring cultural thrust that follows girls into whatever social and public spaces they occupy. Tween girls' position on the line between childhood and adulthood is precarious and characterized by dominant, contradictory ideas of girlhood that position tween girls as both innocent/virginal and hypersexual/sexually threatening. Perceptions of "bad girls" and "at-risk" girls (Harris 2004a) can be mapped onto specific kinds of social media content girls are posting, including any kind of content construed as sexualized (revealing clothing, body exposure, suggestive body movements, etc.) or especially personal, revealing details about home life, friends, or school (Shields Dobson 2015). Tween girls must be careful in how they present themselves online, and they learn a great deal about how to be careful by internalizing the media-driven moral panic and adult-centered fears described here.

Parental Involvement: Internalizing Fear, Following Rules

Part of learning to post content on personal social media profiles is understanding the potential consequences and risks associated with posting. Tween girls are learning the social media terrain via participation and recognizing norms of online behavior among their age demographic. All twenty-six of the tween girls I interviewed indicated some form of communication with their parents or other trusted adults about social media use, with most telling me that their parents set limits on use, establish rules about what kinds of content they can post, and engage them in regular discussions about social media. An attribute I found salient in all this, though, is that the tween girls I talked with used fear-centered and safety-centered language when discussing how their parents play a part in mediating their social media participation. My findings suggest that parents, whether consciously or not, engage fear and danger as primary socializers in teaching girls about social media and the constructed gendered risks associated with it.

Jazz is particularly adamant about girls needing to protect themselves online. It is clear she has internalized a lot of the adult-centered fear that informs feelings about tween girls on social media. In our interview, this talkative and lively ten-year-old Black girl takes on an advisory role. She uses a second-person point of view when discussing safety on social media. Toward the middle of our interview, Jazz starts talking about how social media can be both a good and a bad thing. She appreciates that she can communicate with friends and family from far away, but she has a lot of misgivings and negative feelings about social media. I ask her to tell me about them.

JAZZ: I'm not sure how to say this.

KP: That's okay. Take your time.

JAZZ: So, like if you wanted to text your friends and everything, somebody randomly could just like, text you, and then you would be like, "What is this?" You open the text and then maybe see something bad. That's when you know you have to delete it, but you can't. How are you going to talk to your friends?

KP: Do you mean like a stranger could text you something bad?

JAZZ: Yeah, they could like, hack you or something. Like, get that information on you.

KP: Oh, okay. I see. Can you say more about what something bad might be?

JAZZ: Like, maybe curse words. Or like they say weird things or want to friend you or meet you or something. So that's one of the problems with [social media].

KP: Has that ever happened to you?

JAZZ: No. But people my age, like, I think they should make sure that your mom, or like your parents, anybody who you live with, make sure that they are keeping an eye on what you're doing, like what you're listening to and what you are watching. Make sure that your parents are doing that, like, make sure they are keeping an eye on you because you need to be protected at all times, even if you are some girl, like cute and safe. It can never always be safe. It's not always safe so you need to make sure that you're in contact with your mom and everything. Make sure that your mom knows what you are doing so that you won't end up with all these things happening. You need to make sure that your parents are always with you, and you are in contact with them.

Jazz mentions getting hacked and getting her information stolen by a potential stranger online. She expresses concern about not being able to communicate with her friends if her information gets used, which I interpret as fear of not being able to use her phone in the same way if a stranger tries to contact her. She sees the possibility of getting hacked as interrupting her ability to communicate with her friends.

Jazz uses that second-person point of view and describes a girl being "cute and safe" and "needing to be protected at all times." She reiterates several times that young people need to make sure their parents are monitoring what they are doing online. Not only is the fear narrative internalized here, but it is notably gendered. She sees parents as playing a necessary role in ensuring the safety of young people, but she specifically emphasizes a girl who is "cute and safe," conjuring images of young, White girls in news media stories who have been targets of sexual predation. This speaks to the moral panic associated with the archetype of the young, middle-class, White "future" girl who needs protecting (Banet-Weiser 2018; Cassell and Cramer 2008; Harris 2004a; Thiel-Stern 2014).

Language surrounding parental involvement and social media safety punctuates multiple interviews. Tessy and I watch the sample of Pretty or Ugly YouTube videos together, and part of our discussion afterward focuses on risks associated with the YouTube platform specifically. I ask Tessy, ten years old and White, if she would ever post a Pretty or Ugly video.

TESSY: Oh no. I won't post a video [on YouTube] until I am, like, twenty.

KP: Until you're twenty? Can you tell me why?

TESSY: Because, well, I'm not allowed to yet. Because I'm extremely young, and people could say, like, bad things to me, and it would hurt my feelings really badly. So, my dad wants to protect me and keep me safe for a while.

In a departure from the other girls I interviewed, who tended to set themselves apart from the Pretty or Ugly trend using "Girl Power!" rhetoric, Tessy instead reasons that she would not post a Pretty or Ugly video because of her age and the possibility of receiving comments that could harm her or hurt her feelings. As outlined in Chapter Four, various interviewees responded to Pretty or Ugly videos using these same ideas from protectionist discourse but still Othered the girls in the YouTube trend by suggesting that girls should not be making themselves available online in that way and that they would never post a video like that. Tessy does not necessarily separate herself from the trend in such staunch terms. In this instance, safety goes beyond predatory behavior and the impression that girls are targets for sexualization (Cassell and Cramer 2008; Sales 2016; APA 2008). Rather, Tessy's dad wants to protect her from getting her feelings hurt, pointing to fears of social media as a space where cyberbullying and other forms of online harassment are a prevalent possibility. However, Tessy also continues to say,

> There are usually stalkers on YouTube that watch people. And like they know where people live, and they go up to houses and start things and stuff. And my dad doesn't want that to happen, and I don't like people like that. I don't like to socialize with people like that. And usually when somebody scares me, I accidentally, like, hurt them. Like one time my sister tried to scare me and then I kicked her on accident. (laughs) So yeah.

I chuckle in response because Tessy presents this anecdote in an amusing and lighthearted way, but underneath that lightheartedness is an internalized fear of online stalkers, and more than that, a sense that this kind of predatory behavior could happen to her. She references her dad again and his role in protecting her from being stalked. Tessy evokes mass media and news media images of stalkers who use online information to find out where people are in physical space.

Similarly, Pepper, another ten-year-old White girl, talks to me about how her dad intervenes in her social media use to maintain her safety. She explains,

> I use my dad's iPad, and every once in a while, he checks my social media, to check it for anything like, inappropriate. Which I don't do. I'm just saying. [But] I've had it happen a couple times, where people have tried to follow me and like, if I ask them who they are, they'll be like "You don't know me." And it's kind of creepy. But then I end up blocking them or something. And sometimes my dad steps in and helps me out with it.

While Pepper's dad does monitor her social media use to some degree, Pepper notably plays an active role in her own protection and privacy, blocking people she does not know and seeking support and assistance from a parent when she needs it.

One of the central aspects of the moral panic surrounding girls' bodies is that a boundary between digital and physical space will be crossed. In other words, a fear of online predators is that predatory behavior will not remain online, that girls will be tricked or persuaded into meeting up with strangers offline. Tween girls do not internalize this fear necessarily or solely based on personal experiences of solicitations for sexually explicit content from strangers online. Of the twenty-six girls I interviewed, Pepper is the only one who indicates having been directly contacted by a stranger in a way that made her feel unsafe (i.e., it was "creepy"). Rather, these internalized fears are based on parental concerns and magnified by mass media coverage of sexual predators and stalkers targeting young girls via social media and pushed into a feedback loop. The girls I interviewed internalized the image of the creepy adult man, and that fear makes its way into how they structure online behavior and control information output.

Other girls reveal how their parents have made them delete social media accounts over concerns of safety and well-being. Michelle and I have our conversation after school on a chilly, fall day. A quiet, eleven-year-old Black girl, Michelle fiddles with her phone on the table while we talk about social media. She is on Snapchat and has a Twitter account. I inquire about Facebook and Instagram, and she tells me she's not allowed to have an Instagram account yet.

KP: Why not?

MICHELLE: Well, I had an Instagram before. It was just when my mom found out, and then she made me get rid of it.

KP: Really? Did she tell you why she didn't want you to have it?

MICHELLE: Because my mom said that she read on the news website that a little girl who was on Instagram, well, she was my age, and she was kind of snapping pictures. And she was in Chicago, and um, this guy was following her that she didn't know, and random people can just follow you. So, he followed her. And then he tried to grab her and stuff, but everybody was watching and stuff, and the mom called the police and they got there and then they stopped him. So, my mom got kind of worried that I would start [Instagram], and like random people would start following me.

Here is a clear instance of adult-centered fears and moral panic directly influencing social media behaviors and practices for a tween girl. Michelle seems to conflate or at least not directly distinguish between the girl in the story being followed on social media and followed in physical space, further emphasizing the fear of predatory behavior crossing over from the digital to the physical. Michelle seems passive about her mom making her delete her Instagram account. She matter-of-factly shares with me how her mom saw the news story, catalyzing some alarm that a similar occurrence could happen to her daughter, and responded by prohibiting her from using Instagram. Based on what my interviewees told me, their parents communicate with them the potential dangers and risks associated with social media and pred-

146 / CHAPTER 6

atory behavior, often by giving examples from news media. Tween girls' use of language such as "stalkers," "creepy," "random people," and "it can never always be safe" reveals how parents internalize these fears, socializing their children to approach social media with a level of wariness and caution.

"We Would Never See Sunlight"

Another prominent concern that adults have about social media is based on how much time young people spend online (boyd 2014; Marciano et al. 2022; Palfrey and Gasser 2016) and the possibilities of getting addicted to these platforms, engaging in too much social comparison, and being exposed to negative content. I asked the girls during each of our interviews how much time they spend online each day, and there was quite the spectrum of responses, ranging anywhere from twenty minutes to an hour to several hours a day. Only two of my interview respondents, Kendra and Brooklyn, both thirteen years old, indicated to me that they are online for many hours a day (over five hours). Breanna, an eleven-year-old, spends approximately twenty minutes online each day, and the other twenty-three girls in my sample spend one to three hours online each day, with most of that time dedicated to checking or scrolling social media feeds, sharing content such as snaps, stories, or photos, and engaging with other content such as YouTube videos.

The social media behavior of parents and other family members such as older siblings often acts as the primary entry point for tween girls' learning how to use these platforms; knowing what kind of content they are allowed to look at, like, and post; and establishing limits on how often and for how long they are on social media daily (Berson, Berson, and Ferron 2002; Hiniker, Schoenebeck, and Kientz 2016; Kim and Davis 2017). Parents set limits on which platforms are allowed and which are not, along with how much time is reasonable to spend online each day. Parental involvement also involves enforcing boundaries on "too much screen time." Some girls indicate that their parents give them set times of day (e.g., after school and before dinner) or a specified amount of time on social media each day. For example, Pepper, White and ten years old, tells me, "For the school week, my parents let me have one hour a day [online], and on weekends, I get two hours [a day]."

I did discover, however, that a decent majority of the girls I interviewed can use their phones or devices whenever they want, provided they are not "in trouble" and meet their responsibilities at school and at home. In this sense, tween girls are granted some freedom to use social media at their discretion, but they are required to demonstrate their ability to balance multiple responsibilities and be "good" girls (Burke, Adamic, and Marciniak 2021; Kim and Davis 2017; Weisskirch 2011). Starr, a twelve-year-old Black girl, tells me, "I get to use [my phone] whenever I want, as long as I get stuff cleaned, and then

I'm good to have it." Ricki, Black and eleven years old, similarly explains, "I can use [my phone] as much as I want if I get my homework done and read for thirty minutes." I found that when girls do not have set limits on screen time, they often mimic parental behavior and establish limits for themselves in terms of signing off and "unplugging" from social media (Attia 2023; Doucleff 2023). Given my subject position as adult interviewer who did not grow up with social media, there may be some social desirability bias happening in girls' responses, but it appears that parental modeling of social media behavior can translate to self-governance and tween girls' ability to control limits of screen time for themselves.

Tween girls also mention adult-centered anxiety about Internet use and social media participation as potentially addicting or, at minimum, distracting. In my interview with Black thirteen-year-old Chrissy, she tells me her favorite things to do are play football and basketball and hang out with her friends.

> CHRISSY: Oh, and texting people. I love to text with people. (laughs)
> KP: Do you get to use your phone whenever you want to?
> CHRISSY: Yes. But I don't bring it to school. I can't use it during the day, so what's the point?
> KP: Wow, that seems like it would be hard to do.

My own biases and assumptions sneak in; I assume young people would likely feel incomplete without their phone nearby, as though they could not live without it, which, at this point, would be not unlike a significant portion of adults in the United States, 47 percent of whom reportedly "could not live without their smartphones" (Saad 2022; Sbarra, Briskin, and Slatcher 2019). Chrissy goes on to explain how she sees that people at school who break the rules and use their phones during class get distracted more easily and lose sight of other things they need to do, like schoolwork. I ask her, "Do you think people your age use social media too much?" Chrissy considers my question for a moment and seems stuck on her answer. Finally, she says,

> Well, I think it's appropriate for us to have social media, but I don't think, like, we should be on it so much and we should get out more because then we can get addicted and like, some people can't even last without their phone for a whole day and stuff like that. So like, I think we should be able to have them, but not be able to be on them all day because we would get stuck on that. We would never see sunlight.

I was truthfully taken aback to find that girls did not complain to me about parents setting time limits for being online. When parents set limits, the girls appear to generally accept them without much argument (at least, that is what they tell me). My surprise feels connected to how young people have been positioned in news and popular media in essentialist terms, as a generation addicted to social media and unable to disconnect from their devices (Baron 2018; Edwards and Fox 2018; Johnson 2016; Sales 2016). Chrissy iterates this idea in her response by criticizing people's inability to step away from their phones for a period of time and suggesting that, while social media use is appropriate for her age demographic, there needs to be balance in people "getting out more." Her comment about sunlight evokes an image of a young person in a dark room, face lit up by their phone, eyes glued to the screen—an image regularly employed by news media stories about the perils of Internet addiction.

Whether the cause of moral panic is sexual predation, stalkers, strangers, or social media addiction, tween girls demonstrate internalized fears via parental socialization and mediation in social media participation. This internalization translates to how girls characterize the seriousness of staying safe on social media, setting boundaries, and following parental rules and guidelines. Parental involvement is a crucial part of how girls understand and associate potential danger and risk with social media use. Age of a tween girl also matters in further internalizing parental concerns and shapes ideas about what is appropriate versus inappropriate content to engage with or post.

The Age Line and Appropriate versus Inappropriate Content

The Children's Online Privacy Protection Act (COPPA) was passed in 1998 and went into effect in 2000. The purpose of the act is to protect identifying information online of children under the age of thirteen; social media sites including YouTube, TikTok, Snapchat, Instagram, and Facebook must act in compliance with the law in not allowing users under thirteen years of age to set up accounts. For YouTube, tweens between the ages of thirteen and seventeen need permission to start their own channel. On TikTok, you must be sixteen years old to use any direct message feature (direct messaging is disabled for TikTok accounts whose owners are between thirteen and fifteen years old). That said, given that all my interviewees had at least two active social media accounts and most are younger than thirteen, there is little formal oversight into how social media platforms manage legislated age restrictions and usership.

New legislation was introduced by members of Congress in early 2024 to help combat concerns around the well-being of young people online. One bill is the bipartisan-proposed Kids Online Safety Act (KOSA), which puts forth several requests requiring "online services like social media networks, video game sites and messaging apps to take 'reasonable measures' to prevent harm—including online bullying, harassment, sexual exploitation, anorexia, self-harm and predatory marketing—to minors who used their platforms" (Singer 2024:para. 2). There is a notable amount of bipartisan support around many of these bills in Congress. At the time of writing, legislation has not been passed, and civil liberties groups have been active in arguing against said legislation, citing issues with free speech and freedom of expression and concerns over what it might mean in the culture wars, including restricting information on reproductive rights, gender identity, and LGBTQ+ social justice issues (Perrino and King 2023).

Notably, tweens have not been a central part of the conversation because nearly all large-scale data on social media participation is limited to teenagers thirteen years old and older. Even with COPPA as federal law, lack of oversight renders making an account on a social media site as simple as putting in a false birthday or using the information of an older friend or family member to make a profile (Aiken 2016). Some of the younger girls I interviewed appealed to a parent or older sibling to help them set up an account using their information, while others simply indicated a different birth date when activating their accounts. Only one of the girls indicated having a parent use the thirteen-and-older policy to rationalize keeping their daughter offline. Ariel, an inquisitive ten-year-old White girl, tells me, "Most sites you need to be thirteen . . . [and] basically, [my mom] doesn't want us to participate in, like, you-have-to-be-thirteen site things. I did that once and I got, like, really yelled at." But Ariel does have accounts on Snapchat, Musical.ly, and YouTube, which she uses regularly. Parental knowledge or enforcement of the thirteen-and-older policy seems limited, as all the girls, regardless of age, had Snapchat, and several of my younger interviewees also had Musical.ly or Instagram accounts.

Perhaps part of this incongruity of allowing participation on some sites but not others is because these platforms, especially Snapchat and Musical.ly (which became part of TikTok in a merger in 2018), are characterized or understood as more appropriate for younger users than platforms like Facebook and Instagram, given their structure and the kinds of content people share. Facebook is widely considered of less interest for tween users, and Instagram is geared toward visually oriented content such as selfies that may be seen by a larger audience. Snapchat is arguably more intimate, as tween girls mainly snap friends and peers they know in physical space and have established relationships with. Musical.ly is described with levity: it is silly, fun, and playful to post and share videos of singing and dancing. Though Musical.ly merged with TikTok in 2018, the app was already established as more attractive to users under the legal age limit of thirteen (De Leyn et al. 2021; Herrman 2016).

Another consideration could be parents attempting to balance the desire to protect their children with the reality that social media is a normal aspect of tween life. And insofar as there are potential risks associated with participating on social media, there are also potential consequences of barring girls from being active on it, including impacting their connections with their peer communities and excluding them from important processes of social and emotional development through these interactions (Farrell 2022; Gordon 2019; Nesi, Mann, and Robb 2023; Anderson and Jiang 2018b).

Compiled data from studies on social media usership and age demographics indicate that there are quite literally millions of American girls under the age of thirteen with personal accounts on social media platforms (Canales 2022; Beilinson 2014; Thorn Report 2021). I found that tween girls, via the internalization of parental concerns and the language of appropriateness, have developed a values system of certain social media platforms being more appropriate than others. This values system is necessarily adjudicated by age.

During the interview process, an age line became apparent in multiple ways conceptually and practically dividing twelve- and thirteen-year-olds from ten- and eleven-year-olds. Twelve- and thirteen-year-olds have a pronounced sense of authority about their social media use and a self-proclaimed maturity that younger girls do not have. They generally agree that a ten- or eleven-year-old would not, or should not, need to use social media yet. Many of the older girls feel that social media use is more relevant for them overall. Noelle, the smart and sharp-witted thirteen-year-old Black girl who loves nail art, has a lot to say about younger girls being on social media. She explains,

> I mean, young people, if you're like ten or twelve, you don't need social media because you're just on your cell phone and you really need to focus on school. Now if you are thirteen and up, yeah, of course you have social media. Yes, you are more mature . . . [Like] if you're ten, you don't need a website because when you get to thirteen, then you're going to have all the websites and you're going to be happy. Because if you get it now, then you're not going to be in contact with nobody, because they won't have it until they get older.

Noelle feels that younger tweens should be focusing their attention on school rather than on social media use, but for girls her age (thirteen and older), social media use is assumed. She says, "Of course you have social media" when you get to be her age. Her reasoning suggests that older tween girls (thirteen and up) have had more time to mature, are able to balance their responsibilities of school and social life more effectively, and are more likely to have friends and peers who are also using these platforms once they reach that age, making it more appropriate for them to have social media accounts.

Meanwhile, the younger tween girls I talked with were more likely to express ideas about appropriate versus inappropriate content and spoke often about the role of parents in overseeing their social media use. The younger girls also appeared more likely to be influenced by how their parents use social media and set time limits for themselves on social media compared to the older girls (Kim and Davis 2017; Kroger 2007; Weisskirch 2011). This difference may occur because peer influence is not as strong for younger girls at this point in adolescent development, and they place more emphasis on modeling parent behavior rather than peer behavior (Brown, Clasen, and Eicher 1986; Steinberg and Monahan 2007). A twelve- or thirteen-year-old girl may also be more apt to experience gender-related pressures and expectations associated with body and beauty, which may drive more of her behavior on social media in terms of time spent online, kinds of content engaged with (both looked at and posted), and appearance-related social capital (Farrell 2022; Nilan et al. 2015; Vandenbosch and Eggermont 2012).

My interviewee Ariel, White and ten years old, draws distinct lines along which social media sites are appropriate for which ages. She feels strongly that platforms such as Facebook and Instagram are only appropriate for girls thirteen and older. She says, "I'm too young for that stuff. I don't need it yet." Interestingly, Ariel qualifies her lack of participation on these platforms using the same language as Noelle when she talks about how younger girls have no need for social media accounts. Ariel sees Facebook and Instagram as the province of older tweens and teens, but she does have accounts on Snapchat, Musical.ly, and YouTube. Other girls in the younger interviewee age bracket reinforce Ariel's perspective. My interviewee Ricki, a White eleven-year-old, talks at length about how she uses Snapchat, but Instagram is not appropriate for her or people her age.

> RICKI: A lot of people at my school are on [social media], I know that. Because they're always talking about it at school, like all the sites they have that I don't. I only have Snapchat and Musical.ly and stuff. And they have like, Instagram. I don't have Instagram. But I don't want it because my mom said it's like Facebook, and Facebook is not appropriate.
>
> KP: Why are Facebook and Instagram not appropriate?
>
> RICKI: It's for like fourteen-year-olds. Teens can do it. But none of my friends are teens and a lot of them still have it. But I don't have it. It can be a bad thing. But it depends on how they use it, I guess. They can post very inappropriate pictures, or they can do good stuff.
>
> KP: What would be an example of something good that someone posts on Instagram?

RICKI: Like, they can draw pictures or post pictures of their families, and they just want a lot of people to see it and get a lot of likes.

KP: Would you like to have an Instagram account in the future?

RICKI: Yeah, one day when I'm older. But I think it looks kind of boring. (laughs) It's just people posting pictures. Right now, like, a couple of my friends wish they had it. But they got to, like . . . they got to earn it to have it.

KP: Can you share more about what you mean by "earn it"?

RICKI: Like you got to be good on social media. You got to show your mom that you are mature enough to have it.

"Earn it" is compelling word choice. Ricki's statement about earning the opportunity to be on Instagram by being mature and demonstrating maturity to a parent aligns with the maturity Noelle articulates. This maturity firmly relates to the ability to stay safe on social media, only post certain kinds of content, keep information private, and deal with the possibility of being confronted with inappropriate content. Inappropriate content, in the purview of the girls I talk with, includes curse words, sexual imagery and language, and depictions of violence. These are the kinds of online content tween girls actively work to avoid.

Jazz, Black and ten years old, has stalwart ideas of what people her age should or should not be looking at or engaging with on social media. She discusses how she is not supposed to look at inappropriate content and references videos with curse words in them specifically as what she understands to be inappropriate. She is cautious about social media and relies heavily on parental involvement and oversight to feel safe online. She says, "It's easy for you to find something that you're not supposed to see, like, you say, 'I know I'm not supposed to see that.' And then you just delete it because you think it's bad for you." Jazz tells me that she runs everything by her mom before she posts it on social media. She adopts an "I know it when I see it" approach to inappropriate content, which seems to be mainly learned through parental influence and regular discussions with her mom about how to avoid, delete, or block content she should not see.

Tessy, White and ten years old, buttresses this theme of age-related risk negotiation and navigating what is appropriate on social media and what is not. She uses Instagram, Snapchat, and Musical.ly but does not use Facebook or Twitter. In our interview, she says, "Children should not be able to have a Twitter or Facebook, definitely not Facebook . . . [Because] there's usually like inappropriate things on Facebook that children shouldn't see." Tessy and I talk about the differences between Snapchat, Instagram, Facebook, and Twitter. She has a hard time articulating exactly what makes one platform more appropriate for her age group versus another, only that Facebook and

Twitter are meant for adults and that Instagram is "okay, kind of." This suggests to me that some tween girls are adopting the language of appropriate and inappropriate mainly from how their parents talk to them about social media, but they are not necessarily able to qualify or define what it means for themselves. Further research on how parents perceive tween girls' social media participation is necessary to understand if and how dominant media narratives of social media as dangerous for girls influence how parents talk to their tween girls about it (Barry et al. 2017; Brito 2012; Coyne et al. 2017; De Leyn et al. 2021; Jeffery 2020; Savic, McCosker, and Geldens 2016; Shin, Huh, and Faber 2012).

In my interview with Dominique, a Black eleven-year-old, we talk a lot about what is appropriate for girls her age in terms of social media use. I ask her which social media sites she thinks are okay for people her age to use.

DOMINIQUE: Well, like Facebook, everyone wants it. Like all my friends and stuff, we want it. But it's too inappropriate so I don't like that people post inappropriate stuff.

KP: If you are comfortable with it, can you share an example of something that might be inappropriate for someone your age to see?

DOMINIQUE: My friend has [a Facebook account] and she was showing them and she saw something very inappropriate. It was like a picture of a boy and a girl, and it was very inappropriate. And that's why I told her she should get off of it. [And] it really depends on who your friends are too.

KP: Can you tell me more about that?

DOMINIQUE: On Facebook. Like, yeah, I just think it's inappropriate. I'm not allowed to have one because of the inappropriate stuff. Like, at first, I used to not understand why I can't, but now it's just like, okay, I can't have one, so.

KP: Do you think you might want [a Facebook account] when you get a bit older?

DOMINIQUE: Yeah. Depending on who's my friends. I don't want like random people, like people I don't know and stuff like that . . . [People] can probably like hack you down or something like that. And I think it's unsafe. So, I don't really want to be friends with anyone I don't know because it's very unsafe . . . [I'd] rather just be friends with my friends.

Dominique's comment about strangers "hacking you down" conjures fears of how private or personal information can be lifted, stolen, and/or circulated in online spaces. She consistently uses the words *inappropriate* and *unsafe* but again has a somewhat difficult time defining or explaining what she means.

She references an image she saw on a friend's Facebook account of a boy and a girl, but even with gentle prompting, she does not go into more detail.

As both Tessy and Dominique demonstrate, tween girls assign a values system to different platforms based on what they have been taught is appropriate and inappropriate. Snapchat and Musical.ly are the most popular among all the girls, and most of my participants have accounts on both. Instagram use tends to be more delineated by age, with most twelve- and thirteen-year-olds indicating they have accounts on the platform and most of the younger girls not using it, whether by choice or because they are not allowed to due to parents' views on it being inappropriate. Facebook is viewed by the younger girls as inappropriate, so there is more caution exercised toward this platform, and while some of the younger girls may have a desire to have an account on Facebook, they also generally accept that they are too young.

The older tween girls have Facebook accounts but have less desire to use Facebook primarily because they view it as generating drama or as an outdated form of social media meant for adults. Recent survey data backs this up, suggesting interest in Facebook among Gen Zers has fallen drastically in the last decade (Vogels and Gelles-Watnick 2023; Vogels, Gelles-Watnick, and Massarat 2022). Noelle, Black and thirteen years old, refers to Facebook during our interview as "social media for old people," to which I cannot help but laugh. The popularity of platforms shifts and evolves over time. In the early 2000s, Myspace was among the most popular social media sites, and it is now essentially obsolete. Facebook remains popular with American adults, but it is viewed by younger tweens and teens as one of the least desirable social media platforms in terms of routine participation, dropping from a 71 percent usage rate in 2014/2015 to a reported 32 percent usage rate among surveyed thirteen- to seventeen-year-olds (Vogels and Gelles-Watnick 2023). Aggregate data for the tween age category for social media use across platforms remains elusive.

In various ways, age mediates and facilitates social media experiences for tween girls, connecting with how tween girls internalize parental concerns, as well as what parents teach their children directly about identifying appropriate versus inappropriate content and which platforms are acceptable for girls to use. Younger tween girls are more apt to follow parental guidelines and articulate strong feelings about certain social media platforms being more inappropriate than others, while older tween girls embody and emphasize maturity and an understanding that social media participation is more important and expected for people their age. Girls learn how to use social media from parents, other family members, and peers, but they further their knowledge through participation as they navigate risks associated with visibility, prioritize privacy, and maintain personal safety and boundaries in digital space.

Prioritizing Privacy

Scout is a huge personality in a small package. This ten-year-old White girl is one of my most enthusiastic interview participants. When I arrive at the after-school site on a late October day and greet the group of girls sitting down for a snack, Scout immediately pushes back from the table and demands to be the first interview of the day. Among the twenty-six girls I interview, Scout stands out as exceptionally spirited and remarkably self-aware. She eagerly informs me of a variety of things in quick succession. She just got her own phone; she loves playing games online, going to her grandmother's house, and Snapchatting with family and friends from her class. Her demeanor changes when I bring up Facebook. While Scout is very comfortable using Snapchat, she is wary of other social media sites, Facebook among them. She tells me a story about how her sister, a twelve-year-old, posted an image of Scout on Facebook when she was younger. Scout articulates some anger and frustration about this.

> SCOUT: She needs my permission to do that.
>
> KP: Can you tell me why it made you angry that she did that?
>
> SCOUT: [Facebook] can be bad because there isn't very much privacy.
>
> KP: Does that bother you?
>
> SCOUT: I think it can be a bad thing. You can go on [social media] and people can look at you, and maybe they know you from school. You might do something bad on it. And they could judge you for it.
>
> KP: Can you tell me what something bad might be?
>
> SCOUT: Like, if you make a singing video and they've never heard you singing, they could think it's really weird. They could call you names and stuff like that.
>
> KP: Oh, I see. Do you think that happens a lot on social media?
>
> SCOUT: Yeah, it can. So like, you know the videos you showed me?
>
> KP: The Pretty or Ugly videos?
>
> SCOUT: Yes. Those girls, it's just, maybe they think they are pretty enough to do that. And they are, they are. I'm not saying they're ugly. But they can get judged, you know? People can say mean things about them.
>
> KP: You don't like that about social media? That people can be mean to other people?
>
> SCOUT: I just don't think it's necessary, to like, post your face on like Instagram where everybody in the world can see it . . . [I] like to keep my face to my family and my friends.

My interview findings track with recent scholarship exploring perceptions of privacy among tweens and the importance of privacy while engaging in self-representation practices on social media (Balleys and Coll 2017; Davis and Carrie 2013; De Leyn et al. 2019; De Leyn et al. 2021; Jeffery 2020). How young people interact in the creation and navigation of digitally networked publics catalyzes concern, especially from parents and adult stakeholders, who may presume reckless online behavior among youth, particularly around disclosing personal information (boyd 2007; De Leyn et al. 2019; De Leyn et al. 2021; De Wolf and Joye 2019; Marwick 2008). Parental concern itself signals an ongoing preoccupation with girls' bodies, appearances, and digital socialization, none of which exist in a social media vacuum or separate from historical meaning and political systems. Principles of protectionism, which have over time constructed ideas about tween girls' bodies in this liminal space between childhood and adulthood, are deeply entrenched in centuries-old, cis-heteronormatively structured familial instinct (especially on the part of fathers) to protect girl children from boys and men.

Throughout our conversation, Scout prioritizes privacy on social media and makes values-based statements about posting pictures and videos to public sites. Yet rather than emphasizing disquiet about sexual predators and strangers online, as tend to be of central concern to adults, Scout seems much more attuned to how people at school might be able to look at what she posts and judge or make fun of her based on that content, which speaks to some of the aforementioned pressures girls feel about making themselves visible in certain ways (Banet-Weiser 2014; Butkowski et al. 2020; Elias and Gill 2018; Fardouly, Willburger, and Vartanian 2018; Shields Dobson 2015; Yau and Reich 2019). Her experiences with peers at school have the potential to cross the line into digital space. She feels a sense of insecurity about posting something "bad" or "weird" on social media and how it could incite negative responses, notably from people she knows (Gill 2021). Scout's concern translates into how she maintains her online presence; she keeps her content private, only sharing posts with friends and family and most commonly using Snapchat to communicate with a close circle of friends. She does not like more public sites such as Facebook, Instagram, and YouTube. As she says, she likes to keep her face to her family and friends, and she is bothered that her sister posted an image of her without her permission. Scout's feelings about social media and visibility suggest she has a strong sense of bodily autonomy, as she purposefully keeps her social media activity more private.

I had discussions with all my interviewees about privacy and staying safe online. Girls brought it up on their own in our conversations, framing it as simply part of what they must do as they participate on social media and produce digital girlhoods. Their actual practices of maintaining privacy and protecting themselves are filtered through internalized fears of what could happen to them in online space and through the role parents play in mediating and overseeing social media use. This everyday self-surveillance and prioritizing of privacy are reified by the line of what is considered age appropriate in terms of specific apps and content, as referenced in the previous section of this chapter. As De Leyn et al. note in their research on tween and parent perceptions of privacy on TikTok,

> Parents first and foremost aim to protect their children from "external" privacy threats (e.g., strangers) and from future "adolescent" disclosures, while being less concerned over tweens' present "playful" and "innocent" disclosures on TikTok. Drawing from their developmental understandings of tweenhood, parents furthermore describe tweens as less capable than older age groups to understand the implications of participating in TikTok's networked environment (2021:25).

Pepper, ten years old and White, is very clear about keeping her accounts private. She explains,

> I don't talk to strangers at all, really. I really talk to my friends and that's it. Unless there is a person that tries to follow me, because I have a private account. So, if someone tries to follow me, and I don't recognize them at first, I might ask them who they are. And if I don't know who they are, I won't let them follow me. All my accounts are private.

Pepper is diligent about who she accepts as a friend or follower, and she keeps her social media circle tight, restricting it mainly to friends and family members she knows in physical space.

Noelle, Black and thirteen years old, is also judicious with how she approaches friend and follower requests. During our interview, I ask Noelle about how she decides whether to accept a friend request.

> NOELLE: Well, my accounts are private. Nobody can even see my Snapchat story unless I follow them or add them. But if they don't have Snapchat, they can't see my story unless I actually show it to them on my phone.
>
> KP: Can you tell me more about what your Snapchat story is?
>
> NOELLE: It's just stuff about my day. And when I put stuff on my story, like, the people that follow me can see it. It's like what I do on In-

stagram too. I post pictures of myself, and I post pictures about my family, and what I'm all about and what I do in life. That's what I post on my page.

As we talk more about privacy on social media, Noelle also indicates, "I have my accounts on private because whenever anybody requests to follow me, first I look through their page to see if they're appropriate for me or if there is anything I don't like. And if they're fine, I'll just accept it." For Noelle, part of how she thinks about risk online and protects herself is about determining what content is appropriate for her to see and engage with.

Alarm about strangers makes its way into the processes of girls managing the privacy and publicity of their social media accounts. I talk to Jessie, Black and twelve years old, about whether her accounts are public or private and with whom she tends to interact on these platforms.

> JESSIE: Instagram is a mixture of [strangers and people I know], but I don't have any strangers on Snapchat. I had strangers on Snapchat, but then one of them texted me somehow and I got scared so I blocked them, and then I never added any strangers as a friend, and I never added any strangers back if they tried to follow me.
> KP: Wow. So is Instagram different from Snapchat like, in terms of adding people or following people you don't know?
> JESSIE: Part of it is just about what you post. Like I post silly or weird stuff on Snapchat to my friends. I just post a lot of pictures on Instagram. But I don't just make mine public. Mine aren't just like, all public [for anyone to see]. I don't want like, random people that I don't know just like, looking at it. If you think about it, it could be a grown man and then I'll just get creeped out.

The figure of the creepy, strange man informs how Jessie thinks about and manages privacy and publicity on various social media platforms. And for Jessie, it matters what the content is and the platform in question. Snapchat is about communicating with friends she knows. Instagram is a mixture of people she knows and strangers who follow her, but she keeps the account private in the sense that followers need to be approved by her first. Jessie is the interviewee who has a YouTube channel dedicated to dance and choreography. Her YouTube channel is public, and strategically so, because she wants to be seen and noticed for her dancing. By making her YouTube channel public, Jessie knowingly increases her chances of gaining likes, followers, and subscribers—as well as trolls. She manages the risks associated with visibility, balancing the desire to be seen by making her YouTube account public and dedicating it to her passion and interest in dance while keeping her other social media accounts largely private. Bulger et al. speak to this balance in the *Missing Middle* report, suggesting,

> Communication platforms that offer a space in between being fully private and fully public tend to mirror the developmental stage that tweens and teens are in as they transition from more protected on-line spaces to negotiating what it means to manage their own identity online. The different platforms that they choose to engage with inform their sense of representation, agency, and perceived ability to contribute their voices and opinions on the issues that matter to them (2021:28).

Except in the handful of cases where girls are trying to showcase their interests and increase their social capital via public content on YouTube, such as Jessie, or having fun making dances on Musical.ly, like Brooklyn, my data shows that girls are not blindly accepting followers or friend requests from people they do not know. They are either A) only interacting on social media platforms with people they know in real life and blocking or deleting requests from people they do not know, or B) closely inspecting the social media content of the person who requested to follow or friend them before hitting the accept button. The girls I interviewed adapt several different online privacy rules and, as I mention in the previous chapter, create in-group strategies among online friend groups to maintain and strengthen friendship connections. While they certainly emphasize a desire to be safe, they also emphasize a desire to have fun, wanting their friends to see their content and strategically controlling how, where, and with whom they share their digital girlhoods.

Conclusions: Signing on and Staying Safe

In my interview with Maya, an eleven-year-old Latina girl, it is brought home how the cultural model of innocent girls in need of protection runs deep in individual tween girls' narratives of self-representation. She tells me, "Girls already know that you got, well, that they need to be protected about their self, and about sharing their photos online." Tween girls are indoctrinated with adult-centered fears of social media, which are often driven by dominant media narratives and characterized by parents' desire to protect their children, whether from online predators, cyberbullying, or social media addiction. As I argue in this chapter, however, tween girls primarily keep their content private, interact online with people they know, follow parental guidelines, model parental behavior on social media, and importantly, internalize what their parents teach them in terms of approaching social media with a certain level of fear and caution, as well as recognizing and articulating what is considered age appropriate content.

The onus is placed on girls to adjust their behavior and, as demonstrated, to approach social media with fear and caution, which may concurrently work to protect tween girls and constrict and dampen their self-expressions, embodied online behaviors, political actions, and creation of digital girlhoods. Societally speaking, we have conditioned girls to police themselves and their behavior rather than having the culture at large confront social ills that have continually functioned to normalize male aggression and societal derision toward young girls.

Moral panic often comes from misunderstanding, in addition to highly sensationalized, trumped-up versions of sexually predatory and cyberbullying stories proliferated by the media. However, when adult authorities and youth have conversations and are open about these dialogues, building a level of trust with one another, social media may not need to incite such fear among adults. As danah boyd suggests,

> Adults justify the exclusion of youth as being for their own good or as a necessary response to their limited experience and cognitive capacity. . . . [It] is easy to make technology the target of our hopes and anxieties. . . . [Collaboratively], adults and youth can help create a networked world that we all want to live in (2014:213).

Cassell and Cramer similarly argue,

> [When] a new communication technology is introduced, upper middle-class Americans become afraid for their children—especially afraid about the noxious effects on girls. This is particularly the case when those technologies permit a kind of metaphoric mobility on the part of girls—movement outside the sphere of adult control. And in each case, whereas initially the anxiety is leveled at bad and transgressive predators, it quickly becomes displaced to the girls themselves who use technology. . . . [However,] participation in social networking sites can fulfill some key developmental imperatives for young women, such as forming their own social networks outside of the family, and exploring alternate identities (2008:70).

I do not to suggest that there is no risk associated with tween girls producing digital girlhoods and making themselves visible on social media, but for as many reasons as there are to worry, there are reasons not to. Even in cases of high incidence of daily use, the nature of the content a tween girl is engaging in, as well as how much time she spends self-monitoring, matters in determining negative impacts (Markey and Daniels 2022; Salomon 2017), and most girls are not using social media to an extreme degree in terms of amount of daily use (Nesi, Mann, and Robb 2023; Vogels and Gelles-Watnick 2023).

Recent findings demonstrate that the majority of young people feel social media has either a positive or neutral effect on their lives (Anderson et al. 2022; Anderson and Jiang 2018a; Nesi, Mann, and Robb 2023; Vogels, Gelles-Watnick, and Massarat 2022) and that they use social media for multiple reasons, including connecting with community, finding social support, engaging politically, sharing interests, and developing themselves and their social networks (boyd and Ellison 2007; boyd 2014; Cassell and Cramer 2008; Gordon 2019; Lenhart et al. 2015; Preston-Sidler 2015). As Farrell writes in her work on teenage girls, social media, and identity development, "these platforms have become socially vital for teenage girls providing an ecosystem for dynamic peer communications, a space to connect, building relationship, plan social gatherings and construct and affirm their identities (Metcalfe and Llewellyn 2020; Ringrose et al. 2013)" (2022:1).

While public, news, and popular media often present stories of girls putting themselves at risk online and the sometimes dire consequences, rarely do we hear stories about how tween girls are using social media to connect, express themselves, engage in their interests, support other girls, and create social change. But those stories are there, and they are worth telling.

7

"My Life, My Body, My YouTube Channel"

American Girlhoods for the Digital Age

"When they make media, girls explode limitations imposed by gender constructs and social norms; in fact, they may be the only ones who can."
—PRESTON-SIDLER 2015:202

The titular quote for this final chapter comes from a Pretty or Ugly video made by June, a twelve- or thirteen-year-old White girl who films her video in a bathroom. While June does ask the pretty or ugly question in her video, she also champions social media as a space for her and other girls to share what they are really feeling. Speaking their truths and staying connected to each other and to their own thoughts and feelings are manifestations of courage and resistance for tween girls (hooks 1989; Sullivan, Taylor, and Gilligan 1995). June sums it up succinctly in her YouTube video: "It's my life, my body, my YouTube channel."

For the better part of a decade, I have been thinking about, investigating, and reflecting on what social media means for tween girls in the contemporary United States. Questions about girls online and the state of girlhood in America today are timely. In 2023, several public and news media articles circulated in response to a Centers for Disease Control and Prevention report that states that more than 60 percent of U.S. girls indicate feeling persistent sadness or hopelessness (CDC 2023). The *Washington Post* declares a "crisis in American girlhood" (St. George, Lewis, and Bever 2023); the *Associated Press* asks, "Why Are Teen Girls in Crisis? It's Not Just Social Media" (Tanner and Wang 2023). *PBS NewsHour* offers, "Analysis: There's a Mental Health Crisis among Teen Girls. Here Are Some Ways to Support Them" (Englander and McCoy 2023). Social media could have quickly been assumed the primary culprit behind the mental health crisis of American girls, but the various commentary and op-eds offer a refreshing and nuanced take on the matter, some working to emphasize the voices of girls, who point to pressures, expectations, contradictions, and issues that influence their mental well-being. As the title of the *Associated Press* article suggests, "it's not just social media."

Author Alexe Bernier at *The Conversation* writes the following in response to the 2023 CDC report:

> I am a former community social worker with experience working directly with girls between the ages of 10 and 18 years old. My current doctoral research focuses on girls between the ages of eight and 12 years old who engage in activism, exploring ways that adults can better listen and support them when they tell us what they want for their lives and their worlds. I have heard countless stories from girls themselves about when they had felt dismissed by adults. This dismissal was often directly tied to their identities as girls, attributed to claims that girls were just going through a phase, not accurately sharing what had happened or that they were being dramatic. Put simply, when girls tell us what is happening in their lives, we have a tendency not to believe them (2023:para. 8).

In my own research, I set out to understand some of the social and cultural meanings tween girls are making via their creation of digital girlhoods and their characterizations of and relationships with social media. I found that these meanings are complex and complicated, but, for better or worse, social media is a crucial part of American tween girls' lives, and they are hard pressed to imagine existence without it.

No one book or piece of research stands alone in encapsulating the matter of tween girls on social media. The recent uptick in public and news media response is focused more on the well-being of teenage girls rather than the tween demographic. Yet this liminal space between childhood and adulthood, between empowerment and disempowerment, the "becoming" and process of "doing tween girlhoods" demands fervent attention. The tween years are the life stage during which many American girls make their forays into digital worlds. Though my research here provides only a small glimpse of understanding into a much larger, dynamic, shifting tapestry of inquiry, one thing is abundantly clear: American tween girls today navigate their lives, both offline and online, with the use of social media.

This work sheds light on the paradoxes of tween girlhood in the contemporary United States and seeks to understand how tween girls themselves negotiate and embody these paradoxes through social media participation. In examining a prominent contemporary example of digital girlhoods with the Pretty or Ugly YouTube trend and talking with tween girls about their experiences on social media, I argue that social media is not the cause of the social ills that plague American girlhood (negative body image, self-doubt, mental health issues, bullying, etc.). These issues have been prevalent far longer than social media has been a part of tween girl lives. Rather, how girls characterize their experiences on social media is an important reflection of the dominant, enduring, competing cultural models of innocent girls in need of protection and "Girl Power!" that precariously and continuously position girls on the fitful edge between empowerment and disempowerment. While social media is certainly not devoid of risk, these platforms, and the digital girlhoods American tween girls are creating within them, are salient cultural artifacts that reveal much about the importance of social media in self-representation, social capital, authenticity, self- and social development, engagement with interests, community building, and connection with friends. Social media is also a tool tween girls use to disrupt dominant, prescribed narratives of girlhood and create and define new tween girl digital cultures and subjectivities for themselves.

The user-generated nature of social media, its possibilities for self-representation, social capital, control over content, creative production, connection, and community building with other girls, all serve as meaningful grounds for why tween girls participate so prolifically on these platforms (Anderson et al. 2022; Nesi, Mann, and Robb 2023). As the Preston-Sidler (2015) quote that opens this chapter suggests, tween girls have the power and potential via social media visibility and further production of digital girlhoods to challenge, resist, and subvert dominant paradigms and reveal more nuanced realities of American girlhoods, establishing new understandings of what it means to be a tween girl coming of age in the "in between"—the blurred lines between offline and online space. For American youth, the line demarcating the realms of digital and physical has been all but blurred to indistinguishable (boyd 2014; Buckingham 2013b; Farrell 2022; Palfrey and Gasser 2016). Tween girls today move seamlessly between offline and online. Their experiences in physical spaces are a crucial impetus for why they use social media and are readily reflected in how they use these platforms.

Much of the public discourse surrounding tween girls' use of social media is defined by adult anxieties and desires to protect them from online predators, stalkers, cyberbullies, and other possible harms such as social comparison, poor mental health, and Internet addiction. While these are sincere and valid concerns, my findings demonstrate that tween girls have concerns as well. They internalize adult concern as part of how they engage in social media participation. They set limits for themselves. They are aware of and feel the pull of social media addiction and its potential negative impacts. They know they need to be cautious about strangers online and about seeing and sharing particularly harmful or negative content. Tween girls value privacy and are keen to protect themselves online while balancing a desire and thrust toward visibility. They seek out content deemed appropriate for people their age. And they mostly interact with people they already know online. Recent research surrounding girls on social media affirms these findings (Bennett 2023; Farrell 2022; Malvini Redden and Way 2017; Nesi, Mann, and Robb 2023; Vogels, Gelles-Watnick, and Massarat 2022).

We need to trust tween girls' abilities as digital vanguards and active agents more readily in producing digital girlhoods and listen to what they tell us about the role social media plays in their lives. This trust may be meaningfully cultivated through adult authorities and stakeholders in tween girls' lives not taking harmful and limiting media representations of tween and teen girls at face value, instead creating opportunities for dialogue with the tween girls they know and care about—talking about what girls like and dislike about social media, asking questions about their self-representations, and continuing to help them develop practical and safe tools for exercising caution online without exigently essentializing social media as something girls should fear. Girls should be at the center of the research about their lives; their participation and their voices are vital (Mitchell and Reid-Walsh 2008; Vanner 2019).

Tween girls do rely on parents and adult authority figures to help facilitate their experiences on social media, but much of this reliance is marked by how tween girls internalize historically cyclical and well-established adult-centered moral panics surrounding their bodies in public spaces. To best support tween girls as they start to navigate social media and enter the online world, "adults and stakeholders invested in [girls'] well-being need to be slow and cautious in judgment, as the meanings, values, and significance of new digital cultures and media practices emerge" (Shields Dobson 2015:165).

I argue that contemporary American tween girlhoods are delineated by two competing cultural models: innocent girls in need of protection and "Girl Power!" The concurrent existence of these models generates contradiction and impossible expectations for tween girls to be at once empowered and disempowered, self-confident and self-deprecating, sexually desirable and sexually innocent, sure of themselves and consumed by self-doubt. To be a girl in the United States today is to be in a constant state of dilemma. At intersections of identity including race, class, ability, size, sexuality, and gender expression, the paradoxes of ideal girlhood compound.

These competing models are a result of the proliferation of enduring raced and classed protectionist discourses, postfeminist sensibilities, and a surge of popular feminist rhetoric within consumer culture. Tween girls' body and sexuality narratives are made legible by notions of individual empowerment through "choice," which is neoliberalism-driven consumption, capitalism, and self-improvement via body and beauty work. The distracting and flattening nature of the "Girl Power!" model is tied to how women and girls have historically been corporally objectified and sexualized in the public imagination and how girls' bodies and sexualities have been routinely restricted in their available and acceptable expressions within a White supremacist, capitalist, ableist, cis-het normative system. Entrenched, gendered moral panics about girls' bodies in public spaces are recycled over time, reemerging with each novel technological development or popular culture craze, manifesting as old stories in new bindings. Young girls on social media are the most recent iteration of this panic. Like panics in decades past, the onus is placed on girls to take responsibility for their bodies and behaviors (Thiel-Stern 2014) and balance expectations of self-exposure and digital visibility with staying safe amid various, and notably feminized, threats and risks associated with social media participation.

Gendered Politics of Visibility

Within a postfeminist digital culture (Banet-Weiser 2018; Shields Dobson 2015), the promise of self-empowerment is enacted through emphasis on visibility. Visibility on social media has become a tremendously important part of how tween girls "do gender" (Currie, Kelly, and Pomerantz 2009; Schilt and Westbrook 2009; West and Zimmerman 1987) in the contemporary digital age. While tween girls are expected to make themselves visible on social media in socially and culturally acceptable ways aligned with raced and classed iterations of ideal femininity, my research shows that they also give meaning to aspects of online visibility that grant opportunities for controlling self-representation and engaging their interests. They must balance this desire and expectation to be seen with a gendered politics of visibility and the enduring cultural and social imperative to protect girls' bodies and restrict them from public spaces.

Some of the benefits and rewards of social media visibility include tween girls being able to make themselves seen in ways they want to be seen. They can explore different digital mediums and learn how to use various software and applications, building their knowledge and skill sets and increasing digital adeptness. They can be creative, silly, social, and have fun playing with identities on various platforms. Jessalynn Keller writes,

> [Girls] are savvy social media users, demonstrating keen knowledge about the platforms they regularly use and how they work. They make conscious decisions about what to post and where, weighing issues like public visibility, peer support, anonymity, and social privacy before they upload content (2019:9).

They connect with other people and gain followers and supporters of the digital girlhoods they produce. They explore their interests in deep and purposeful ways. Social media helps tween girls expose themselves to new ideas and different modes of being. If they do not see themselves readily represented in popular media—or accurately represented, as is so often the case (Bulger et al. 2021; Hill 2017; Hill Collins 1990; Smith et al. 2017)—they can represent themselves and find others who identify and express themselves in similar ways, which promotes feelings of validation and acceptance (Berger et al. 2021; Erigha and Crooks-Allen 2020; Farrell 2022; Hill 2017; Wade 2019b).

Conversely, however, making their bodies visible online renders tween girls more vulnerable, particularly as they reckon with the protectionist discourses and social structures that inform their daily lives. Gendered power dynamics are not absent from social media; gradations of these dynamics manifest online as tween girls keenly balance the desire for visibility through contemporary forms of social capital explored in previous chapters with the associated risks, largely related to constructions of race, gender expression, sexuality, and ability, and adult-centered fears of girls' risky online behavior—sharing too much information, creating and sharing sexualized content, engaging with strangers, or making themselves targets for sexual predation or cyberbullying. In response to this, tween girls learn from parents, peers, and through their own participation, developing practices and strategies that help them manage their visibility and center how they hope to benefit from social media participation (e.g., control over how they are seen, increased self-esteem, building social capital) while prioritizing privacy and protection.

Further related to this gendered politics of visibility on social media as a new and meaningful form of social capital, I found that while girls in a post-feminist digital context are being called to visibility and self-exposure in ways readily aligned with "ideal femininity" (e.g., appearance-related content, hetero-sexiness, self-effacing authenticity), the tween girls I interviewed are largely not ascribing to this push. Rather, they set themselves apart from this kind of social media content and emphasize a desire for online visibility and resultant social capital specifically related to their interests and passions, such as dance, art, and computer coding. Even tween girls who make and post Pretty or Ugly videos demonstrate resistance to constructions of ideal femininity in notable ways. The trend itself invites questions of how tween girls are discursively constructing new meanings of girlhood through public digital performances. Tween girls who exist outside of normative standards of body and beauty may also employ self-representation on social media to challenge those standards and incite conversation about a broader multiplicity of girlhood identities and embodied experiences. As one example of this, Sarah Hill's work on girlhoods and disability suggests that disabled girls' online self-representation practices, such as producing selfies and other forms of self-representation, enable them to gain visibility in a distinctly heteronormative and ableist mediascape and also allows them to engage in a form of advocacy through challenging stereotypes and ideas about disability (2017:118).

Though my sample is small and not generalizable, I see the production of different kinds of digital girlhoods as having the potential to confront impossible notions of ideal femininity that demand hetero-sexiness and conventional standards of body and beauty in the same measure that tween girls today are expected to just "be empowered." Tween girls are seeing through some of these contradictions and exercising control over their digital girlhoods and online self-representations in exciting, emboldening, and politically significant ways. Tween girl digital cultures will continue to shift and evolve, taking on meanings from the sociopolitical contexts of which they are a part, and tween girls' production of digital girlhoods will continue to be an essential site of sociological inquiry.

Too often tween girls are dismissed for having shallow interests or disdained for being petty or catty with other girls, but we need to take a critical look at *why* tween girls are framed in this way and what tween girls themselves bring to the fore in challenging these simplistic framings. American society does not frame girls in this way because social media exists or because girls are avid users of these platforms. Legacies of girls' gendered oppression runs deep. That said, as scholar Kimberly Hall suggests, "[young girls] represent the new vanguard of political action; dismissing them risks missing significant dynamics of power and capital within neoliberal culture as it manifests as the very affective condition of everyday life" (2015:140). A selfie is not just a selfie. A Pretty or Ugly YouTube video is not just a Pretty or Ugly YouTube video. Tween girls are social and political actors who use social media to critically engage with and create their own meanings of girlhoods.

Connection and Community

Along with controlling self-representations and creating digital content related to their lives and interests, tween girls cite wanting to connect with friends and peer groups as much as possible as a primary motivation for how and why they use social media (Boudreau 2007; Ging and O'Higgins Norman 2016; Kennedy and Lynch 2016; Lenhart et al. 2015; Malvini Redden and Way 2017; Spies Shapiro and Margolin 2014). Though girls express complicated feelings about social media in terms of pressures of social comparison and negative relational behavior such as bullying and drama, they also emphasize how maintaining friend communities in digital space is a decisive source of homosocial support and affirmation. In some cases, social media can operate as a haven and crucial site of respite from elements of toxic girl culture and other modes of social oppression. In her work on Black girlhoods and digital cultures, scholar Ashleigh Greene Wade writes that "digital spaces create more possibilities for black girls to form support networks and exercise an agency to control space often denied them in their everyday school and home environments" (2019a:81). Establishing support networks and exercising agency online may be particularly important for American tween girls who are multiply marginalized, including but certainly not limited to Black, Brown, and Indigenous girls, queer, trans, and fat girls, girls with disabilities, girls who are foreign-born or second-generation immigrants, and undocumented girls—girls embodying any number of these identities.

A large part of this desire for continual connection to friend groups online is that girls feel like themselves in their digital communities, which matters significantly because of how contradiction and (mis)representation so readily structure the social and cultural conditions of their lives. Many of the girls I interviewed directly expressed a very real concern associated with no longer having access to these support systems, these platforms for visibility, expression, and connection. When I asked my interviewees how they would feel if social media suddenly disappeared and they could not use it anymore, they reacted in telling ways:

Genie, White and ten years old, emphatically groans, "Nooooooo."
Marcie, White and ten years old, states plainly, "I would freak out."
Noelle, Black and thirteen years old, explains, "If I didn't have [social media], oh my lord, I just need social media. I would be so *bored*! I would probably have a heart attack."
Sierra, Black and ten years old, quietly says, "If someone took my phone away, I would not survive."
And Chrissy, Black and thirteen years old, explains, "It would be, like, so hard. Like, changing my whole life."

Cassell and Cramer write, "The important identity construction, self-efficacy, and social network production work that [girls] do online is not only largely ignored, but too often condemned" (2008:54). In a cultural epoch defined by deeply contradictory narratives of girlhood, an epoch in which achieving "successful" girlhood is a true dilemma due to competing cultural models, the ability for a tween girl to go online, make herself seen in ways that feel authentic to her, create content, be creative, and foster and maintain positive, supportive relationships with other girls is powerful.

Other research shows that spending time on social media benefits youth by strengthening communication, social connection, and digital skills, as well as offering more abstract benefits of greater understanding of self, community, and the broader world (Anderson et al. 2022; boyd 2014; Buckingham 2013b; Bulger et al. 2021; Farrell 2022; Ito et al. 2009; Knorr 2017; Palfrey and Gasser 2016). Regarding further research, continued intersectional inquiry is necessary to examine and unpack the intricacies and nuances of American tween girls' social media participation, the skills it can build, and the opportunities it presents to tween girls as active agents in navigating, challenging, and changing the social, cultural, and political conditions that inform their experiences and opportunities for inclusion.

Limitations and Future Directions

This research is part of a growing body of work centered on theorizing the role that social media plays in the lives of American tween girls. As consequential users of various platforms (YouTube, TikTok, Snapchat, Instagram, etc.), American tween girls can create space not only for themselves but also for broader understandings and imaginings of who American tween girls are—their desires, motivations, interests, concerns, and contributions. Referencing Cassell and Cramer once again,

> For young women, the Internet appears to be a way to explore aspects of identity that may not be welcome in the real world, to project more forceful agentive personalities than they feel at liberty to do in the physical world, and to explore their technological prowess (2008:68).

There are many significant avenues of continued critical investigation into tween girls' experiences and production on social media, how they navigate "doing girlhood" through the creation of digital girlhoods. Future research must consider how American tween girls who do *not* engage with social media, willingly or unwillingly, experience and create girlhoods within postfeminist digital confidence culture and economies of visibility (Banet-Weiser 2018; Orgad and Gill 2022). Given how I recruited for this study, with social media use being a necessary component of inclusion, every tween girl I interviewed was active on multiple social media sites. I did not speak to tween girls who choose not to use, or are restricted from using, social media with as much or any frequency. There remains a significant need for empirical investigation into the experiences of tween girls who do not use social media and what this means for their self- and social development.

Existing literature on the social media participation gap (Jenkins 2009) suggests that in addition to having potentially harmful impacts on digital literacy skills and knowledge of digital media, a lack of social media participation may have consequences for social development. As is the case with some of my interview subjects, a tween girl may only be using Snapchat to interact with friends and family she knows in her physical social world, and no longer having that outlet for connection may have meaningful, and possibly detrimental, impacts on her. This was particularly the case amid the COVID-19 pandemic, especially the first two years, 2020 and 2021, as digital participation became the primary or even sole mode of connection and socializing for a massive number of American youth (Bennett 2023; Bulger et al. 2021; Rideout et al. 2021). The girls I interviewed indicated that most people their age they know have social media and use it regularly. Someone not having it is viewed as an aberrant occurrence and considered abnormal. Though the vast majority of teens are active on at least one social media account at any given time (Nesi, Mann, and Robb 2023; Vogels and Gelles-Watnick 2023), there is still a percentage who do not participate; we have even less data on the tween demographic because they are technically not supposed to have accounts on social media if younger than thirteen years old. Only by understanding the realities of those social conditions, how tween girls who do not have social media experience their social worlds today, can we garner a fuller sense of the overall impact that social media has on this population.

The American-centric nature of my research and the bounded geography of my interview participants are weighty limitations. The qualitative study design offers rich perspective on how girls feel about and use social media, but these findings are from a small group. That said, the interest in gender, power, girlhoods, and impacts and potentials of social media around the world continues to deepen and expand. Recent scholarship has asked questions about girls online from Belgium to India (De Leyn et al. 2021; Subramanian 2021; Vyas et al. 2020), China to Pakistan (Abbasi and Huang 2020; Chang and Tian 2021; Liu and Li 2024; Shahid, Kauser, and Zulqarnain 2018), Saudi Arabia to Nigeria (Dunmade and Tella 2023; Gangwani, Alruwaili, and Al Safar 2021; Kutbi 2015), Australia to Brazil, and beyond (Castilho and Romancini 2017; Farrell 2022; Marôpo, Jorge, and Tomaz 2020; Papageorgiou, Fisher, and Cross 2022).

Sociological inquiry that brings together intersectional and transnational feminist frameworks around specific regional and spatial landscapes, geopolitical realities, and cultural constructions of girlhoods in digital space has yielded seminal scholarship on transnational girlhoods and girlhoods in global context at different axes of identity (Berents 2016; Erevelles and Nyugen 2016; Field and Simmons 2022; Mitchell and Rentschler 2016). Catherine Vanner implores us to continue to center girls' voices in our efforts toward learning more about what girls need, suggesting,

Adults working to strengthen transnational girlhood need to examine how our efforts genuinely connect girls from different localities and build from the experiences they choose to share. We must consider how we frame these experiences in an intersectional analysis that privileges the voices of girls who have been the most overlooked, mobilizing with them to enact structural changes that create a better world in which to be a girl (2019:128).

What does girls' participation on social media mean across various global contexts? What do the digital girlhoods they are creating tell us about processes of girlhood in those places? What possibilities are there for girls' political resistance and transformation online? The work being done in this arena is exciting, innovative, and timely.

There remains a dearth of research on intersectional explorations of social media participation and its impacts on girls. Questions of how tween girls at various intersections of identity relate to and characterize their experiences on social media are vital. More sociological inquiry into queer girlhoods online is a fruitful area of research, as existing literature on LGBTQIA+ youth online suggests that social media can all at once heighten experiences of discrimination, harassment, bullying, and violence as well as be a refuge, providing access to resources and community and creating space for people to express themselves in authentic ways (Austin et al. 2020; Craig et al. 2015; Kuper, Adams, and Mustanski 2018; McInroy 2019). An avenue worthy of thoughtful exploration is how new media behaviors among girls may contribute to broader representation and understanding of varied girlhood sexual subjectivities, resistance to prescribed notions of hetero-sexiness, and the queering of girlhoods. Discursive constructions of American tween girls in public and popular media deploy controlling images of appropriate or acceptable expressions of body and sexuality for tween girls, begging important questions about how content creation may disrupt and subvert those images. Additionally, as social media has contributed to increased representation and visibility of gender and sexual diversity, I wonder how queer girls may experience phenomena such as gatekeeping, policing, and surveillance surrounding queer authenticity in their performances in digital space. Would a digital values system of authenticity like what is exhibited in reaction to the Pretty or Ugly YouTube trend find parallel with questions of whether girls are being "queer enough" online?

Regarding girls with disabilities, none of the tween girls I interviewed had a visible disability, and I did not explicitly ask about disabilities, visible or invisible. I also could not reasonably assess whether the girls in the Pretty or Ugly YouTube videos identify with having a disability unless explicitly mentioned. If disability is mentioned, it is not necessarily framed that way, as tween girls in the videos reference anxiety, depression, and/or neurodiversity in a way that is usually uncritical or unattached to conceptualizations of disability as political category. Stienstra asks,

> Why does disability as a problem or lack figure so prominently in the stories of girls with disabilities? Does disability substantively and negatively alter all experiences of girls? How do experiences of disability interact with global location, minority culture or being Indigenous for girls? (2015:55).

Because of the vastness and multiplicity of disability as identity, social construct, and political category (Kafer 2013; Wendell 1997), intersections of disability and girlhood embodiments require much more attention, especially as disability often supersedes girlhood as an identity category (Erevelles and Mutua 2005), marring the unique and varied gendered embodied experiences of girls with disabilities in digital space (Hill 2017; Hill 2023).

Investigating further gendered dynamics of social media use, I note that tween girls routinely brought up differences in how girls and boys use social media from their perspectives during our interviews. Research that does not lump all youth together is necessary to explore how gender scripts and norms are enacted on social media and how tween boys characterize their experiences on social media in terms of gendered expectations and gender performances. Additionally, the politics of racial performance require more fervent investigation. I did not put substantial emphasis on racial identity and racialized experiences of social media in my interview guide, as it was not a central part of my research design. While this was a missed opportunity, my interview sample was predominantly Black and Latina girls (accounting for sixteen of the twenty-six girls I interviewed). What they shared with me during the interview process showcases the intricacies, overlaps, and divergences of digital girlhoods, invaluable in illuminating nuanced, everyday experiences of tween girls online.

Additionally, the interview findings offer a compelling interplay with how the Pretty or Ugly YouTube trend is overwhelmingly White in its makeup. Racial performance was a narrow thread of analysis in my exploration of the Pretty or Ugly YouTube trend. I primarily looked at how many White girls in the trend co-opt elements of Black culture and features of Black beauty and how some Black girls demonstrate performances of "ideal femininity" (i.e., Whiteness) in their videos. Existing literature on tween and teen girls and the politics of race online is fecund and growing (Barner 2016; Erigha and Crooks-Allen 2020; Hill 2019; Hobson 2016; Lindsey 2013; Wade 2019a; Wade 2024). More thorough exploration of racial performance and performativity (Butler 1990; Markus and Moya 2010) in the Pretty or Ugly YouTube trend, in addition to continued qualitative investigation into how racial identity mediates experiences on social media for tween girls, is a crucial area of inquiry. As Wade argues, "racially nuanced understandings of girlhood can lead to more expansive imaginings of what the Internet can do in the realm of social justice" (2019a:iii).

Deepening Inquiry into the Pretty or Ugly Question

The pretty or ugly question being asked on public digital platforms offers many continued veins of analysis, whether furthering analysis of the YouTube trend itself or furthering understanding of iterations of the trend on other social media platforms. Because I was most interested in analyzing Pretty or Ugly videos as a prominent example of contemporary digital girlhoods in and of themselves, I was less focused on the social meanings of the comments posted on the videos. And because of the tremendous volume of these videos and the incredible range of number of views and comments across the trend, I did not include a systematic analysis of number of views and content of comments on videos when designing this research project. We know virtually nothing about how the tween girls making these videos respond to and/or internalize comments, and contacting subjects of these videos brings up dubious ethical quandaries. Given the widespread media condemnation of the trend, as well as the significant number of response videos that popped up in reaction to it, it is fair to suggest we assume the worst as far as how girls might interact with comments on their content. But there is also the possibility of increased self-esteem and positive self-feeling inspired by affirming comments and likes (Cipolletta et al. 2020; Davis 2013). Viewer comments and Pretty or Ugly response videos warrant further study, especially as iterations of this trend and the question "Am I pretty or ugly?" have popped up on other social media platforms.

Additionally, I recommend investigation into the Pretty or Ugly trend surrounding identity development, psychoanalysis, and the unique and important function of the web camera as a mirror. Pretty or Ugly videos are a digital version of an explicitly gendered mirror stage. Jacques Lacan (1968) theorizes the mirror stage as a mode of development for identity and subjectivity—a child learns to identify himself in a mirror as an Other, able to see the body as an object outside of himself, giving way to a psychic representation of the self, or *I*. Catherine Driscoll (2002) offers a more gendered approach to the mirror stage. She writes, "If something approximating the mirror stage is necessary to the formation of body image, feminine adolescence might locate processes comparable to the mirror stage" (2002:238). Pretty or Ugly videos are an example of this process. Through use of a web camera, whether on a computer, tablet, or mobile phone, girls see, watch, and assess themselves before ever posting a video for public consumption. This policing via the web camera (which literally acts as a mirror) works to construct a body image and visual representation of the self that is Othered through the screen. Self-assessment occurs first, and girls then make the choice to post these videos on YouTube. The question of pretty or ugly is not as simple as girls asking and getting answers from viewers; the fact that they are seeing themselves during the making of the video matters immensely.

In coding the Pretty or Ugly memos, it became readily apparent that most girls are not looking at the web camera as they record their videos; they are plainly looking at themselves on the screen. Often, they will move their faces and bodies and position themselves at different angles, playing with their hair and pursing their lips just as they might when looking in a mirror. A significant number of the videos in the sample do not have any verbal language or script. Rather, the viewer is only made aware of the intent of the video through the title and tagline at the bottom of the screen. Sonia's video is a clear example. For approximately thirty seconds, the viewer watches Sonia (White and approximately eleven or twelve years old), smile into the screen, tilting and shifting her head to various angles and running her fingers through her hair. She is looking at herself, not at the camera. The only way a viewer would know to comment on her appearance is because the video, titled "Pretty or Ugly?" has a tagline below that reads, "Please tell me what you think! Am I pretty or ugly?" An investigation of the more abstract meanings and possibilities of the Pretty or Ugly trend through a framework of psychoanalytic feminist theory could yield compelling empirical and theoretical contributions to girlhood studies and questions of identity development.

Though the Pretty or Ugly YouTube trend raises several other questions, a final one I wish to highlight is around the blurred boundary between the physical and the digital and what it might mean for American tween girls to situate themselves as sexual subjects on YouTube. Many of the videos I analyzed (41 of the 260) are coded as "sexy"—coded as such because the video subject in question positions herself in ways that align with heteronormative scripts and constructions of what is considered sexy appearance and behavior within a cis-hetero normative patriarchal social order. In some videos, girls are in various states of undress, contorting their bodies in ways that emphasize legs, torsos, and breasts. They smile coyly at the web camera, bite their lips, play with their hair, and perform their bodies in ways that resemble Western pornified images from popular men's magazines and media. In these videos, the tensions of tweenhood are amplified.

I paid close attention to my own reactions to these videos coded as sexy, and I understood just how entrenched our cultural notions of girls as pure and innocent and as objects of desire are. My instinct was not to celebrate what these tween girls are doing but rather to cringe, suck in my breath, and hope that they are being careful with how they make themselves available to viewers. I question these seemingly inherent feelings of fear and horror and how my reaction would change if these video subjects were in any way different from how I perceive them in terms of age, race, gender, and so on. I see these videos as negotiating a cultural landscape of American girlhood that presumes innocence while also presuming the power of girls' bodies as distracting and enticing to men and boys (Doyle 2019; Renold and Ringrose 2011). And I see that maybe through all the contradictions that tell these girls who they are supposed to be, what they are supposed to look like, and how they are supposed to behave, girls are making a justified choice, a valid choice, in playing with the public and private, playing with intimate space by making it visible (Ashton and Patel 2020; Kearney 2011; Kennedy 2020; McRobbie and Garber 2006), expressing and playing with sexuality via digital girlhoods.

Some of these Pretty or Ugly performances can be categorized as what Shields Dobson calls "hot and hostile" (2015:67): girls gazing directly at the camera with assertive body language, baring parts of their bodies while covering others. Feminist logic is present in these performances in strange and novel ways. Because tween girls are the producers of these videos and images, they can present themselves as sexual beings while maintaining a barrier between themselves and a viewer who may desire to do more than gaze. In the fluid space of the digital, girls can create and perform while troubling the cultural weight of the male gaze (Mulvey 1975).

Compulsory visibility on social media, how tween girls perform their bodies online, is inherently connected to sexuality. Though not as central to my analysis as questions of authenticity, social capital, and homosocial relationships, the push-pull between desperation and desire that shows up in the Pretty or Ugly YouTube trend intrigues me. It is difficult to parse what might be exploitation versus empowerment for a tween girl living in a heteronormative, masculine hegemonic culture. Girls do not exist in a vacuum; they are influenced by the culture in which they live and must reckon with heteronormative expectations, both overt and covert. Girls are not supposed to come off as desperate, and yet they are often categorized as such by viewers in comments on videos and images. They are also not supposed to come across as openly confident, overtly sexual, or desirous. Culturally speaking, we flatten girls as being desirable, as objects of desire, even as we provide them with endless consumer options to present themselves as empowered, even sexually empowered. That empowerment, within the "Girl Power!" model of contemporary American girlhood, remains heavily constrained by persistent oppressive gendered norms. Preston-Sidler writes, "Girlhood, especially the transition to womanhood, is a negotiation of the tension between cultural imperatives and individual and collective desires" (2015:199).

There are some feminist empirical studies of girls' sexualities, but questions of where and how tween girl sexualities interact with the digital must be substantially deepened. Sexual desires are complex feelings for adolescent and teenage girls (Fine 1988; Fine and McClelland 2007; French 2013; McRobbie 1993; Orenstein 2016; Renold and Ringrose 2013; Tolman 1994; Tolman 2005). In her work on adolescent female sexuality and desire, Deborah Tolman (1994) suggests that during adolescence, girls lose touch with embodied desires and start to view themselves from the perspectives of men. Historically, women and girls have been theorized as sexually passive—ideal femininity has traditionally been linked with passivity, while masculinity is associated with the active in sexual relations (Bordo 1993; Brumberg 1997; Tolman 1994). The idea that tween girls can and do desire sex remains abstract and distressing in the American cultural imagination. The "Girl Power!" model of contemporary girlhood has put emphasis on empowerment through sexy femininity, but the protectionist imperative is still alive and well. Shields Dobson explains:

> Feminist scholars have acknowledged the contradictions girls and young women face to present themselves as "sexy," but not "slutty" or "sexualized." At the same time, young women are called to present their identities in line with the girl-powered neoliberal ideals discussed of girls as confident, strong, capable, fun, and up for a good time. They are called toward public self-representation, visibility, and self-exposure (2015:40).

There is work being done in academia and some forms of media to change this long-accepted convention of passive feminine sexuality, but I suggest that tween girls, amongst the top users of visibility-oriented social media sites, are doing the most groundbreaking and important work of dismantling social and cultural restrictions on their sexualities via online visibility and body performances, and it is worthy of attention.

Recommendations and Signing Off

American society is still grappling with social media becoming a normalized part of everyday life. Only within the last fifteen years or so has social media really proliferated and youth participation on social media exploded. The most popular platforms among tween girls today (YouTube, TikTok, Instagram, Snapchat) are being used for different purposes, whether for creating a video demonstrating an interest, sharing selfies, documenting daily life, building social capital, engaging in self-expression, or connecting with friends. Given how new social media is in the scope of everyday life for American youth, continued sociological investigation of and phenomenological approaches to the digital arena are prudent.

The onset of social media use among adolescents to such a significant degree mobilizes cultural anxieties and persistent questions. But social media is something we are all navigating, adults included, and we are still learning what its impacts are, both good and bad. Tween girls may be figuring out who they are online as they are in the physical spaces they move through, but to suggest that they are *only* vulnerable, *only* at risk, implies that social media is not for them, when really, girls have been on social media from the beginning and have made social media what it is.

As a society, we cannot discount the voices of American tween girls that characterize the why and how behind their social media use or dismiss the digital girlhoods that constitute contemporary tween girl digital cultures and the issues they bring to the fore. This research finds that tween girls have complicated relationships with social media but deeply value and give powerful meaning to their ability to control how they are seen and who can see them; to create content that they believe in, that they are passionate about, and that makes them feel good; and to connect with friends and foster digital interactions centered on homosocial support and affirmation.

Popular and public media that frames girls as irresponsible online participants, shallow consumers, narcissists, or passive victims of online predatory behavior do not reflect what is going on with American tween girls online. Societal focus should not be on restricting tween girls' social media use in a bid to protect them from predators and preserve their culturally constructed innocence. Girls deserve to be safe, and they deserve our attention, but so often the response to their social media use is either dismissive of girls as vapid or panicked that girls are going to behave recklessly and therefore experience harm. Too often, girls are dismissed simply because they are girls. I do not suggest that we do nothing in the face of tween girls experiencing harm on social media, but I implore us to consider how we frame the solution as individualized, positioning girls as personally responsible for how others engage with them online, or as self-regulation, which I learned tween girls are already doing to a significant degree, primarily in prioritizing privacy and personal safety on these platforms.

Education and social practice should be geared toward safe and responsible use, but I think it needs to be framed as a collective enterprise and an evolving conversation between and among tween girls and adult stakeholders that continually recognizes tween girls as agential subjects across social arenas, including on social media. Cyber safety programming should strive for mixed methods research and various modes of knowledge production toward a more holistic understanding of social media participation, in particular privileging the voices of youth who are using these platforms daily.

The sociocultural landscape is ever shifting, and digital challenges young people face are context specific and change over time.

Relatedly, response to tween girl social media use should be sensitive to the discursive positioning of the tween age category. Tween girls demonstrate familial dependence (socially, emotionally, materially, etc.), but they are coming into themselves in a new way, developing independence and autonomy and engaging in self- and social development in both physical and digital space (Nesi, Choukas-Bradley, and Prinstein 2018; Abiala and Hernwall 2013). Tween girls should be supported in their experimentation and play online, and resources for ensuring harm reduction on social media must be attuned to the realities of American tween girls as a tremendously heterogeneous group of humans (Livingstone 2009). Channeling more resources into education and programming that teaches critical thought, and critical social media literacies specifically (Pangrazio and Cardozo Gaibisso 2020), can help tween girls self-reflect, connect to broader social and political realities, and consider the role of their digital girlhoods in the production of new tween girl digital cultures.

Emphasis on diverse experience and identities can also help foster inclusion and create equitable opportunities for young people in utilizing digital space. Tween girls are open to these messages and desire to stay safe online. Actively listening to tween girls, centering their voices as expert digital stakeholders, and looking at what they produce online as sources of valuable knowledge about contemporary digital girlhoods can work toward dismantling the social ills that plague American girlhoods.

While social media reflects these ills, I argue that the competing cultural models of innocent girls in need of protection and "Girl Power!" have buoyed heteronormative patriarchal structures, mobilized toxic girl culture, spurred and naturalized girls bullying girls, and reinforced girlhood confusion, self-doubt, negative body image, and dangerous associated behaviors such as eating disorders and self-harm. A surge of body-positive rhetoric online has primarily served to bolster neoliberal, individualized efforts toward the empowered body as capitalist consumer project and product. It has not meaningfully disrupted or transformed the systems that reproduce and reify gender-based oppressions. Confidence culture (Orgad and Gill 2022) has fostered conditions for American women that suggests they can have it all, but they also need to do it all. This translates to how American tween girls are growing up and negotiating contradiction both online and offline. American girlhoods are not monolithic. They are informed by identity politics, sociopolitical realities, economics, and cultural expectations.

Through the normalized production of digital girlhoods on visibility-oriented platforms and the cultivation of meaningful digital communities, American tween girls have found ways to make social media their own and have granted us the opportunity to get to know them better by engaging with them and what they create online. Tween girls may be hearts, stars, rainbows, flowers, and bubblegum. They may be princess crowns, disco balls, lip gloss, glitter, peace signs, and smiley faces. If we devalue these things, it is only because they are associated with conventional femininity, which we have theorized as shallow and material. Tween girls claim it as their own while also demonstrating their dynamic interests and values online. So yes, they are all those things. Those things are awesome. And they are also coders, artists, athletes, entrepreneurs, poets, dancers, musicians, bakers, chefs, activists, crafters, creatives, and comedians.

Palfrey and Gasser suggest that "as a culture of fear emerges around the online environment, we must put these real threats into perspective; our children and future generations have tremendous opportunities in store for them, and not in spite of the digital age, but because of it" (2016:9). The onus should not be on tween girls to keep themselves offline for fear of voyeurs and trolls; indeed, if that fear is the grounds on which we are restricting girls, we need to seriously consider the foundations of that fear, the histories and cultural incongruities that champion a girls' ability to be and do anything but keep her suppressed in practice. Rather, it is our responsibility, as the people invested in the well-being of our girls, to open further avenues of communication and investigation so that tween girls, in all their identities, intersections, and nuance, may continue to play, create, explore, act, participate, build community, and take full advantage of all the contemporary digital landscape has to offer them.

Notes

CHAPTER 1

1. There is social, cultural, and political debate on the recommendation of using uppercase *B* versus lowercase *b* when referring to Black subjects. My original feeling in formatting the text was that *Black* should be capitalized. Historically and in much of the social science and feminist scholarship I have read, *Black* has been capitalized and *white* remains lowercase. This formatting feels correct to me. Yet there are arguments to be made that keeping *white* lowercase allows white people to be understood as individuals, normalizing whiteness as somehow devoid of racial meaning or categorization, especially within white supremacist systems. I also want to be mindful of how the *w* in *white* has at times been capitalized and weaponized as violence to assert white dominance. The ASA style guide indicates racial groups should be lowercase, while the APA guide follows principles of capitalization for racial groups and identities. Though there are multiple ways to go about this, I have made the decision to capitalize all references to racial categories and identities (Black, White, Latina, etc.) to emphasize the weight that racial identities and embodiments hold in shaping experiences of tween girls, both online and offline, and to underscore the crucial politics and histories of racialization as they intersect with girlhood embodiments. Exceptions are made for direct quotes from works by other authors.

2. Social media and its impacts on populations is far from fully understood (Anderson et al. 2022; Valkenburg, Meier, and Beyens 2022; Valkenburg et al. 2022). Social media platforms shift and expand, and their utilization is context driven and specific. As Papacharissi writes, "our understanding of social media is temporally, spatially, and technologically sensitive—informed but not restricted by the definitions, practices, and materialities of a single time period or locale. How we have defined social media in societies has changed, and will continue to change" (2015:1). For clarity, I use the following definition of social media in this work: "Social media are web-based services that allow individuals, communities, and organizations to collaborate, connect, interact, and build

community by enabling them to create, co-create, modify, share, and engage with user-generated content that is easily accessible" (McCay-Peet and Quan-Haase 2017:17).

3. A *New York Times* article published in March of 2022 lays out recent data from a survey study conducted by the nonprofit organization Common Sense Media, in particular commenting on increasing amounts of screen time among children during the COVID-19 pandemic. The survey collected data from an eight- to twelve-year-old demographic but was not able to pinpoint use of specific platforms among this demographic because it is a protected class. The article notes the difficulty of situating this data in broader social context, as federal law (Children's Online Privacy Protection Act, or COPPA) prohibits companies from collecting data of children under the age of thirteen, the established minimum age for young people to create accounts on social media platforms such as Instagram, Snapchat, and TikTok. This age restriction is not regularly enforced, as children younger than thirteen are highly visible users of social media platforms. Yet they are also an invisible demographic online given the limited data available on their use of social media.

4. I opted to give Pretty or Ugly video subjects pseudonyms for the analysis not only for the sake of clarity in referring to various videos throughout the book but also because, even though these videos are public and available to view on YouTube and to use in academic research via the fair use doctrine (Stim 2019), I deemed it important to offer an added layer of protection to the girls who may use channels that are not their own, make videos without parental/guardian permission, or want to maintain some level of anonymity, not expecting their video to extend beyond friends and family in terms of viewership. Because it was not ethically or logistically feasible to reach out to video subjects directly, I felt it best to use less direct identifying information and use pseudonyms across the entirety of the study, for both Pretty or Ugly video subjects as well as the tween girls I interviewed.

5. In videos in which a subject does not articulate a specific gender identity, I assumed a gender category of *girl* by assessing whether subjects are wearing feminine-coded clothing, speaking and gesturing in feminine ways, and exhibiting other markers that indicate a girlhood identity. I estimated tween age category and assumed racial and gender categories for inclusion in the sample for the textual analysis. I fully recognize the limitations of this subjective estimation. Ideally, each video subject would identify themselves in terms of age, race, and gender so that if others were to watch and analyze the same set of YouTube videos, recognition of the subjects therein would be consistent. I was not able to reach out to video subjects individually for multiple reasons. According to fair use legal doctrine, YouTube videos can be reused for academic purposes (YouTube Copyright and Fair Use; Stim 2019). For my research, I looked at and analyzed YouTube videos as public content, but because I could not be certain whether specific YouTube channels posting Pretty or Ugly videos belonged to the video subject, a family member, or another party entirely, I could not ensure direct outreach to video subjects. Furthermore, given that the video subjects are minors, the ability to obtain parental consent to speak with girls directly was outside of feasibility for this project. I could not contact parents/guardians of the tween girls in the videos because the only point of contact would be through the YouTube channel itself. The ethical considerations of trying to contact video subjects through YouTube were questionable and could have put the girls at risk. I was most interested in analyzing the Pretty or Ugly trend broadly and at face value and felt the best option was to make certain defensible assumptions about the identities of the video subjects.

CHAPTER 3

1. I was not entirely familiar with the function of this social media app at the start of my research and subsequently learned that Musical.ly shut down after its merger with TikTok, which was the most downloaded app in the United States in 2018 and rapidly grew to be the social media platform du jour during the COVID-19 pandemic in 2020. At the time of writing, TikTok remains the most popular app among tween girls second only to YouTube (Kennedy 2020; Perez 2020).

References

Abbasi, Nosharwan Arbab, and Huang, Dianlin. 2020. "Digital Media Literacy: Social Media Use for News Consumption among Teenagers in Pakistan." *Global Media Journal* 18(35): 1–7.

Aberg, Erica, and Koivula, Aki. 2022. "The Ouroboros of Seeking Validation? Exploring the Interconnection of Appearance (Dis)satisfaction and Content Creation on Social Media." In *Appearance as Capital*, edited by Outa Sarpila, Iida Kukkonen, Tero Pajunen, and Erica Aberg, 117–134. Bingley, UK: Emerald.

Aberg, Erica, and Solonen, Laura. 2021. "Well-Beshaved Women Rarely Make History—Exploring the Contestation of the Hairless Beauty Ideal with Case #Januhairy." In *Appearance as Capital*, edited by Outa Sarpila, Iida Kukkonen, Tero Pajunen, and Erica Aberg, 149–164. Bingley, UK: Emerald.

Abiala, Kristina, and Hernwall, Patrik. 2013. "Tweens Negotiating Identity Online—Swedish Girls' and Boys' Reflections on Online Experiences." *Journal of Youth Studies* 16(8): 951–969.

Abidin, Crystal. 2018. *Internet Celebrity: Understanding Fame Online*. Bingley, UK: Emerald.

Abidin, Crystal. 2020. "Mapping Internet Celebrity on TikTok: Exploring Attention Economies and Visibility Labours." *Cultural Science* 12(1): 77–103.

Abitbol, A., and Sternadori, M. 2016. "You Act like a Girl: An Examination of Consumer Perceptions of 'Femvertising.'" *Quarterly Review of Business Disciplines* 3(2): 117–138.

Abrams, L. S. 2003. "Contextual Variations in Young Women's Gender Identity Negotiations." *Psychology of Women Quarterly* 27(1): 64–74.

Adams, Natalie, and Bettis, Pamela. 2003. "Commanding the Room in Short Skirts: Cheering as the Embodiment of Ideal Girlhood." *Gender & Society* 17(1): 73–91.

Adamson, Maria. 2017. "Postfeminism, Neoliberalism, and a 'Successfully' Balanced Femininity in Celebrity CEO Autobiographies." *Gender, Work, and Organization* 24(3): 314–327.

Adler, Patricia, and Adler, Peter. 2011. *The Tender Cut: Inside the Hidden World of Self-Injury*. New York: New York University Press.

Ahn, June. 2011. "Digital Divides and Social Network Sites: Which Students Participate in Social Media?" *Journal of Educational Computing Research* 45(2): 147–163.

Aiken, Mary. 2016. *The Cyber Effect: A Pioneering Cyberpsychologist Explains How Human Behavior Changes Online*. New York: Random House.

Alavi, N., Roberts, N., Sutton, C., Axas, N., and Repetti, L. 2015. "Bullying Victimization (Being Bullied) among Adolescents Referred for Urgent Psychiatric Consultation: Prevalence and Association with Suicidality." *Canadian Journal of Psychiatry* 60(10): 427–431.

Albury, Kath, and Crawford, Kate. 2012. "Sexting, Consent and Young People's Ethics: Beyond *Megan's Story*." *Continuum* 26(3): 463–473.

Alter, A. L., Stern, C., Granot, Y., and Balcetis, E. 2016. "The 'Bad Is Black' Effect: Why People Believe Evildoers Have Darker Skin Than Do-Gooders." *Personality and Social Psychology Bulletin* 42(12): 1653–1665.

Anderson, Monica. 2018. "A Majority of Teens Have Experienced Some Form of Cyberbullying." *Pew Research Center*. Retrieved July 11, 2019. (https://www.pewinternet.org/2018/09/27/a-majority-of-teens-have-experienced-some-form-of-cyberbullying/).

Anderson, Monica, and Jiang, J. 2018a. "Teens, Social Media & Technology." *Pew Research Center*. Retrieved July 15, 2019. (https://www.pewresearch.org/internet/2018a/05/31/teens-social-media-technology-2018/).

Anderson, Monica, and Jiang, J. 2018b. "Teens' Social Media Habits and Experiences." *Pew Research Center*. Retrieved July 15, 2019. (https://pewresearch.org/internet/2018b/11/28/teens-social-media-habits-and-experiences/).

Anderson, Monica, Vogels, Emily, Perrin, Andrew, and Rainie, Lee. 2022. "Connection, Creativity, and Drama: Teen Life on Social Media in 2022." *Pew Research Center*. November 16. Retrieved January 17, 2024. (https://www.pewresearch.org/internet/2022/11/16/connection-creativity-and-drama-teen-life-on-social-media-in-2022/).

Anderson, Tammy L., Grunert, Catherine, Katz, Arielle, and Lovascio, Samantha. 2010. "Aesthetic Capital: A Research Review on Beauty Perks and Penalties." *Sociology Compass* 4(8): 464–575.

Ang, R. P., and Goh, D. H. 2010. "Cyberbullying among Adolescents: The Role of Affective and Cognitive Empathy, and Gender." *Child Psychiatry & Human Development* 41(4): 387–397.

APA. 2008. "Report of the APA Task Force on the Sexualization of Girls." *American Psychological Association*. February 1. Retrieved November 4, 2013. (http://www.apa.org/pi/women/programs/girls/report.aspx).

Ashton, Daniel, and Patel, Karen. 2020. "Girls' Bedroom Cultures." *International Encyclopedia of Gender, Media, and Communication*. Retrieved August 12, 2023. (https://doi.org.10.1002/9781119429128.iegmc214).

Attia, Sharon. 2023. "Adults Are Panicked about Teens and Social Media. These Girls Have Advice." *New York Times*. September 22. Retrieved January 26, 2024. (https://www.nytimes.com/2023/09/20/well/family/social-media-teens-adults.html).

Attrino, Anthony. 2019. "Family Catches Online Predator Trying to Lure 12-Year-Old N.J. Girl for Sex Through Social Media, Prosecutor Says." *NJ.com*. May 15. Retrieved June 8, 2019. (https://www.nj.com/bergen/2019/05/family-catches-online-predator-trying-to-lure-12-year-old-nj-girl-for-sex-through-social-media-prosecutor-says.html).

Attwood, Feona. 2007. "Sluts and Riot Grrrls: Female Identity and Sexual Agency." *Journal of Gender Studies* 16(3): 233–247.

Attwood, Feona, Hakim, Jamie, and Winch, Alison. 2017. "Mediated Intimacies: Bodies, Technologies and Relationships." *Journal of Gender Studies* 26(3): 1–5.

Austin, Ashley, Craig, Shelley L., Navega, Nicole, and McInroy, Lauren B. 2020. "It's My Safe Space: The Life-Saving Role of the Internet in the Lives of Transgender and Gender Diverse Youth." *International Journal of Transgender Health* 21(1): 33–44.

Avery, Lanice R., Stanton, Alexis G., Ward, L. Monique, Cole, Elizabeth R., Trinh, Sarah L., and Jerald, Morgan C. 2021. "'Pretty Hurts': Acceptance of Hegemonic Feminine Beauty Ideals and Reduced Sexual Well-Being among Black Women." *Body Image* 38(3): 181–190.

Azzarito, Laura. 2009. "The Panopticon of Physical Education: Pretty, Active, and Ideally White." *Physical Education and Sport Pedagogy* 14(1): 19–39.

Bailey, J., and Steeves, V. 2015. *eGirls, eCitizens: Putting Technology, Theory and Policy into Dialogue with Girls' and Young Women's Voices*. Ottawa, Canada: University of Ottawa Press.

Bailey, J., Steeves, V., Burkell, J., and Regan, P. 2013. "Negotiating with Gender Stereotypes on Social Networking Sites: From 'Bicycle Face' to Facebook." *Journal of Communication Inquiry* 37(2): 91–112.

Bailey, Moya. 2021. *Misogynoir Transformed: Black Women's Digital Resistance*. New York: New York University Press.

Balanda, Marisa E. 2020. "Bodies without the Burden: White Appropriation and Exploitation of Black Appearance and Culture." *Student Publications* 857. (https://cupola.gettysburg.edu/student_scholarship/857).

Balleys, C., and Coll, S. 2017. "Being Publicly Intimate: Teenagers Managing Online Privacy." *Media, Culture, and Society* 39(6): 885–901.

Balt, Elias, Mérelle, Saskia, Robinson, Jo, Popma, Arne, Creemers, Daan, van den Brand, Isa, van Bergen, Diana, Rasing, Sanne, Mulder, Wico, and Gilissen, Renske. 2023. "Social Media Use of Adolescents Who Died by Suicide: Lessons from a Psychological Autopsy Study." *Child and Adolescent Psychiatry and Mental Health* 17(48): 1–11.

Banet-Weiser, Sarah. 2012. *Authentic™: The Politics of Ambivalence in a Brand Culture*. New York: New York University Press.

Banet-Weiser, Sarah. 2014. "Am I Pretty or Ugly? Girls and the Market for Self-Esteem." *Girlhood Studies* 7(1): 83–101.

Banet-Weiser, Sarah. 2015. "Keynote Address: Media, Markets, Gender; Economies of Visibility in a Neoliberal Moment." *Communication Review* 18(1): 53–70.

Banet-Weiser, Sarah. 2017. "'I'm Beautiful the Way I Am': Empowerment, Beauty, and Aesthetic Labour." In *Aesthetic Labour: Rethinking Beauty Politics in Neoliberalism*, edited by Ana Sofia Elias, Rosalind Gill, and Christina Scharff, 265–282. London: Palgrave Macmillan.

Banet-Weiser, Sarah. 2018. *Empowered: Popular Feminism and Popular Misogyny*. Durham, NC: Duke University Press.

Barnard, Stephen R. 2016. "Spectacles of Self(ie) Empowerment? Networked Individualism and the Logic of the (Post)Feminist Selfie." In *Communication and Information Technologies Annual (Studies in Media and Communications 11)*, 63–88. Leeds, UK: Emerald Group Publishing Limited.

Barner, Briana. 2016. "The Creative (and Magical) Possibilities of Digital Black Girlhood." Master's thesis. University of Texas at Austin.

Baron, Mendi. 2018. "Is My Teen Really Addicted to Social Media?" *Psychology Today*. July 24. Retrieved May 8, 2019. (https://www.psychologytoday.com/us/blog/the-verge/201807/is-my-teen-really-addicted-social-media).

Barrense-Dias, Y., Berchtold, A., Surís, J. C., and Akre, C. 2017. "Sexting and the Definition Issue." *Journal of Adolescent Health* 61(5): 544–554.

Barry, Christopher T., Sidoti, Chloe L., Briggs, Shanelle M., Reiter, Shari R., and Lindsey,
Rebecca A. 2017. "Adolescent Social Media Use and Mental Health from Adolescent
and Parent Perspectives." *Journal of Adolescence* 61: 1–11.

Bartky, Sandra L. 1988. "Foucault, Femininity and the Modernization of Patriarchal Power." In *Feminism and Foucault: Reflections on Resistance*, edited by Irene Diamond
and Lee Quinby, 61–87. Boston: Northeastern University Press.

Bauman, S., Toomey, R. B., and Walker, J. L. 2013. "Associations among Bullying, Cyberbullying, and Suicide in High School Students." *Journal of Adolescence* (2): 341–350.

Beauvoir, Simone de. 1949. *Le Deuxieme Sexe: Vol. 1, Les faits et les mythes*. Paris: Gal-
limard.

Becker-Herby, Elisa. 2016. "The Rise of Femvertising: Authentically Reaching Female
Consumers." University of Minnesota Digital Conservancy. Thesis. University of Minnesota. (https://hdl.handle.net/11299/181494).

Beckman, Linda, Hagquist, Curt, and Hellström, Lisa. 2013. "Discrepant Gender Patterns
for Cyberbullying and Traditional Bullying—An Analysis of Swedish Adolescent Data."
Computers in Human Behavior 29(5): 1896–1903.

Beilinson, Jeremy. 2014. "What 12-Year-Olds Do on Social Media." *Consumer Reports*.
October 17. Retrieved April 10, 2016. (https://www.consumerreports.org/cro/news
/2014/10/kids-on-social-media/index.htm).

Bennett, Jessica. 2023. "Being 13." *New York Times*. September 20. Retrieved January 26,
2024. (https://www.nytimes.com/interactive/2023/09/20/well/family/13-year-old-girls
-social-media-self-esteem.html).

Berents, Helen. 2016. "Hashtagging Girlhood: #IAmMalala, #BringBackOurGirls and
Gendering Representations of Global Politics." *International Feminist Journal of Politics* 18(4): 513–527.

Berger, M. N., Taba, M., Marino, J. L., Lim, M. S. C., and Skinner, S. R. 2022. "Social Media
Use and Health and Well-Being of Lesbian, Gay, Bisexual, Transgender, and Queer
Youth: Systematic Review." *Journal of Medical Internet Research* 24(9): e38449.

Bernier, Alexe. 2023. "Girls Are in Crisis—And Their Mental Health Needs to Be Taken
Seriously." *The Conversation*. May 22. Retrieved July 24, 2023. (https://theconversation
.com/girls-are-in-crisis-and-their-mental-health-needs-to-be-taken-seriously-205177).

Berson, Ilene R., Berson, Michael J., and Ferron, John M. 2002. "Emerging Risks of Violence in the Digital Age." *Journal of School Violence* 1(2): 51–71.

Best, Joel, and Bogle, Kathleen. 2014. *Kids Gone Wild: From Rainbow Parties to Sexting,
Understanding the Hype over Teen Sex*. New York: New York University Press.

Bettie, Julie. 2003. *Women Without Class: Girls, Race, and Identity*. Oakland: University
of California Press.

Birkett, M., and Espelage, D. L. 2015. "Homophobic Name-Calling, Peer-Groups, and
Masculinity: The Socialization of Homophobic Behavior in Adolescents." *Social Development* 24(1): 184–205.

Bishop, Sophie. 2021. "Influencer Management Tools: Algorithmic Cultures, Brand Safety, and Bias." *Social Media + Society* 7(1):1–13.

Blaikie, Fiona. 2018. "Habitus, Visual and Cultural Identity: *Mean Girls*' Hyperfeminine
Performances as Burlesque Pastiche and as Archetypal Female Pariahs." *Studies in
Art Education* 59(3): 215–227.

Bobel, Chris, and Kwan, Samantha. 2011. *Embodied Resistance: Challenging the Norms,
Breaking the Rules*. Nashville, TN: Vanderbilt University Press.

Bobel, Chris, and Kwan, Samantha. 2019. *Body Battlegrounds: Transgressions, Tensions, and Transformations*. Nashville, TN: Vanderbilt University Press.

Bogle, D. 2001. *Toms, Coons, Mulattoes, Mammies, and Bucks: An Interpretive History of Blacks in American Films*. 4th ed. New York: Continuum.

Bordo, Susan. 1993. *Unbearable Weight: Feminism, Western Culture, and the Body*. Berkeley: University of California Press.

Bordo, Susan. 2000. *The Male Body: A New Look at Men in Public and in Private*. New York: Farrar, Straus, and Giroux.

Borrelli, Anthony. 2018. "Online Predators: They Hunted Girls. They Lied to Girls. They Manipulated Girls." *Press Connects USA Today*. December 3. Retrieved April 6, 2019. (https://www.pressconnects.com/story/news/public-safety/2018/12/03/online-predators-internet-sexual-enticement-children-cyber-crime-protect/1820834002/).

Boudreau, K. 2007. "The Girls' Room: Negotiating Schoolyard Friendships Online." In *Growing Up Online*, edited by S. Weber and S. Dixon, 69–81. New York: Palgrave Macmillan.

Boursier, V., Gioia, F., and Griffiths, M. D. 2020. "Selfie-Engagement on Social Media: Pathological Narcissism, Positive Expectation, and Body Objectification—Which Is More Influential?" *Addict Behav. Rep* 11: 100263.

Bowen, Sesali. 2021. *Bad Fat Black Girl: Notes from a Trap Feminist*. New York: Amistad.

boyd, danah. 2007. "Why Youth (Heart) Social Network Sites: The Role of Networked Publics in Teenage Social Life." *MacArthur Foundation Series on Digital Learning–Youth, Identity, and Media Volume*. Cambridge, MA: MIT Press. 119–142.

boyd, danah. 2010. "Social Network Sites as Networked Publics: Affordances, Dynamics, and Implications." In *Networked Self: Identity, Community, and Culture on Social Network Sites*, edited by Zizi Papacharissi, 39–58. London: Routledge.

boyd, danah. 2014. *It's Complicated: The Social Lives of Networked Teens*. New Haven, CT: Yale University Press.

boyd, danah, and Ellison, Nicole. 2007. "Social Network Sites: Definition, History, and Scholarship." *Journal of Computer Mediated Communication* 13(1): 210–230.

Brailovskaia, Julia, Teismann, Tobias, and Margraf, Jürgen. 2018. "Cyberbullying, Positive Mental Health and Suicide Ideation/Behavior." *Psychiatry Research* 267: 240–242.

Brandes, S. B., and Levin, D. 2014. "'Like My Status': Israeli Teenage Girls Constructing Their Social Connections on the Facebook Social Network." *Feminist Media Studies* 14(5): 743–758.

Brickman, Barbara Jane. 2019. "Queering Girlhood." *Girlhood Studies* 12(1): vi+.

Briggs, Bill. 2012. "Cyberbullying Not as Rampant as Thought, Study Suggests." *NBC News*. August 10. Retrieved April 17, 2019. (https://www.nbcnews.com/health/health-news/cyberbullying-not-rampant-thought-study-suggests-flna1b5307590).

Brito, P. Q. 2012. "Tweens' Characterization of Digital Technologies." *Computers & Education* 59(2): 580–593.

Brown, B. Bradford, Clasen, Donna R., and Eicher, Sue A. 1986. "Perceptions of Peer Pressure, Peer Conformity Dispositions, and Self-Reported Behavior among Adolescents." *Developmental Psychology* 22(4): 521–530.

Brown, Lyn Mikel. 2003. *Girlfighting: Betrayal and Rejection among Girls*. New York: New York University Press.

Brown, Lyn Mikel, and Gilligan, Carol. 1992. *Meeting at the Crossroads: Women's Psychology and Girls' Development*. Cambridge, MA: Harvard University Press.

Brown, Ruth Nicole. 2013. *Hear Our Truths: The Creative Potential of Black Girlhood*. Chicago: University of Illinois Press.

Brown, Wendy. 2003. "Neo-liberalism and the End of Liberal Democracy." *Theory and Event* 7(1): 1–19.

Brumberg, Joan Jacobs. 1997. *The Body Project: An Intimate History of American Girls.* New York: Vintage.

Buckingham, David. 2008. *Youth, Identity, and Digital Media.* Boston: MIT Press.

Buckingham, David. 2013a. *Beyond Technology: Children's Learning in the Age of Digital Culture.* Malden, MA: Polity Press.

Buckingham, David. 2013b. "Making Sense of the 'Digital Generation': Growing up with Digital Media." *Self & Society* 40(3): 7–15.

Buckingham, David, Bragg, Sara, and Kehily, Mary, eds. 2014. *Youth Cultures in the Age of Global Media.* Studies in Childhood and Youth. Basingstoke: Palgrave Macmillan.

Buckingham, David, Willett, Rebekah, Bragg, Sara, and Russell, Rachel. 2010. "Sexualised Goods Aimed at Children: A Report to the Scottish Parliament Equal Opportunities Committee." Scottish Parliament Equal Opportunities Committee, Edinburgh, UK.

Bulger, Monica, Madden, Mary, Sobel, Kiley, and Davison, Patrick. 2021. *The Missing Middle: Reimagining a Future for Tweens, Teens, and Public Media.* New York City: Joan Ganz Cooney Center at Sesame Workshop.

Burgess, Jean, and Green, Joshua. 2018. *YouTube: Online Video and Participatory Culture.* Cambridge: Polity Press.

Burke, M., Adamic, L., and Marciniak, K. 2021. "Families on Facebook." *Proceedings of the International AAAI Conference on Web and Social Media* 7(1): 41–50.

Burnette, C. Blair, Kwitowski, Melissa A., and Mazzeo, Suzanne E. 2017. "'I Don't Need People to Tell Me I'm Pretty on Social Media': A Qualitative Study of Social Media and Body Image in Early Adolescent Girls." *Body Image* 23(4): 114–125.

Burns, Anne. 2015. "Self(ie)-Discipline: Social Regulation as Enacted through the Discussion of Photographic Practice." *International Journal of Communication* 9: 1716–1733.

BusinessWire. 2022. "Skin Lighteners Global Markets Report." August 3. Retrieved December 1, 2022. (https://www.businesswire.com/news/home/20220803005583/en/Skin -Lighteners-Global-Market-Reports-2022-Rising-Interest-of-Men-in-Beauty-and-Cos metic-Products-Presents-Lucrative-Growth-Opportunities---ResearchAndMarkets .com).

Butkowski, C. P., Dixon, T. L., Weeks, K. R., and Smith, M. A. 2020. "Quantifying the Feminine Self(ie): Gender Display and Social Media Feedback in Young Women's Instagram Selfies." *New Media & Society* 22(5): 817–837.

Butler, Jess. 2013. "For White Girls Only? Postfeminism and the Politics of Inclusion." *Feminist Formations* 25(1): 35–58.

Butler, Judith. 1990. *Gender Trouble: Feminism and the Subversion of Identity.* New York: Routledge.

Byer, Nicole. 2020. *#VERYFAT #VERYBRAVE: The Fat Girl's Guide to Being #Brave and Not a Dejected, Melancholy, Down-in-the-Dumps Weeping Fat Girl in a Bikini.* Kansas City, MO: Andrews McMeel.

Callen, Anthea. 2018. *Looking at Men: Anatomy, Masculinity and the Modern Male Body.* New Haven, CT: Yale University Press.

Camero, Katie. 2024. "Young Girls Are Flooding Sephora in What Some Call an 'Epidemic.' So We Talked to Their Moms." *USA Today.* January 19. Retrieved February 2, 2024. (https://www.usatoday.com/story/life/health-wellness/2024/01/19/sephora-kids -makeup-preteen-moms/72267089007/).

Campbell, Marilyn. 2005. "Cyber Bullying: An Old Problem in a New Guise?" *Australian Journal of Guidance and Counselling* 15(1): 68–76.

Canales, Katie. 2022. "Silicon Valley Says Kids over the Age of 13 Can Handle the Big, Bad World of Social Media. Experts Say That's the Result of a 'Problematic' 1990s Internet Law." *BusinessInsider.* January 14. Retrieved September 10, 2023. (https://www.businessinsider.com/why-you-must-be-13-facebook-instagram-problematic-law-coppa-2022-1).

Carter Andrews, D. J., Brown, T., Castro, E., and Id-Deen, E. 2019. "The Impossibility of Being 'Perfect and White': Black Girls' Racialized and Gendered Schooling Experiences." *American Educational Research Journal* 56(6): 2531–2572.

Cassell, Justine, and Cramer, Meg. 2008. "High Tech or High Risk: Moral Panics about Girls Online." In *Digital Youth, Innovation, and the Unexpected*, edited by Tara McPherson, 53–76. Cambridge, MA: MIT Press.

Castilho, F., and Romancini, R. 2017. "'Fight Like a Girl': Virtual Bedroom Culture in Public School Occupations in Brazil." *Catalan Journal of Communication & Cultural Studies* 9(2): 303–320.

Cavalcante, Andre. 2016. "'I Did It All Online': Transgender Identity and the Management of Everyday Life." *Critical Studies in Media Communication* 33(1): 109–122.

CDC. 2022. "New CDC Data Illuminate Youth Mental Health Threats during the COVID-19 Pandemic." *Centers for Disease Control and Prevention.* March 31. Retrieved on June 23, 2023. (https://www.cdc.gov/media/releases/2022/p0331-youth-mental-health-covid-19.html).

CDC. 2023. "U.S. Teen Girls Experiencing Increased Sadness and Violence." *Youth Risk Behavior Survey: Centers for Disease Control and Prevention.* February 13. Retrieved June 24, 2023. (https://www.cdc.gov/media/releases/2023/p0213-yrbs.html).

Chang, Jiang, and Tian, Hao. 2021. "Girl Power in Boy Love: Yaoi, Online Female Counterculture, and Digital Feminism in China." *Feminist Media Studies* 21(4): 604–620.

Chang, Yuanyuan. 2021. "Do Boys and Girls Behave Differently Online? A Review of Gender Differences in Cyberbullying." *Advances in Social Science, Education, and Humanities Research* 554. In *Proceedings of the 7th International Conference on Humanities and Social Science Research*. Amsterdam, Netherlands. 819–824.

Chen, X., Luo, Yj., and Chen, H. 2020. "Body Image Victimization Experiences and Disordered Eating Behaviors among Chinese Female Adolescents: The Role of Body Dissatisfaction and Depression." *Sex Roles* 83(7/8): 442–452.

Cherid, Maha Ikram. 2021. "'Ain't Got Enough Money to Pay Me Respect': Blackfishing, Cultural Appropriation, and the Commodification of Blackness." *Cultural Studies, Critical Methodologies* 21(5): 359–364.

Cherlin, Andrew. 2010. *The Marriage Go Round: The State of Marriage and the Family in America Today.* New York: Vintage.

Chesney-Lind, Meda, Morash, Merry, and Irwin, Katherine. 2007. "Policing Girlhood? Relational Aggression and Violence Prevention." *Youth Violence and Juvenile Justice* 5(3): 328–345.

Choukas-Bradley, S., Roberts, S. R., Maheux, A. J., and Nesi, J. 2022. "The Perfect Storm: A Developmental–Sociocultural Framework for the Role of Social Media in Adolescent Girls' Body Image Concerns and Mental Health." *Clinical Child and Family Psychology Review* 25(4): 681–701.

Chua, T. H. H., and Chang, L. 2016. "Follow Me and Like My Beautiful Selfies: Singapore Teenage Girls' Engagement in Self-Presentation and Peer Comparison on Social Media." *Computers in Human Behavior* 55(Part A): 190–197.

Cipolletta, S., Malighetti, C., Cenedese, C., and Spoto, A. 2020. "How Can Adolescents Benefit from the Use of Social Networks? The iGeneration on Instagram." *International Journal of Environmental Research on Public Health* 17(19): 6952.

Cohen, R., Newton-John, T., and Slater, A. 2018. "'Selfie'-Objectification: The Role of Selfies in Self-Objectification and Disordered Eating in Young Women." *Computers in Human Behavior* 79(2): 68–74.

Cohen, R., Newton-John, T., and Slater, A. 2021. "The Case for Body Positivity on Social Media: Perspectives on Current Advances and Future Directions." *Journal of Health Psychology* 26(13): 2365–2373.

Cohen, Stanley. 1972. *Folk Devils and Moral Panics: The Creation of the Mods and Rockers*. New York: Routledge.

Common Sense Media. 2018. "Social Media, Social Life: Teens Reveal Their Experiences." September 10. Retrieved June 7, 2019. (https://www.commonsensemedia.org/research/social-media-social-life-teens-reveal-their-experiences-2018).

Common Sense Media. 2024. "Parents' Ultimate Guide to Snapchat." January 12. Retrieved February 1, 2024. (https://www.commonsensemedia.org/articles/parents-ultimate-guide-to-snapchat).

Connell, R. W. 1987. *Gender and Power*. Stanford: Stanford University Press.

Connell, R. W., and Messerschmidt, James. 2005. "Hegemonic Masculinity: Rethinking the Concept." *Gender and Society* 19(6): 829–859.

Cook, Daniel Thomas, and Kaiser, Susan B. 2004. "Betwixt and Be Tween: Age Ambiguity and the Sexualization of the Female Consuming Subject." *Journal of Consumer Culture* 4(2): 203–227.

Coontz, Stephanie. 1993. *The Way We Never Were: American Families and the Nostalgia Trap*. New York: Basic Books.

Cooper, Charlotte. 2016. *Fat Activism: A Radical Social Movement*. Bristol, UK: HammerOn Press.

Coulter, Natalie. 2021. "'Frappés, Friends, and Fun': Affective Labor and the Cultural Industry of Girlhood." *Journal of Consumer Culture* 21(3): 487–500.

Cox, Joy Arlene Renee. 2020. *Fat Girls in Black Bodies: Creating Communities of Our Own*. Berkeley, CA: North Atlantic Books.

Coyne, S. M., Radesky, J., Collier, K. M., Gentile, D. A., Linder, J. R., Nathanson, A. I., Rasmussen, E. E., Reich, S. M., and Rogers, J. 2017. "Parenting and Digital Media." *Pediatrics* 140(2): S112–S116.

Craig, Shelley L., McInroy, Lauren, McCready, Lance T., and Alaggia, Ramona. 2015. "Media: A Catalyst for Resilience in Lesbian, Gay, Bisexual, Transgender, and Queer Youth." *Journal of LGBT Youth* 12(3): 254–275.

Crann, S. E. 2017. "Rewriting Girlhood: Gendered Subjectivities among Girls and Young Women Attending a Girls' Empowerment Program in a Rural Canadian Community." Doctoral dissertation. University of Guelph. (https://atrium.lib.uoguelph.ca/xmlui/handle/10214/10323).

Crawford Robert. 1980. "Healthism and the Medicalization of Everyday Life." *International Journal of Health Services* 10(3): 365–388.

Crenshaw, Kimberlé. 1989. "Demarginalizing the Intersection of Race and Sex: A Black Feminist Critique of Antidiscrimination Doctrine, Feminist Theory and Antiracist Politics." *University of Chicago Legal Forum* 1989(1): 139–167.

Cristo, Isabel. 2023. "Women in Retrograde." *The Cut*. December 19. Retrieved January 4, 2024. (https://www.thecut.com/article/girl-culture.html).

Currie, Dawn, Kelly, Deirdre, and Pomerantz, Shauna. 2007. "'The Power to Squash People': Understanding Girls' Relational Aggression." *British Journal of Sociology of Education* 28(1): 23–37.

Currie, Dawn, Kelly, Deirdre, and Pomerantz, Shauna. 2009. *'Girl Power': Girls Reinventing Girlhood*. New York: Peter Lang.

Davis, Katie. 2010. "Coming of Age Online: The Developmental Underpinnings of Girls' Blogs." *Journal of Adolescent Research* 25(1): 145–171.

Davis, Katie. 2012. "Friendship 2.0: Adolescents' Experiences of Belonging and Self-Disclosure Online." *J Adolesc*. 35(6): 1527–1536.

Davis, Katie. 2013. "Young People's Digital Lives: The Impact of Interpersonal Relationships and Digital Media Use on Adolescents' Sense of Identity." *Computers in Human Behavior* 29(6): 2281–2293.

Davis, K., and Carrie, J. 2013. "Tweens' Conceptions of Privacy Online: Implications for Educators." *Learning, Media and Technology* 38(1): 4–25.

De Leyn, Tom, De Wolf, Ralf, Vanden Abeele, Mariek, and De Marez, Lieven. 2019. "Reframing Current Debates on Young People's Online Privacy by Taking into Account the Cultural Construction of Youth." In *SMSociety '19 Proceedings of the 10th International Conference on Social Media & Society*, 174–183. New York: Association for Computing Machinery.

De Leyn, Tom, De Wolf, Ralf, Vanden Abeele, Mariek, and De Marez, Lieven. 2021. "In between Child's Play and Teenage Pop Culture: Tweens, TikTok & Privacy." *Journal of Youth Studies* 25(8): 1–18.

Demby, Gene. 2013. "The Truth behind the Lies of the Original Welfare Queen." *Code Switch: National Public Radio*. December 20. Retrieved January 12, 2019. (https://www.npr.org/sections/codeswitch/2013/12/20/255819681/the-truth-behind-the-lies-of-the-original-welfare-queen).

De Ridder, S., and Van Bauwel, S. 2015. "The Discursive Construction of Gay Teenagers in Times of Mediatization: Youth's Reflections on Intimate Storytelling, Queer Shame and Realness in Popular Social Media Places." *Journal of Youth Studies* 18(6): 777–793.

De Wolf, R., and Joye, S. 2019. "Control Responsibility: The Discursive Construction of Privacy, Teens, and Facebook in Flemish Newspapers." *International Journal of Communication* 13: 5505–5524.

Diamond, Irene, and Quinby, Lee. 1988. *Feminism and Foucault: Reflections on Resistance*. Boston: Northeastern University Press.

Dionne, Evette. 2019. "Here's What Fat Acceptance Is—And Isn't." *Yes Magazine*. June 24. Retrieved August 15, 2019. (https://www.yesmagazine.org/social-justice/2019/06/24/fat-acceptance-movement).

Dorol-Beauroy-Eustache, Ophely, and Mishara, Brian L. 2021. "Systematic Review of Risk and Protective Factors for Suicidal and Self-Harm Behaviors among Children and Adolescents Involved with Cyberbullying." *Preventive Medicine* 152(1): 106684.

Doucleff, Michaeleen. 2023. "Teens Say Social Media Is Stressing Them Out. Here's How to Help Them." *NPR All Things Considered*. May 17. Retrieved January 19, 2024. (https://www.npr.org/sections/health-shots/2023/05/17/1176452284/teens-social-media-phone-habit).

Douglas, Mary. 1970. *Natural Symbols*. London: Barrie and Rockliff.

Downe, Pamela. 2005. "Aboriginal Girls in Canada: Living Histories of Dislocation, Exploitation, and Strength." In *Girlhood: Redefining the Limits*, edited by Yasmin Jiwani, Candis Steenbergen, and Claudia Mitchell, 1–14. Montreal: Black Rose.

Doyle, Sady. 2019. *Dead Blondes and Bad Mothers: Monstrosity, Patriarchy, and the Fear of Female Power*. New York: Melville House.

Draper, Nora R. A. 2012. "Is Your Teen at Risk? Discourses of Adolescent Sexting in United States Television News." *Journal of Children and Media* 6(2): 221–236.

Driscoll, Catherine. 2002. *Girls: Feminine Adolescence in Popular Culture and Cultural Theory*. New York: Columbia University Press.

Driscoll, Catherine, and Gregg, Melissa. 2008. "Broadcast Yourself: Moral Panic, Youth Culture, and Internet Studies." In *Youth, Media, and Culture in the Asia Pacific Region*, edited by Usha Rodriguez and Belinda Smaill, 71–86. Newcastle upon Tyne, UK: Cambridge Scholars Press.

Driver, Susan. 2007. *Queer Girls and Popular Culture: Reading, Resisting, and Creating Media (Mediated Youth)*. New York: Peter Lang.

Dubrofsky, Rachel, and Wood, Megan. 2014. "Posting Racism and Sexism: Authenticity, Agency, and Self-Reflexivity in Social Media." *Communication and Critical/Cultural Studies* 11(3): 282–287.

Duffy, Brooke Erin. 2015. "The Romance of Work: Gender and Aspirational Labour in the Digital Culture Industries." *International Journal of Cultural Studies* 19(4): 1–17.

Duffy, Brooke Erin, and Hund, Emily. 2015. "'Having It All' on Social Media: Entrepreneurial Femininity and Self-Branding among Fashion Bloggers." *Social Media and Society* 1(2): 1–11.

Dunmade, Aderinola, and Tella, Adeyinka. 2023. "Social Media Use and Its Implications on Cyberethical Behaviour in Nigeria: Perspectives of Generation Z Girls." *Journal of Cyberspace Studies* 7(1): 23–44.

Dunne, A., Lawlor, M., and Rowley, J. 2010. "Young People's Use of Online Social Networking Sites—A Uses and Gratifications Perspective." *Journal of Research in Interactive Marketing* 4(1): 46–58.

Durham, D. 2017. "Elusive Adulthoods: Introduction." In *Elusive Adulthoods: The Anthropology of New Maturities*, edited by D. Durham and J. Solway, 1–38. Bloomington: Indiana University Press.

Durham, M. Gigi. 2008. *The Lolita Effect: The Media Sexualization of Young Girls and What We Can Do about It*. New York: Abrams Press.

Dvorak, John C. 2013. "Last Word." *PC Magazine*. December 2013.

Ebert, Roger. 2007. *Your Movie Sucks*. Kansas City, MO: Andrews McMeel.

Edwards, Erika, and Fox, Maggie. 2018. "More Teens Addicted to Social Media, Prefer Texting to Talking." *NBC News*. September 10. Retrieved July 9, 2019. (https://www.nbcnews.com/health/health-news/moreteens-addicted-social-media-say-they-re-wise-distractions-n908126).

Egan, R. Danielle. 2013. *Becoming Sexual: A Critical Appraisal of the Sexualization of Girls*. Cambridge: Polity Press.

Ehrenreich, Sam. 2020. "What Do Parents Need to Know about Teens and Sexting?" *NEVADAToday*. February 10. Retrieved March 5, 2022. (https://www.unr.edu/nevada-today/news/2020/atp-teen-sexting).

Eisenstein, Hester. 2010. *Feminism Seduced: How Global Elites Use Women's Labor and Ideas to Exploit the World*. Boulder, CO: Paradigm.

Elgersma, Christine. 2017. "The Facts about Online Predators Every Parent Should Know." *Common Sense Media*. July 25. Retrieved February 4, 2019. (https://www.commonsensemedia.org/articles/the-facts-about-online-predators-every-parent-should-know).

Elgin, Jenna. 2014. "Examining the Relationships between Suicidal Ideation, Substance Use, Depressive Symptoms, and Educational Factors in Emerging Adulthood." Doctoral dissertation. University of Washington. 1–88.

Elias, A. S., and Gill, R. 2018. "Beauty Surveillance: The Digital Self-Monitoring Cultures of Neoliberalism." *European Journal of Cultural Studies* 21(1): 59–77.

Englander, Elizabeth, and McCoy, Meghan K. 2023. "Analysis: There's a Mental Health Crisis among Teen Girls. Here Are Some Ways to Support Them." *PBS Newshour.* February 24. Retrieved July 8, 2023. (https://www.pbs.org/newshour/health/analysis-theres-a-mental-health-crisis-among-teen-girls-here-are-some-ways-to-support-them).

Erdman Farrell, Amy. 2011. *Fat Shame: Stigma and the Fat Body in American Culture.* New York: New York University Press.

Erevelles, Nirmala, and Mutua, Kagendo. 2005. "'I Am a Woman Now!' Rewriting Cartographies of Girlhood from the Critical Standpoint of Disability." In *Geographies of Girlhood: Identities In-between*, edited by Pamela J. Bettis and Natalie J. Adams, 253–269. New York: Routledge.

Erevelles, Nirmala, and Nguyen, Xuan Thuy. 2016. "Disability, Girlhood, and Vulnerability in Transnational Contexts." *Girlhood Studies* 9(1): 3–20.

Erigha, Maryann, and Crooks-Allen, Ashley. 2020. "Digital Communities of Black Girlhood: New Media Technologies and Online Discourses of Empowerment." *Black Scholar* 50(4): 66–76.

Farady, Michael. 2010. "The Girl-Crisis Movement: Evaluating the Foundation." *Review of General Psychology* 14(1): 44–55.

Fardouly, J., Diedrichs, P. C., Vartanian, L. R., and Halliwell, E. 2015. "Social Comparisons on Social Media: The Impact of Facebook on Young Women's Body Image Concerns and Mood." *Body Image* 13(C): 38–45.

Fardouly, J., and Vartanian, L. R. 2016. "Social Media and Body Image Concerns: Current Research and Future Directions." *Current Opinion in Psychology* 9(3): 1–5.

Fardouly, J., Willburger, B. K., and Vartanian, L. R. 2018. "Instagram Use and Young Women's Body Image Concerns and Self-Objectification: Testing Mediational Pathways." *New Media & Society* 20(4): 1380–1395.

Farman, Jason. 2012. *Mobile Interface Theory.* New York: Routledge.

Farrell, Christina. 2022. *Teenage Girls' Experiences on Social Media: A Discursive Exploration of Institutional Power and Identity Formation.* Doctoral thesis. Charles Stuart University.

Favaro, Laura. 2017. "'Just Be Confident Girls!': Confidence Chic as Neoliberal Governmentality." In *Aesthetic Labour: Rethinking Beauty Politics in Neoliberalism*, edited by Ana Sofia Elias, Rosalind Gill, and Christina Scharff, 283–300. London: Palgrave Macmillan.

Febos, Melissa. 2021. *Girlhood.* New York: Bloomsbury.

Felmlee, Diane, and Faris, Robert. 2016. "Toxic Ties: Networks of Friendship, Dating, and Cybervictimization." *Social Psychology Quarterly* 79(3): 243–262.

Feltman, C., and Szymanski, D. 2018. "Instagram Use and Self-Objectification: The Roles of Internalization, Comparison, Appearance Commentary, and Feminism." *Sex Roles* 78(56): 311–324.

Field, Corinne T., and Simmons, LaKisha Michelle, eds. 2022. *The Global History of Black Girlhood.* Champaign: University of Illinois Press.

Fields, Jessica. 2008. *Risky Lessons: Sex Education and Social Inequality.* New Brunswick, NJ: Rutgers University Press.

Fine, Michelle. 1988. "Sexuality, Schooling, and Adolescent Females: The Missing Discourse of Desire." *Harvard Educational Review* 58(1): 29–54.

Fine, Michelle, and McClelland, Sara I. 2007. "The Politics of Teen Women's Sexuality: Public Policy and the Adolescent Female Body." *Emory Law Journal* 56(4): 995–1038.

Foucault, Michel. 1976. *History of Sexuality*. Vol. I, *An Introduction*. New York: Random House.

Fox 13 Tampa Bay. 2016. "PSA: Kids Easily Targeted by Sexual Predators Online." April 27. Retrieved October 12, 2017. (https://www.fox13news.com/news/psa-kids-easily -targeted-by-sexual-predators-online).

French, B. H. 2013. "More Than Jezebels and Freaks: Exploring How Black Girls Navigate Sexual Coercion and Sexual Scripts." *Journal of African American Studies* 17(1): 35–50.

Gallo, Amanda. 2013. "Am I Pretty or Ugly?" *The Argus*. December 9. Retrieved September 20, 2015. (http://thesheaf.com/2013/12/09/am-i-pretty-or-ugly/).

Gangwani, S., Alruwaili, N., and Al Safar, S. 2021. "Social Media Usage and Female Empowerment in Saudi Arabia." *Academy of Strategic Management Journal* 20(4): 1–8.

García-Gómez, Antonio. 2011. "Regulating Girlhood: Evaluative Language, Discourses of Gender Socialization and Relational Aggression." *European Journal of Women's Studies* 18(3): 243–264.

García-Gómez, Antonio. 2018. "From Selfies to Sexting: Tween Girls, Intimacy, and Subjectivities." *Girlhood Studies* 11(1): 43–58.

Garcia-Rapp, Florencia. 2017. "'Come Join and Let's BOND': Authenticity and Legitimacy Building on YouTube's Beauty Community." *Journal of Media Practice* 18(2): 120–137.

Gerhardt, Linda. 2020. "The Rebellious History of the Fat Acceptance Movement." *Center for Discovery Eating Disorder Treatment*. Retrieved September 2021. (https://center fordiscovery.com/blog/fat-acceptance-movement/).

Gill, Rosalind. 2007. "Postfeminist Media Culture: Elements of a Sensibility." *European Journal of Cultural Studies* 10(2): 147–166.

Gill, Rosalind. 2021. "Being Watched and Feeling Judged on Social Media." *Feminist Media Studies* 21(8): 1387–1392.

Gill, Rosalind, and Orgad, Shani. 2017. "Confidence Culture and the Remaking of Feminism." *New Formations* 2017(91): 16–34.

Gill, Rosalind, and Scharff, Christina. 2011. "Introduction." In *New Femininities: Postfeminism, Neoliberalism and Subjectivity*, edited by Rosalind Gill and Christina Scharff, 1–19. Basingstoke: Palgrave Macmillan.

Ging, Debbie, and O'Higgins Norman, James. 2016. "Cyberbullying, Conflict Management, or Just Messing? Teenage Girls' Understandings and Experiences of Gender, Friendship, and Conflict on Facebook in an Irish Second-Level School." *Feminist Media Studies* 16(5): 1–17.

Giovanelli, Dina, and Ostertag, Stephen. 2009. "Controlling the Body: Media Representations, Body Size, and Self-Discipline." In *The Fat Studies Reader*, edited by Esther Rothblum and Sondra Solovay, 289–296. New York: New York University Press.

Glassner, Barry. 1999. *The Culture of Fear: Why Americans Are Afraid of the Wrong Things*. New York: Basic Books.

Goetzman, Amy. 2014. "'Dance Hall to Facebook' Calls for More Measured Media Coverage of Young People." *MinnPost*. Retrieved July 13, 2018. (https://www.minnpost.com /books/2014/09/dance-hall-facebook-calls-more-measured-media-coverage-young -people/).

Gonick, Marnina. 2003. *Between Femininities: Ambivalence, Identity, and the Education of Girls.* Albany, NY: SUNY Press.

Gonick, Marnina. 2006. "Sugar and Spice and Something More Than Nice? Queer Girls and Transformations of Social Exclusion." In *Girlhood: Redefining the Limits*, edited by Yasmin Jiwani, Candis Steenbergen, and Claudia Mitchell, 122–137. Montreal: Black Rose Books.

Gonick, Marnina, and Gannon, Susanne. 2014. *Becoming Girl: Collective Biography and the Production of Girlhood.* Toronto: Women's Press of Canada.

Gonick, Marnina, Renold, Emma, Ringrose, Jessica, and Weems, Lisa. 2009. "Rethinking Agency and Resistance: What Comes after Girl Power?" *Girlhood Studies* 2(2): 1–9.

Gordon, Aubrey. 2020. *What We Don't Talk about When We Talk about Fat.* Boston: Beacon Press.

Gordon, Aubrey. 2023. *You Just Need to Lose Weight: And 19 Other Myths about Fat People.* Boston: Beacon Press.

Gordon, Sherri. 2019. "Surprising Ways Your Teen Benefits from Social Media." *Very Well Family.* July 9. Retrieved August 4, 2019. (https://www.verywellfamily.com/benefits-of-social-media-4067431).

Gordon-Messer, D., Bauermeister, J. A., Grodzinski, A., and Zimmerman, M. 2013. "Sexting among Young Adults." *Journal of Adolescent Health* 52(3): 301–306.

Graham, Anne, Powell, Mary Ann, Taylor, Nicola, Anderson, Donnah, and Fitzgerald, Robyn. 2013. *Ethical Research Involving Children.* Florence: UNICEF Office of Research Innocenti.

Gray, Emma. 2012. "'Am I Ugly?' Videos: Young Teens Ask YouTube Users Whether They're Pretty or Not." *Huffpost.* February 21. Retrieved July 10, 2024. (https://www.huffpost.com/entry/am-i-ugly-or-pretty-videos-youtube-teens_n_1292113).

Greig, A., Taylor, J., and MacKay, T. 2013. *Doing Research with Children.* Thousand Oaks, CA: SAGE.

Griffith, R. Marie. 2004. *Born Again Bodies: Flesh and Spirit in American Christianity.* Berkeley: University of California Press.

Guba, E. G., and Lincoln, Y. S. 1994. "Competing Paradigms in Qualitative Research." In *Handbook of Qualitative Research*, edited by N. K. Denzin and Y. S. Lincoln, 105–117. Thousand Oaks, CA: SAGE.

Hackley, C., and Hackley, R. A. 2015. "Marketing and the Cultural Production of Celebrity in the Era of Media Convergence." *Marketing Management* 31(5–6): 461–477.

Hadley, Martha. 2003. "Relational, Indirect, Adaptive, or Just Mean: Recent Work on Aggression in Adolescent Girls—Part I." *Studies in Gender and Sexuality* 4(4): 367–394.

Hadley, Martha. 2004. "Relational, Indirect, Adaptive, or Just Mean: Recent Studies on Aggression in Adolescent Girls—Part II." *Studies in Gender and Sexuality* 5(3): 331–350.

Hall, Kimberly Ann. 2015. "The Authenticity of Social-Media Performance: Lonelygirl15 and the Amateur Brand of Young-Girlhood." *Women & Performance: A Journal of Feminist Theory* 25(2): 128–142.

Hamilton, Maggie. 2008. *What's Happening to Our Girls.* Camberwell, Victoria: Viking.

Hammond, Simon P., Cooper, Neil, and Jordan, Peter. 2018. "Social Media, Social Capital and Adolescents Living in State Care: A Multi-perspective and Multi-method Qualitative Study." *British Journal of Social Work* 48(7): 2058–2076.

Harris, Anita. 2004a. *Future Girl: Young Women in the Twenty-First Century.* New York: Routledge.

Harris, Anita. 2004b. *All about the Girl: Culture, Power, and Identity.* New York: Routledge.

Harrison, Da'Shaun L. 2021. *Belly of the Beast: The Politics of Anti-fatness as Anti-Blackness.* Berkeley, CA: North Atlantic Books.

Hart, Laurel, and Mitchell, Claudia. 2015. "From Spaces of Gender-Based Violence to Sites of Networked Resistance: Reimagining Social Media Technologies." *Perspectives in Education* 33(4): 135–150.

Hasinoff, Amy A. 2013. "Sexting as Media Production: Rethinking Social Media and Sexuality." *New Media & Society* 15(4): 449–465.

Hasinoff, Amy A. 2015. *Sexting Panic: Rethinking Criminalization, Privacy, and Consent.* Champaign, IL: University of Chicago Press.

Hearn, A. 2008. "'Meat, Mask, Burden': Probing the Contours of the Branded 'Self.'" *Journal of Consumer Culture* 8(2): 197–217.

Herring, Susan C., and Kapidzic, Sanja. 2015. "Teens, Gender, and Self Presentation in Social Media." In *International Encyclopedia of Social and Behavioral Sciences*, 2nd ed., edited by J. D. Wright, 146–152. Oxford: Elsevier.

Herrman, John. 2016. "Who's Too Young for an App? Musical.ly Tests the Limits." *New York Times.* September 16. Retrieved on July 3, 2019. (https://www.nytimes.com/2016/09/17/business/media/a-social-network-frequented-by-children-tests-the-limits-of-online-regulation.html).

Hesse-Biber, Sharlene N. 2006. *The Cult of Thinness.* New York: Oxford University Press.

Hey, Valerie. 1997. *The Company She Keeps: An Ethnography of Girls' Friendships.* Buckingham: Open University Press.

Hill, Dominique C. 2018. "Black Girl Pedagogies: Layered Lessons on Reliability." *Curriculum Inquiry* 48(3): 383–405.

Hill, Dominique C. 2019. "Blackgirl, One Word: Necessary Transgressions in the Name of Imagining Black Girlhood." *Cultural Studies ↔ Critical Methodologies* 19(4): 275–283.

Hill, Sarah. 2017. "Exploring Disabled Girls' Self-Representational Practices Online." *Girlhood Studies* 10(2): 114–130.

Hill, Sarah. 2023. "Navigating Visibility and Risk: Disabled Young Women's Self-Presentation Practices on Social Media." *Journal of Gender Studies* 33(5): 1–12.

Hill Collins, Patricia. 1990. *Black Feminist Thought.* New York: Routledge.

Hinduja, Sameer, and Patchin, Justin. 2010. "Bullying, Cyberbullying, and Suicide." *Archives of Suicide Research* 14(3): 206–221.

Hinduja, Sameer, and Patchin, Justin. 2015. *Bullying beyond the Schoolyard: Preventing and Responding to Cyberbullying.* Thousand Oaks, CA: Corwin.

Hinduja, Sameer, and Patchin, Justin. 2016. "Cyberbullying Identification, Prevention, and Response." *Cyberbullying Research Center.* Retrieved October 12, 2018. (cyberbullying.org).

Hinduja, Sameer, and Patchin, Justin. 2018. "Connecting Adolescent Suicide to the Severity of Bullying and Cyberbullying." *Journal of School Violence* 18(3): 1–14.

Hiniker, Alexis, Schoenebeck, Sarita Y., and Kientz, Julie A. 2016. "Not at the Dinner Table: Parents' and Children's Perspectives on Family Technology Rules." In *Proceedings of the 19th ACM Conference on Computer-Supported Cooperative Work and Social Computing*, 1376–1389. New York: Association for Computing Machinery.

Hinkelman, Lisa. 2017. "The Girls' Index: New Insights into the Complex World of Today's Girls." Columbus, OH: Ruling Our eXperiences.

Hlavka, H. R. 2014. "Normalizing Sexual Violence: Young Women Account for Harassment and Abuse." *Gender & Society* 28(3): 337–358.

Hobbes, Michael. 2018. "Everything You Know about Obesity Is Wrong." *HuffPost*. September 19. Retrieved December 12, 2019. (https://highline.huffingtonpost.com/articles/en/everything-you-know-about-obesity-is-wrong/).

Hobson, Janell. 2016. "Black Beauty and Digital Spaces: The New Visibility Politics." *Ada: A New Journal of Gender, New Media, and Technology* 10: 1–20.

Holland, G., and Tiggemann, M. 2016. "A Systematic Review of the Impact of the Use of Social Networking Sites on Body Image and Disordered Eating Outcomes." *Body Image* 17(2): 100–110.

hooks, bell. 1981. *Ain't I a Woman: Black Women and Feminism*. Cambridge, MA: South End Press.

hooks, bell. 1984. *Feminist Theory: From Margin to Center*. Cambridge, MA: South End Press.

hooks, bell. 1989. *Talking Back: Thinking Feminist, Thinking Black*. Cambridge, MA: South End Press.

hooks, bell. 1992. *Black Looks: Race and Representation*. Cambridge, MA: South End Press.

Horak, Laura. 2014. "Trans on YouTube Intimacy, Visibility, Temporality." *TSQ: Transgender Studies Quarterly* 1(4): 572–585.

Howard, Jacqueline. 2018. "The History of the 'Ideal' Woman and Where That Has Left Us." *CNN Health*. March 9. Retrieved August 8, 2019. (https://www.cnn.com/2018/03/07/health/body-image-history-of-beauty-explainer-intl/index.html).

Irigaray, Luce. 1985. *The Sex Which Is Not One*. Ithaca, NY: Cornell University Press.

Italie, Leanne. 2012. "YouTube Phenomenon Has Girls Asking: Am I Pretty?" *New Haven Register*. (https://www.nhregister.com/news/article/YouTube-phenomenon-has-girls-asking-Am-I-pretty-11494795.php).

Ito, M., Baumer, S., Bittanti, M., boyd, d., Cody, R., and Herr-Stephenson, B. 2009. *Hanging out, Messing around, and Geeking out: Kids Living and Learning with New Media*. Cambridge, MA: MIT Press.

Jackson, J. B. 2021. "On Cultural Appropriation." *Journal of Folklore Research* 58(1): 77–122.

Jackson, S., and Vares, T. 2015. "'Too Many Bad Role Models for Us Girls': Girls, Female Pop Celebrities and 'Sexualization.'" *Sexualities* 18(4): 480–498.

Jakes, Lara. 2021. "Pandemic Lockdown Aided Predators Worldwide, Especially Online, U.S. Says." *New York Times*. July 1. Retrieved August 13, 2023. (https://www.nytimes.com/2021/07/01/us/politics/coronavirus-lockdown-online-exploitation.html).

Jarman, H. K., Marques, M. D., McLean, S. A., Slater, A., and Paxton, S. J. 2021. "Social Media, Body Satisfaction and Well-Being among Adolescents: A Mediation Model of Appearance-Ideal Internalization and Comparison." *Body Image* 36(1): 139–148.

Jeffery, C. P. 2020. "Parenting in the Digital Age: Between Socio-biological and Sociotechnological Development." *New Media & Society* 23(5): 1045–1062.

Jenkins, Henry. 2009. *Confronting the Challenges of Participatory Culture: Media Education for the 21st Century*. Cambridge, MA: MIT Press.

Jennings, Rebecca. 2019. "TikTok, Explained." *Vox*. July 12. Retrieved June 23, 2023. (https://www.vox.com/culture/2018/12/10/18129126/tiktok-app-musically-meme-cringe).

Jennings, Rebecca. 2021. "The $5,000 Quest for the Perfect Butt." *Vox*. August 2. Retrieved March 8, 2022. (https://www.vox.com/the-goods/22598377/bbl-brazilian-butt-lift-miami-cost-tiktok).

Jenzen, Olu. 2017. "Trans Youth and Social Media: Moving between Counterpublics and the Wider Web." *Gender, Place & Culture* 24(11): 1626–1641.

Jerslev, Anne. 2016. "In the Time of the Microcelebrity: Celebrification and the YouTuber Zoella." *International Journal of Communication* 10(1): 5233–5251.

Johnson, Judith. 2016. "Teens Addicted to Social Media." *Huffpost*. April 15. Retrieved January 5, 2019. (https://www.huffpost.com/entry/teens-addicted-to-social_b_9696378).

Jones, Lisa, Mitchell, Kimberly, and Finkelhor, David. 2012. "Trends in Youth Internet Victimization: Findings from Three Youth Internet Safety Surveys 2000–2010." *Journal of Adolescent Health* 50(2): 179–186.

Jong, S. T., and Drummond, M. J. N. 2016. "Hurry up and 'Like' Me: Immediate Feedback on Social Networking Sites and the Impact on Adolescent Girls." *Asia-Pacific Journal of Health, Sport, and Physical Education* 7(3): 251–267.

Kafer, Alison. 2013. *Feminist, Queer, Crip*. Bloomington: Indiana University Press.

Kahn, Mattie. 2023a. *Young and Restless: The Girls Who Sparked America's Revolutions*. New York: Viking.

Kahn, Mattie. 2023b. "Girlhood Is Trending, but Actual Girlhood Has Never Been More Fraught." *InStyle*. September 14. Retrieved on January 8, 2024. (https://www.instyle.com/girlhood-trend-failing-real-girls-7964043).

Kanai, Akane. 2019a. "On Not Taking the Self Seriously: Resilience, Relatability and Humour in Young Women's Tumblr Blogs." *European Journal of Cultural Studies* 22(1): 67–77.

Kanai, Akane. 2019b. *Gender and Relatability in Digital Culture: Managing Affect, Intimacy and Value*. Cham, Switzerland: Palgrave Macmillan.

Kearney, Mary Celeste. 2006. *Girls Make Media*. New York: Routledge.

Kearney, Mary Celeste. 2007. "PRODUCTIVE SPACES." *Journal of Children and Media* 1(2): 126–141.

Kearney, Mary Celeste. 2011. *Mediated Girlhoods: New Explorations of Girls' Media Culture*. New York: Peter Lang.

Kedzior, Richard, and Allen, Douglas. 2016. "From Liberation to Control: Understanding the Selfie Experience." *European Journal of Marketing* 50(9/10): 1893–1902.

Keles, B., McCrae, N., and Grealish, A. 2020. "A Systematic Review: The Influence of Social Media on Depression, Anxiety and Psychological Distress in Adolescents." *International Journal of Adolescence and Youth* 25(1): 79–93.

Keller, Jessalynn. 2016. *Girls' Feminist Blogging in the Postfeminist Age*. New York: Routledge.

Keller, Jessalynn. 2019. "'Oh, She's a Tumblr Feminist': Exploring the Platform Vernacular of Girls' Social Media Feminisms." *Social Media + Society* 5(3): 1–27.

Keller, Jessalynn, and Ryan, Maureen, eds. 2018. *Emergent Feminisms: Complicating a Postfeminist Media Culture*. Philadelphia: Routledge.

Kelly, Lauren Leigh. 2018. "A Snapchat Story: How Black Girls Develop Strategies for Critical Resistance in School." *Learning, Media and Technology* 43(4): 374–389.

Kelly, Yvonne, Zilanawala, Afshin, Booker, Cara, and Sacker, Amanda. 2018. "Social Media Use and Adolescent Mental Health: Findings from the UK Millennium Cohort Study." *EClinical Medicine* 6(4): 59–68.

Kennedy, J., and Lynch, H. 2016. "A Shift from Offline to Online: Adolescence, the Internet and Social Participation." *Journal of Occupational Science* 23(2): 156–167.

Kennedy, Lesley. 2013. "The Sad Question Young Girls Are Asking on YouTube." *TODAY*. October 31. Retrieved December 3, 2013. (https://www.today.com/parents/girls-ask-youtube-am-i-pretty-or-ugly-I551374).

Kennedy, Melanie. 2018. *Tweenhood: Femininity and Celebrity in Tween Popular Culture*. London: Bloomsbury Academic.

Kennedy, Melanie. 2020. "'If the Rise of TikTok Dance and e-Girl Aesthetic Has Taught Us Anything, It's That Teenage Girls Rule the Internet Right Now': TikTok Celebrity, Girls and the Coronavirus Crisis." *European Journal of Cultural Studies* 23(6): 1069–1076.

Kennedy, Melanie, and Coulter, Natalie. 2018. "Locating Tween Girls." *Girlhood Studies* 11(1): 1–7.

Khan, F., Limbana, T., Zahid, T., Eskander, N., and Jahan, N. 2020. "Traits, Trends, and Trajectory of Tween and Teen Cyberbullies." *Cureus* 12(8): e9738.

Kim, A. S., and Davis, K. 2017. "Tweens' Perspectives on Their Parents' Media-Related Attitudes and Rules: An Explanatory Study in the US." *Journal of Children and Media* 11(3): 358–366.

Kim, Y. S., and Leventhal, B. 2008. "Bullying and Suicide: A Review." *International Journal of Adolescent Medicine and Health* 20(2): 133–154.

King, Angela. 2004. "The Prisoner of Gender: Foucault and the Disciplining of the Female Body." *Journal of International Women's Studies* 5(2): 29–39.

Kirkland, Anna. 2011. "The Environmental Account of Obesity: A Case for Feminist Skepticism." *Signs* 36(2): 463–485.

Klettke, B., Hallford, D. J., and Mellor, D. J. 2014. "Sexting Prevalence and Correlates: A Systematic Literature Review." *Clinical Psychology Review* 34(1): 44–53.

Klomek, A. Brunstein, Sourander, A., and Gould, M. 2010. "The Association of Suicide and Bullying in Childhood to Young Adulthood: A Review of Cross-Sectional and Longitudinal Research Findings." *Canadian Journal of Psychiatry* 55(5): 282–288.

Knorr, Caroline. 2017. "How Girls Use Social Media to Build up, Break down Self-Image." *Common Sense Media*. January 12. Retrieved July 17, 2019. (https://www.cnn.com/20 17/01/12/health/girls-social-media-self-image-partner/index.html).

Kofoed, Jette, and Ringrose, Jessica. 2012. "Travelling and Sticky Affects: Exploring Teens and Sexualized Cyberbullying through a Butlerian-Deleuzian-Guattarian Lens." *Discourse: Studies in the Cultural Politics of Education* 33(1): 5–20.

Kowalski, Robin M., Limber, Susan P., and McCord, Annie. 2019. "A Developmental Approach to Cyberbullying: Prevalence and Protective Factors." *Aggression and Violent Behavior* 45(1): 20–32.

Kroger, J. 2007. *Identity Development: Adolescence through Adulthood*. 2nd ed. Thousand Oaks, CA: Sage.

Kuper, L. E., Adams, N., and Mustanski, B. S. 2018. "Exploring Cross-Sectional Predictors of Suicide Ideation, Attempt, and Risk in a Large Online Sample of Transgender and Gender Nonconforming Youth and Young Adults." *LGBT Health* 5(7): 391–400.

Kutbi, Alaa Ibraheem. 2015. "How Undergraduate Female Students in the Kingdom of Saudi Arabia Perceive Social Media as a Learning Tool: An Exploratory Study." *Electronic Theses and Dissertations* 5290. Master's thesis. University of Windsor.

Lacan, Jacques. 1968. "The Mirror Stage." *New Left Review* 1(51): 63–77.

Laine Talley, Heather. 2014. *Saving Face: Disfigurement and the Politics of Appearance*. New York: New York University Press.

Laukkanen, M. 2007. "Young Queers Online: The Limits and Possibilities of Non-heterosexual Self-Representation in Online Conversations." In *Queer Online: Media Technology and Sexuality*, edited by Kate O'Riordan and David J Philips, 81–100. New York: Peter Lang.

Leaf, M., and Schrock, D. P. 2011. "What I Had to Do to Survive': Self-Injurers' Bodily Emotion Work." In *Embodied Resistance: Challenging the Norms, Breaking the Rules*, edited by C. Bobel and S. Kwan, 156–166. Nashville, TN: Vanderbilt University Press.

LeBlanc, John C. 2012. "Cyberbullying and Suicide: A Retrospective Analysis of 22 Cases." *American Academy of Pediatrics*. National Conference and Exhibition. October 20.

Lenhart, Amanda. 2007. "Cyberbullying and Online Teens." *Pew Internet and American Life Project: Pew Research Center.* (https://www.pewresearch.org/internet/2007/06/27/cyberbullying/).

Lenhart, Amanda, Fallows, Deborah, and Horrigan, John B. 2004. "Content Creation Online." *Pew Research Center.* (https://www.pewresearch.org/internet/2004/02/29/content-creation-online/).

Lenhart, Amanda, Smith, A., Anderson, M., Duggan, M., and Perrin, A. 2015. "Teens, Technology, and Friendships: Video Games, Social Media and Mobile Phones Play an Integral Role in How Teens Meet and Interact with Friends." *Pew Research Center.* (https://www.pewresearch.org/internet/2015/08/06/teens-technology-and-friendships).

Letendre, Joan. 2007. "'Sugar and Spice Not Always Nice': Gender Socialization and Its Impact on Development and Maintenance of Aggression in Adolescent Girls." *Child and Adolescent Social Work Journal* 24(4): 353–368.

Levin, Diane, and Kilbourne, Jean. 2008. *So Sexy so Soon: The New Sexualized Childhood and What Parents Can Do to Protect Their Kids.* New York: Ballantine Books.

Limber, S. P., and Small, M. A. 2003. "State Laws and Policies to Address Bullying in Schools." *School Psychology Review* 32(3): 445–455.

Lindsey, Treva. 2013. "'One Time for My Girls': African-American Girlhood, Empowerment, and Popular Visual Culture." *Journal of African American Studies* 17(1): 22–34.

Lippman, Julia R., and Campbell, Scott W. 2014. "Damned If You Do, Damned If You Don't . . . If You're a Girl: Relational and Normative Contexts of Adolescent Sexting in the United States." *Journal of Children and Media* 8(4): 371–386.

Liu, Yuanhang, and Li, Xinjian. 2024. "'Pale, Young, and Slim' Girls on Red: A Study of Young Femininities on Social Media in Post-Socialist China." *Feminist Media Studies* 24(4): 744–759.

Livingstone, Sonia. 2009. *Children and the Internet: Great Expectations, Challenging Realities.* Cambridge: Polity.

London, Lela. 2021. "How the What Waist Trainer Outlived the Instagram Trend." *Forbes.* January 8. Retrieved January 3, 2022. (https://www.forbes.com/sites/lelalondon/2021/01/08/how-the-what-waist-trainer-outlived-the-instagram-trend).

Lupton, Deborah. 2014. *Digital Sociology.* New York: Routledge.

Maes, Chelly, and Vandenbosch, Laura. 2022. "Adolescent Girls' Instagram and TikTok Use: Examining Relations with Body Image-Related Constructs over Time Using Random Intercept Cross-Lagged Panel Models." *Body Image* 41(1): 453–459.

Maldonado, Elisha. 2013. "'Am I Ugly?' YouTube Trend Is Disturbing." *New York Post.* October 27. Retrieved December 4, 2013. (https://nypost.com/2013/10/27/girls-shouldnt-be-obsessed-with-physical-beauty/).

Malvini Redden, S., and Way, A. K. 2017. "'Adults Don't Understand': Exploring How Teens Use Dialectical Frameworks to Navigate Webs of Tensions in Online Life." *Journal of Applied Communication Research* 45(1): 21–41.

Marciano, Laura, Ostroumova, Michelle, Schulz, Peter J., and Camerini, Anne-Linda. 2022. "Digital Media Use and Adolescents' Mental Health During Covid-19 Pandemic: A Systematic Review and Meta-analysis." *Frontiers in Public Health* 9: 1–28.

Markey, Charlotte H., and Daniels, Elizabeth A. 2022. "An Examination of Preadolescent Girls' Social Media Use and Body Image: Type of Engagement May Matter Most" *Body Image* 42(1): 145–149.

Markus, Hazel Rose, and Moya, Paula M. L. 2010. *Doing Race: 21 Essays for the 21st Century.* New York: W.W. Norton.

Marôpo, Lidia, Jorge, Ana, and Tomaz, Renata. 2020. "'I Felt Like I Was Really Talking to You!': Intimacy and Trust among Teen Vloggers and Followers in Portugal and Brazil." *Journal of Children and Media* 14(1): 22–37.

Marr, K. L., and Duell, M. N. 2020. "Cyberbullying and Cybervictimization: Does Gender Matter?" *Psychological Reports* 124(2): 577–595.

Marres, Noortje. 2017. *Digital Sociology: The Reinvention of Social Research*. Malden, MA: Polity Press.

Marwick, Alice. 2008. "To Catch a Predator? The Myspace Moral Panic." *First Monday* 13(6): 1–22.

Marwick, Alice. 2013a. "Online Identity." In *Companion to New Media Dynamics*, edited by J. Hartley, J. Burgess, and A. Bruns, 355–364. Chichester, UK: Wiley-Blackwell.

Marwick, Alice. 2013b. *Status Update: Celebrity, Publicity and Branding in the Social Media Age*. New Haven, CT: Yale University Press.

Marwick, Alice, and boyd, danah. 2014. "'It's Just Drama': Teen Perspectives on Conflict and Aggression in a Networked Era." *Journal of Youth Studies* 17(9): 1187–1204.

Mascheroni, G., and Ólafsson, K. 2014. *Net Children Go Mobile: Risks and Opportunities*. 2nd ed. Milano: Educatt.

Mascheroni, G., Vincent, J., and Jimenez, E. 2015. "'Girls Are Addicted to Likes so They Post Semi Naked Selfies': Peer Mediation, Normativity, and the Construction of Identity Online." *Cyberpsychology: Journal of Psychosocial Research on Cyberspace* 9(1): article 5.

Mazzarella, Sharon R. 2010. *Girl Wide Web 2.0: Revisiting Girls, the Internet, and the Negotiation of Identity*. New York: Peter Lang.

Mazzarella, Sharon R., and Pecora, Norma O. 2007. "Girls in Crisis: Newspaper Coverage of Adolescent Girls." *Journal of Communication Inquiry* 31(1): 6–27.

McCain, Abby. 2023. "20 + Trending U.S. Wedding Industry Statistics [2023]: How Big Is the Wedding Industry." *Zippia*. March 14. Retrieved August 1, 2023. (https://www.zippia.com/advice/wedding-industry-statistics/).

McCay-Peet, L., and Quan-Haase, A. 2017. "What Is Social Media and What Questions Can Social Media Research Help Us Answer?" In *The SAGE Handbook of Social Media Research Methods*, edited by L. Sloan and A. Quan-Haase, 13–26. Thousand Oaks, CA: SAGE.

McClain, Colleen, Rainie, Lee, and Bell, Peter. 2023. "Life on Social Media Platforms in Users' Own Words." *Pew Research Center*. June 7. Retrieved September 2, 2023. (https://www.pewresearch.org/internet/2023/06/07/life-on-social-media-platforms-in-users-own-words/).

McClearen, Jennifer. 2023. "'If You Let Me Play': Girls' Empowerment and Transgender Exclusion in Sports." *Feminist Media Studies* 23(4): 1361–1375.

McInroy, L. B. 2019. "Building Connections and Slaying Basilisks: Fostering Support, Resilience, and Positive Adjustment for Sexual and Gender Minority Youth in Online Fan Communities." *Information, Communication and Society* 23(13): 1874–1891.

McInroy, L. B., and Craig, S. L. 2015. "Transgender Representation in Offline and Online Media: LGBTQ Youth Perspectives." *Journal of Human Behavior in the Social Environment* 25(6): 606–617.

McMillan Cottom, Tressie. 2013. "Brown Body, White Wonderland." *Slate Magazine*. August 19. Retrieved June 10, 2015. (https://slate.com/human-interest/2013/08/miley-cyrus-vma-performance-white-appropriation-of-black-bodies.html).

Mcqueeney, Krista, and Girgenti-Malone, Alicia, eds. 2018. *Girls, Aggression, and Intersectionality Transforming the Discourse of "Mean Girls" in the United States*. New York: Routledge.

McRobbie, Angela. 1990. *Feminism and Youth Culture: From Jackie to Just Seventeen*. New York: Routledge.

McRobbie, Angela. 1993. "Shut up and Dance: Youth Culture and Changing Modes of Femininity." *Cultural Studies* 7(3): 406–426.

McRobbie, Angela. 2008. *The Aftermath of Feminism: Gender, Culture, and Social Change*. Los Angeles: Sage.

McRobbie, Angela, and Garber, Jenny. 2006. "Girls and Subcultures." In *Resistance through Rituals: Youth Subcultures in Post-war Britain*, edited by S. Hall and T. Jefferson, 177–188. London: Routledge.

McRobbie, Angela, and Thornton, Sarah L. 1995. "Rethinking 'Moral Panic' for Multi-mediated Social Worlds." *British Journal of Sociology* 46(4): 559–574.

Mendes, Kaitlynn, Ringrose, Jessica, and Keller, Jessalynn. 2019. *Digital Feminist Activism: Girls and Women Fight Back against Rape Culture*. New York: Oxford University Press.

Mercedes, Marquisele. 2020. "Our Fat Bodies Are Not Your Metaphors." *Marquisele Mercedes*. November 29. Retrieved December 12, 2021. (https://www.marquiselemercedes.com/read/metaphors).

Mercedes, Marquisele. 2022. "No Health, No Care: The Big Fat Loophole in the Hippocratic Oath." *Pipe Wrench*. Retrieved July 23, 2023. (https://pipewrenchmag.com/dismantling-medical-fatphobia/).

Metcalfe, S. N., and Llewellyn, A. 2020. "'It's Just the Thing You Do': Physical and Digital Fields, and the Flow of Capital for Young People's Gendered Identity Negotiation." *Journal of Adolescent Research* 35(1): 84–110.

Meyers, Eric M., Erickson, Ingrid, and Small, Ruth V. 2013. "Digital Literacy and Informal Learning Environments: An Introduction" *Learning, Media and Technology* 38(4): 355–367.

Miller, Farah. 2023. "Being 13 Is Hard. Being a Parent Brings It All Back." *New York Times*. September 20. Retrieved January 26, 2024. (https://www.nytimes.com/2023/09/20/well/family/teenagers-adolescence-parenting.html).

Miller, Marissa. 2023. "Hot Girl Walks Are All over TikTok. Here's What You Need to Do One Right." *CNN Underscored*. July 6. Retrieved January 27, 2024. (https://www.cnn.com/cnn-underscored/home/hot-girl-walk-tiktok-trend).

Miller, S. A. 2016. "'How You Bully a Girl': Sexual Drama and the Negotiation of Gendered Sexuality in High School." *Gender & Society* 30(5): 721–744.

Mingoia, John, Hutchinson, Amanda D., Wilson, Carlene, and Gleaves, David H. 2017. "The Relationship between Social Networking Site Use and the Internalization of a Thin Ideal in Females: A Meta-analytic Review." *Frontiers in Psychology* 8: 1–10.

Mishna, F., Schwan, K. J., Birze, A., Van Wert, M., Lacombe-Duncan, A., McInroy, L., and Attar-Schwartz, S. 2020. "Gendered and Sexualized Bullying and Cyber Bullying: Spotlighting Girls and Making Boys Invisible." *Youth & Society* 52(3): 403–426.

Mitchell, Claudia, and Jacqueline Reid-Walsh. 2008. "Girl Method: Placing Girl-Centred Research Methodologies on the Map of Girlhood Studies." In *Roadblocks to Equality: Women Challenging Boundaries*, edited by Jeffrey Klaehn, 214–233. Montreal: Black Rose Books.

Mitchell, Claudia, and Rentschler, Carrie. 2016. *Girlhood and the Politics of Place*. New York: Berghahn Books.

Modglin, Lindsay, and McCormick, April. 2024. "11 Parental Control and Monitoring Apps We Recommend in 2023." *Parents*. January 10. Retrieved February 1, 2024. (https://www.parents.com/parentsirl/best-parental-monitoring-apps/).

Monaghan, Whitney. 2016. *Queer Girls, Temporality, and Screen Media*. London: Palgrave Macmillan.

Mooney, Heather. 2018. "Sad Girls and Carefree Black Girls: Affect, Race, (Dis)Possession, and Protest." *WSQ: Women's Studies Quarterly* 46(3/4): 175–194.

Morris, Monique W. 2015. *Pushout: The Criminalization of Black Girls in Schools*. New York: New Press.

Mosley, A. J., and Biernat, M. 2021. "The New Identity Theft: Perceptions of Cultural Appropriation in Intergroup Contexts." *Journal of Personality and Social Psychology* 121(2): 308–331.

Mulvey, Laura. 1975. "Visual Pleasure and Narrative Cinema." *Screen* 16(3): 6–18.

Murray, Samantha. 2007. "Corporeal Knowledges and Deviant Bodies: Perceiving the Fat Body." *Social Semiotics* 17(3): 361–373.

Nesi, J. 2020. "The Impact of Social Media on Youth Mental Health: Challenges and Opportunities." *North Carolina Medical Journal* 81(2): 116–121.

Nesi, J., Choukas-Bradley, S., and Prinstein, M. J. 2018. "Transformation of Adolescent Peer Relations in the Social Media Context: Part 2—Application to Peer Group Processes and Future Directions for Research." *Clinical Child and Family Psychology Review* 21(3): 295–319.

Nesi, J., Mann, S., and Robb, M. B. 2023. *Teens and Mental Health: How Girls Really Feel about Social Media*. San Francisco, CA: Common Sense.

Nesi, J., and Prinstein, M. J. 2015. "Using Social Media for Social Comparison and Feedback Seeking: Gender and Popularity Moderate Associations with Depressive Symptoms." *Journal of Abnormal Child Psychology* 43(8): 1427–1438.

Nichter, Mimi. 2000. *Fat Talk*. Cambridge, MA: Harvard University Press.

Nicolaou, Elena. 2020. "Social Media Is Having Its Moment on Film and It's Pretty Grim." *Refinery29*. March 4. Retrieved November 3, 2021. (https://www.refinery29.com/en-us/2017/09/173239/social-media-movies).

Nilan, P., Burgess, H., Hobbs, M., Threadgold, S., and Alexander, W. 2015. "Youth, Social Media, and Cyberbullying among Australian Youth: 'Sick Friends.'" *Social Media + Society* 1(2): 1–12.

Nunn, Nia Michelle. 2018. "Super-Girl: Strength and Sadness in Black Girlhood." *Gender and Education* 30(2): 239–258.

Nurka, Camille. 2014. "Public Bodies." *Feminist Media Studies* 14(3): 485–499.

O'Donnell, Brenna. 2021. "Covid-19 and Missing and Exploited Children." *National Center for Missing and Exploited Children*. April 30. Retrieved June 12, 2023. (https://www.missingkids.org/blog/2020/covid-19-and-missing-and-exploited-children/).

Office of the Surgeon General (OSG). 2023. "Social Media and Youth Mental Health: The U.S. Surgeon General's Advisory." Washington, DC: U.S. Department of Health and Human Services.

Olweus, Dan, and Limber, Susan P. 2018. "Some Problems with Cyberbullying Research." *Current Opinion in Psychology* 19: 139–143.

Oppliger, Patrice A. 2008. *Girls Gone Skank: The Sexualization of Girls in American Culture*. Jefferson, NC: McFarland.

Oppliger, Patrice A. 2013. *Bullies and Mean Girls in Popular Culture*. Jefferson, NC: McFarland.

Orben, Amy, and Przybylski, Andrew. 2019. "The Association between Adolescent Well-Being and Digital Technology Use." *Nature Human Behaviour* 3: 173–182.

Orenstein, Peggy. 1994. *Schoolgirls: Young Women, Self Esteem, and the Confidence Gap*. New York: Doubleday.

Orenstein, Peggy. 2016. *Girls and Sex: Navigating the Complicated New Landscape*. New York: HarperCollins.

Orgad, Shani, and Gill, Rosalind. 2022. *Confidence Culture*. Durham, NC: Duke University Press.

Orton-Johnson, Kate, and Prior, Nick, eds. 2013. *Digital Sociology: Critical Perspectives*. New York: Palgrave Macmillan.

Palfrey, John, and Gasser, Urs. 2016. *Born Digital: Understanding the First Generation of Digital Natives*. New York: Basic Books.

Pangrazio, Luci, and Cardozo Gaibisso, Lourdes. 2020. "Beyond Cybersafety: The Need to Develop Social Media Literacies in Pre-teens." *Digital Education Review* 37: 49–63.

Papacharissi, Z. 2015. "We Have Always Been Social." *Social Media + Society* 1(1): 1.

Papageorgiou, A., Fisher, C., and Cross, D. 2022. "'Why Don't I Look Like Her?' How Adolescent Girls View Social Media and Its Connection to Body Image." *BMC Women's Health* 22(261): 1–13.

Pascoe, C. 2013. "Notes on a Sociology of Bullying: Young Men's Homophobia as Gender Socialization." *QED: A Journal in GLBTQ Worldmaking* 1(1): 87–103.

Payne, E. 2010. "Sluts: Heteronormative Policing in the Stories of Lesbian Youth." *Educational Studies* 46(3): 317–336.

Pearson, Catherine. 2023. "What Social Media Does to the Teen Brain." *New York Times*. September 20. Retrieved January 26, 2024. (https://www.nytimes.com/2023/09/20/well/family/social-media-teen-brain-mental-health.html).

Perez, S. 2020. "Kids Now Spend Nearly as Much Time Watching TikTok as YouTube in US, UK and Spain." *TechCrunch*. June 4. Retrieved February 2, 2023. (https://techcrunch.com/2020/06/04/kids-now-spend-nearly-as-much-time-watching-tiktok-as-youtube-in-u-s-u-k-and-spain/).

Perle, Elizabeth. 2013. "What the 'Am I Pretty?' YouTube Trend Is REALLY Saying." *Huffington Post*. November 11. Retrieved September 20, 2015. (https://www.huffpost.com/entry/what-the-am-i-pretty-yout_b_4222947/).

Perrino, John, and King, Jennifer. 2023. "Overcoming Fear and Frustration with the Kids Online Safety Act." *TechPolicy.Press*. November 13. Retrieved February 1, 2024. (https://www.techpolicy.press/overcoming-fear-and-frustration-with-the-kids-online-safety-act/).

Phelps, Katherine. 2019. "Am I Pretty Enough for You Yet?: Resistance through Parody in the Pretty or Ugly YouTube Trend." In *Body Battlegrounds: Transgressions, Tensions, and Transformations*, edited by C. Bobel and S. Kwan, 76–87. Nashville, TN: Vanderbilt University Press.

Phelps-Ward, Robin J., and Laura, Crystal T. 2016. "Talking Back in Cyberspace: Self-Love, Hair Care, and Counter Narratives in Black Adolescent Girls' YouTube Vlogs." *Gender and Education* 28(6): 807–820.

Pipher, Mary. 1994. *Reviving Ophelia: Saving the Selves of Adolescent Girls*. New York: Putnam.

Poggi, Maria Santa. 2024. "Stop Shaming Sephora Kids." *Highsnobiety*. February 7. Retrieved February 8, 2024. (https://www.highsnobiety.com/p/sephora-kids-up-aging/).

Preston-Sidler, Leandra. 2015. "From Cyborgs to Cybergrrrls: Redefining 'Girl Power' through Digital Literacy." In *Difficult Dialogues about Twenty-First Century Girls*, edited by Donna Marie Johnson and Alice E. Ginsberg, 195–206. Albany, NY: State University of New York Press.

Projansky, Sarah. 2014. *Spectacular Girls: Media Fascination and Celebrity Culture*. New York: New York University Press.

Quenqua, Douglas. 2014. "Tell Me What You See, Even If It Hurts Me." *New York Times*. August 1. Retrieved January 10, 2015. (https://www.nytimes.com/2014/08/03/fashion /am-i-pretty-videos-posed-to-the-internet-raise-questions.html).

Quicho, Alex. 2023. "Everyone Is a Girl Online." *Wired*. September 11. Retrieved September 18, 2023. (https://www.wired.com/story/girls-online-culture/).

Rainville, Camille. 2017. "Be a Lady They Said." *Writings of a Furious Woman*. December 9. Retrieved August 20, 2023. (https://writingsofafuriouswoman.wordpress.com/2017 /12/09/be-a-lady-they-said/).

Rainville, Camille. 2020. "Be a Lady They Said." Performed by Cynthia Nixon. *Girls. Girls. Girls. Magazine*. YouTube. (https://www.youtube.com/watch?v=z8ZSDS7zVdU &ab_channel=Girls.Girls.Girls.Magazine).

Ramirez, Fanny, Denault, Vincent, Carpenter, Sarah, and Wyers, Jessica. 2022. "'But Her Age Was Not Given on Her Facebook Profile': Minors, Social Media, and Sexual Assault Trials." *Information, Communication & Society* 25(15): 2282–2298.

Ranney, M. L., Pittman, S. K., Riese, A., Koehler, C., Ybarra, M. L., Cunningham, R. M., Spirito, A., and Rosen, R. K. 2020. "What Counts?: A Qualitative Study of Adolescents' Lived Experience with Online Victimization and Cyberbullying." *Academic Pediatrics* 20(4): 485–492.

Raskauskas, J., and Stoltz, A. D. 2007. "Involvement in Traditional and Electronic Bullying among Adolescents." *Developmental Psychology* 43(3): 564–575.

Raun, Tobias. 2016. *Out Online: Trans Self-Representation and Community Building on YouTube*. London: Routledge.

Reinke, Rachel, and Anastasia Todd. 2016. "'Cute Girl in Wheelchair—Why?' Cripping YouTube." *Transformations: The Journal of Inclusive Pedagogy* 25(2): 93–103.

Reischer, Erica, and Koo, Kathryn S. 2004. "The Body Beautiful: Symbolism and Agency in the Social World." *Annual Review of Anthropology* 33: 297–317.

Remillard, A. M., and Lamb, S. 2005. "Adolescent Girls' Coping with Relational Aggression." *Sex Roles* 53(3–4): 221–229.

Renold, Emma. 2002. "Presumed Innocence: (Hetero)sexual, Heterosexist and Homophobic Harassment among Primary School Girls and Boys." *Childhood* 9(4): 415–434.

Renold, Emma. 2006. "'They Won't Let Us Play . . . Unless You're Going out with One of Them': Girls, Boys and Butler's 'Heterosexual Matrix' in the Primary Years." *British Journal of Sociology of Education* 27(4): 489–509.

Renold, Emma, and Ringrose, Jessica. 2011. "Schizoid Subjectivities?: Re-theorizing Teen Girls' Sexual Cultures in an Era of 'Sexualization.'" *Journal of Sociology* 47(4): 389–409.

Renold, Emma, and Ringrose, Jessica. 2013. "Feminisms Re-figuring 'Sexualisation', Sexuality, and 'The Girl.'" *Feminist Theory* 14(3): 247–254.

Rentschler, Carrie A., and Mitchell, Claudia. 2014. "The Re-description of Girls in Crisis." *Girlhood Studies* 7(1): 1–6.

Rentschler, Carrie, and Mitchell, Claudia. 2016. "The Significance of Place in Girlhood Studies." In *Girlhood and the Politics of Place*, edited by Claudia Mitchell and Carrie Rentschler, 1–17. New York: Berghahn Books.

Rideout, V., Peebles, A., Mann, S., and Robb, M. B. 2021. *Common Sense Census: Media Use by Tweens and Teens, 2021*. San Francisco, CA: Common Sense.

Ringrose, Jessica. 2006. "A New Universal Mean Girl: Examining the Discursive Construction and Social Regulation of a New Feminine Pathology." *Feminism & Psychology* 16(4): 405424.

Ringrose, Jessica. 2011. "Are You Sexy, Flirty, or a Slut? Exploring 'Sexualization' and How Teen Girls Perform/Negotiate Digital Sexual Identity on Social Networking Sites." In *New Femininities: Postfeminism, Neoliberalism and Subjectivity*, edited by Rosalind Gill and Christina Scharff, 99–116. New York: Palgrave Macmillan.

Ringrose, Jessica. 2013. *Postfeminist Education? Girls and the Sexual Politics of Schooling*. London: Routledge.

Ringrose, J., and Harvey, L. 2015. "Boobs, Back-off, Six Packs and Bits: Mediated Body Parts, Gendered Reward, and Sexual Shame in Teens' Sexting Images." *Continuum* 29(2): 205217.

Ringrose, J., Harvey, L., Gill, R., and Livingstone, S. 2013. "Teen Girls, Sexual Double Standards and 'Sexting': Gendered Value in Digital Image Exchange." *Feminist Theory* 14(3): 305–323.

Ringrose, Jessica, and Renold, Emma. 2010. "Normative Cruelties and Gender Deviants: The Performative Effects of Bully Discourse for Girls and Boys in School." *British Educational Research Journal* 36(4): 573–596.

Riordan, Ellen. 2001. "Commodified Agents and Empowered Girls: Consuming and Producing Feminism." *Journal of Communication Inquiry* 25(3): 279–297.

Rodin, J., Silberstein, L., and Striegel-Moore, R. 1984. "Women and Weight: A Normative Discontent." *Nebraska Symposium on Motivation* 32: 267–307.

Rodriguez-Garcia, K. 2023. "The End of the BBL Era, A Return to 90's Thinness." *The Michigan Daily*. February 27. Retrieved July 15, 2024. (https://www.michigandaily.com /arts/style/the-end-of-the-bbl-era-a-return-to-90s-thinness/).

Rogers, O., Mastro, D., Robb, M. B., and Peebles, A. 2021. "The Inclusion Imperative: Why Media Representation Matters for Kids' Ethnic-Racial Development." San Francisco, CA: Common Sense Media.

Rohm Nulsen, Charise. 2023. "A Complete Guide to Potentially Dangerous Apps All Parents Should Be Aware Of." *FamilyEducation*. September 12. Retrieved September 18, 2023. (https://www.familyeducation.com/entertainment-activities/online/a-complete -guide-to-potentially-dangerous-apps-all-parents-should-be-aware-of).

Rosario, R. J., Minor, I., and Rogers, L. O. 2021. "'Oh, You're Pretty for a Dark-Skinned Girl': Black Adolescent Girls' Identities and Resistance to Colorism." *Journal of Adolescent Research* 36(5): 501–534.

Rose, Nikolas. 1999. *Powers of Freedom: Reframing Political Thought*. Cambridge: Cambridge University Press.

Rossie, Amanda. 2015. "Moving beyond 'Am I pretty or Ugly?': Disciplining Girls through YouTube Feedback." *Continuum* 29(2): 230–240.

Rottenberg, Catherine. 2018. *The Rise of Neoliberal Feminism*. New York: Oxford University Press.

Rush, Mariah. 2022. "What Is BeReal? Why the Social Media App All about Authenticity Is Skyrocketing." *TechXplore*. April 7. Retrieved November 27, 2022. (https://tech xplore.com/news/2022-04-bereal-social-media-app-authenticity.html).

Russell, Kim. 2019. "Reading This 'Predator Playbook' Could Help Protect Your Child." *WXYZ Detroit*. June 17. Retrieved July 1, 2019. (https://www.wxyz.com/news/reading -this-predators-playbook-could-help-protect-your-child).

Ryalls, E. 2012. "Demonizing 'Mean Girls' in the News: Was Phoebe Prince 'Bullied to Death?'" *Communication, Culture & Critique* 5(3): 463–481.

Saad, Lydia. 2022. "Americans Have Close but Wary Bond with Their Smartphone." *Gallup*. June 20. Retrieved February 5, 2024. (https://news.gallup.com/poll/393785/amer icans-close-wary-bond-smartphone.aspx).

Saeed, Kim. 2017. "The Brutal Truth about Selfies, Narcissism, and Low Self-Esteem." *PsychCentral*. November 3. Retrieved June 2, 2018. (https://psychcentral.com/blog/liberation/2017/11/the-brutal-truth-about-selfies-narcissism-and-low-self-esteem).

Sales, Nancy Jo. 2016. *American Girls: Social Media and the Secret Lives of Teenagers*. New York: Knopf.

Salomon, Ilyssa P. 2017. "The Selfie Generation: Examining the Relationship between Social Media Use and Early Adolescent Body Image." Theses and dissertations, Psychology. University of Kentucky. 112.

Salter, Michael. 2016. "Privates in the Online Public: Sex(ting) and Reputation on Social Media." *New Media & Society* 18(11): 2723–2739.

Sands, Victoria. 2012. "Neoliberalism, Postfeminism, and Ideal Girls: A Semiotic Discourse Analysis of Successful Girlhood in Seventeen Magazine." Thesis. University of Ottawa.

Savic, M., McCosker, A., and Geldens, P. 2016. "Cooperative Mentorship: Negotiating Social Media Use within the Family." *M/C Journal* 19(2): 1–9.

Sbarra, David A., Briskin, Julia L., and Slatcher, Richard B. 2019. "Smartphones and Close Relationships: The Case for an Evolutionary Mismatch." *Perspectives on Psychological Science* 14(4): 596–618.

Schilt, Kristen, and Westbrook, Laurel. 2009. "Doing Gender, Doing Heteronormativity: 'Gender Normals,' Transgender People, and the Social Maintenance of Heterosexuality." *Gender and Society* 23(4): 440–464.

Schmuck, Desirée. 2021. "Following Social Media Influencers in Early Adolescence: Fear of Missing out, Social Well-Being and Supportive Communication with Parents." *Journal of Computer-Mediated Communication* 26(5): 245–264.

Schonfeld, Ariel, McNiel, Dale, Toyoshima, Takeo, and Binder, Renee. 2023. "Cyberbullying and Adolescent Suicide." *Journal of the American Academy of Psychiatry and the Law* 51(1): 1–8.

Seabrook, E. M., Kern, M. L., and Rickard, N. S. 2016. "Social Networking Sites, Depression, and Anxiety: A Systematic Review." *JMIR Mental Health* 3(4): e50.

Searle, K. A., and Kafai, Y. B. 2012. "Beyond Freedom of Movement: Boys Play in a Tween Virtual World." *Games and Culture* 7(4): 281–304.

Seldin, Melissa, and Yanez, Christina. 2019. *Student Reports of Bullying: Results from the 2017 School Crime Supplement to the National Crime Victimization Survey*. Washington, D.C.: National Center for Education Statistics, U.S. Department of Education.

Selwyn, Neil. 2019. *What Is Digital Sociology?* Malden, MA: Polity Press.

Shackelford, Hunter Ashleigh. 2021. "When You Are Already Dead: Black Fat Being as Afrofuturism." In *The Routledge International Handbook of Fat Studies (1st Ed.)*, edited by Cat Pausé and Sonya Renee Taylor, 253–257. London, UK: Routledge.

Shahid, K., Kauser, S., and Zulqarnain, W. 2018. "Unveiling the Evil: Pakistani Young Girls and Online Harassment." *Journal of Research and Reviews in Social Sciences Pakistan* 1(2): 152–163.

Sheanoda, V., Bussey, K., and Jones, T. 2024. "Sexuality, Gender, and Culturally Diverse Interpretations of Cyberbullying." *New Media and Society* 26(1): 154–171.

Shields Dobson, Amy. 2011. "The Representation of Female Friendships on Young Women's MySpace Profiles: The All-Female World and the Feminine 'Other.'" In *Youth Culture and Net Culture: Online Social Practices*, edited by Elza Dunkels, Gun-Marie Franberg, and Camilla Hallgren, 126–152. Hershey, PA: IGI Global.

Shields Dobson, Amy. 2012. "'Individuality Is Everything': 'Autonomous' Femininity in MySpace Mottos and Self-Descriptions." *Continuum* 26(3): 371–383.

Shields Dobson, Amy. 2014. "Performative Shamelessness on Young Women's Social Network Sites: Shielding the Self and Resisting Gender Melancholia." *Feminism & Psychology* 24(1): 97–114.

Shields Dobson, Amy. 2015. *Postfeminist Digital Cultures: Femininity, Social Media, and Self Representation*. New York: Palgrave Macmillan.

Shin, W., Huh, J., and Faber, R. J. 2012. "Tweens' Online Privacy Risks and the Role of Parental Mediation." *Journal of Broadcasting & Electronic Media* 56(4): 632–649.

Simmons, Rachel. 2002. *Odd Girl Out: The Hidden Culture of Aggression in Girls*. New York: Harcourt.

Simmons, Rachel. 2018. *Enough as She Is: How to Help Girls Move beyond Impossible Standards of Success to Live Healthy, Happy, and Fulfilling Lives*. New York: HarperCollins.

Singer, Natasha. 2024. "Bipartisan Bill Aims to Protect Children Online." *New York Times*. January 31. Retrieved February 1, 2024. (https://www.nytimes.com/2024/01/31/tech nology/congress-social-media-safety.html).

Singh, Halle. 2021. "Method-ological Mapping of Girlhood Studies: The Academic Landscapes of Girlhood." *Girlhood Studies* 14(3): 1–17.

Sloan, L., and Quan-Haase, A. 2016. *The SAGE Handbook of Social Media Research Methods*. Thousand Oaks, CA: SAGE.

Smith, Barbara, Frazier, Demita, and Smith, Beverly. 1977. *The Combahee River Collective Statement*. Archived 2015. United States. Retrieved from the Library of Congress. (https://www.loc.gov/item/lcwaN0028151/).

Smith, Jason A. 2017. "Textual Analysis." In *The International Encyclopedia of Communication Research Methods*, edited by Jörg Matthes, 1–7. Hoboken, NJ: John Wiley & Sons.

Smith, Peter K., Mahdavi, Jess, Carvalho, Manuel, Fisher, Sonja, Russell, Shanette, Tippett, Neil. 2008. "Cyberbullying: Its Nature and Impact in Secondary School Pupils." *Journal of Child Psychology and Psychiatry* 49(4): 376–385.

Smith, S. L., Pieper, K., Choueiti, M., Tofan, A., Depauw, A., and Case, A. 2017. "The Future Is Female? Examining the Prevalence and Portrayal of Girls and Teens in Popular Movies." *Media, Diversity, and Social Change Initiative Report*. Los Angeles: USC Annenberg Press.

Snell, Patricia A., and Englander, Elizabeth K. 2010. "Cyberbullying Victimization and Behaviors among Girls: Applying Research Findings in the Field." *Journal of Social Sciences* 6(4): 510–514.

Sole-Smith, Virginia. 2023. *Fat Talk: Parenting in the Age of Diet Culture*. New York: Henry Holt.

Sorsoli, Lynn, and Tolman, Deborah. 2008. "Hearing Voices: Listening for Multiplicity and Movement in Interview Data." In *Handbook of Emergent Methods*, edited by S. N. Hesse-Biber and P. Leavy, 495–515. New York: Guildford Press.

Spies Shapiro, L. A., and Margolin, G. 2014. "Growing up Wired: Social Networking Sites and Adolescent Psychosocial Development." *Clinical Child and Family Psychology Review* 17(1): 1–18.

Stearns, Peter N. 2002. *Fat History: Bodies and Beauty in the Modern West*. 2nd ed. New York: New York University Press.

Steele, L., and Goldblatt, B. 2020. "The Human Rights of Women and Girls with Disabilities: Sterilization and Other Coercive Responses to Menstruation." In *The Palgrave Handbook of Critical Menstruation Studies*, edited by Chris Bobel, Inga T. Winkler, Breanne Fahs, Katie Ann Hasson, Elizabeth Arveda Kissling, and Tomi-Ann Roberts, 77–91. Singapore: Palgrave Macmillan.

Steinberg, Laurence, and Monahan, Kathryn C. 2007. "Age Differences in Resistance to Peer Influence." *Developmental Psychology* 43(6): 1531–1543.

Steinsbekk, S., Wichstrøm, L., Stenseng, F., Nesi, J., Hygen, B. W., and Skalická, V. 2021. "The Impact of Social Media Use on Appearance Self-Esteem from Childhood to Adolescence—A 3-Wave Community Study." *Computers in Human Behavior* 114(106528): 1–7.

Stern, Susannah. 1999. "Adolescent Girls' Expression on Web Home Pages: Spirited, Somber, and Self-Conscious Sites." *Convergence* 5(4): 22–41.

St. George, Donna, Reynolds Lewis, Katherine, and Bever, Lindsey. 2023. "The Crisis in American Girlhood." *Washington Post*. February 17. Retrieved August 5, 2023. (https://www.washingtonpost.com/education/2023/02/17/teen-girls-mental-health-crisis/).

Stienstra, Deborah. 2015. "Trumping All? Disability and Girlhood Studies." *Girlhood Studies* 8(2): 54–70.

Stim, Richard. 2019. *Getting Permission: How to License & Clear Copyrighted Materials Online & Off*. 7th ed. Berkeley, CA: Nolo Press.

Stokes, Carla. 2007. "Representin' in Cyberspace: Sexual Scripts, Self-Definition, and Hip Hop Culture in Black American Adolescent Girls' Home Pages." *Culture, Health, and Sexuality* 9(2): 169–184.

Strings, Sabrina. 2019. *Fearing the Black Body: The Racial Origins of Fat Phobia*. New York: New York University Press.

Subramanian, Sujatha. 2021. "Bahujan Girls' Anti-caste Activism on TikTok." *Feminist Media Studies* 21(1): 154–156.

Sui, W., Sui, A., and Rhodes, R. E. 2022. "What to Watch: Practical Considerations and Strategies for Using YouTube for Research." *Digital Health* 8: 1–13.

Sullivan, Amy, Taylor, Jill, and Gilligan, Carol. 1995. *Between Voice and Silence: Women and Girls, Race and Relationship*. Cambridge, MA: Harvard University Press.

Swindle, Monica. 2011. "Feeling Girl, Girling Feeling: An Examination of 'Girl' as Affect." *Rhizomes* 1(22): 1–25.

Sylwander, Kim, and Gottzén, Lucas. 2020. "Whore! Affect, Sexualized Aggression and Resistance in Young Social Media Users' Interaction." *Sexualities* 23(5/6): 971–986.

Takayoshi, Pamela. 1999. "No Boys Allowed: The World Wide Web as Clubhouse for Girls." *Computers and Composition* 16(1): 89–106.

Tanenbaum, L. 2015. *I Am Not a Slut: Slut-Shaming in the Age of the Internet*. New York: Harper Perennial.

Tanksley, T. 2016. "Race, Education and Resistance: Black Girls in Popular Instagram Memes." In *Intersectional Internet: Race, Sex, Class and Culture Online*, edited by S. Noble and B. Tynes, 243–259. New York: Peter Lang.

Tanner, Lindsey, and Wang, Angie. 2023. "Why Are Teen Girls in Crisis? It's Not Just Social Media." *Associated Press*. April 17. Retrieved August 9, 2023. (https://apnews.com/article/teens-girls-mental-health-social-media-928d45094e94fccb81e1fa9aca30fcdf).

Tasker, Yvonne, and Negra, Diane. 2007. *Interrogating Postfeminism: Gender and the Politics of Popular Culture*. Durham, NC: Duke University Press.

Tepper, M. S. 2000. "Sexuality and Disability: The Missing Discourse of Pleasure." *Sexuality and Disability* 18(4): 283–290.

Thiel-Stern, Shayla. 2009. "Femininity out of Control on the Internet: A Critical Analysis of Media Representations of Gender, Youth, and MySpace.com in International News Discourses." *Girlhood Studies: An Interdisciplinary Journal* 2(1): 20–39.

Thiel-Stern, Shayla. 2014. *From the Dance Hall to Facebook: Teen Girls, Mass Media, and Moral Panic in the United States, 1905–2010*. Boston: University of Massachusetts Press.

Thompson, Roberta. 2018. "Combatting Online Bullying Is Different for Girls and Boys: Here's Why." *The Conversation*. February 22. Retrieved November 11, 2018. (https://theconversation.com/combatting-online-bullying-is-different-for-girls-and-boys-heres-why-91837).

Thorn Report. 2021. "Responding to Online Threats: Minors' Perspectives on Disclosing, Reporting, and Blocking." February 1. Retrieved April 10, 2023. (chrome-extension://efaidnbmnnnibpcajpcglclefindmkaj/https://info.thorn.org/hubfs/Research/Thorn_ROT_Monitoring_2021.pdf).

Thorne, Barrie. 1993. *Gender Play: Girls and Boys in School*. New Brunswick, NJ: Rutgers University Press.

Tiggemann, M., and Barbato, I. 2018. "'You Look Great!': The Effect of Viewing Appearance Related Instagram Comments on Women's Body Image." *Body Image* 27: 61–66.

Tiggemann, M., and Miller, J. 2010. "The Internet and Adolescent Girls' Weight Satisfaction and Drive for Thinness." *Sex Roles: A Journal of Research* 63(1–2): 79–90.

Tiggemann, M., and Slater, A. 2013. "NetGirls: the Internet, Facebook, and Body Image Concern in Adolescent Girls." *International Journal of Eating Disorders* 46(6): 630–633.

Tiggemann, M., and Wilson-Barrett, E. 1998. "Children's Figure Ratings: Relationship to Self Esteem and Negative Stereotyping." *International Journal of Eating Disorders* 23(1): 83–88.

Tiidenberg, K., and Gómez Cruz, E. 2015. "Selfies, Image and the Re-making of the Body." *Body & Society* 21(4): 77–102.

Toliver, S. R. 2018. "Alterity and Innocence: The Hunger Games, Rue, and Black Girl Adultification." *Journal of Children's Literature* 44(2): 4–15.

Tolman, Deborah. 1994. "Doing Desire: Adolescent Girls' Struggles for/with Sexuality." *Gender and Society* 8(3): 324–342.

Tolman, Deborah. 2005. *Dilemmas of Desire: Teenage Girls Talk about Sexuality*. Cambridge, MA: Harvard University Press.

Turner, G. 2004. *Understanding Celebrity*. London: SAGE.

Twenge, Jean. 2023. *Generations: The Real Differences Between Gen Z, Millennials, Gen X, Boomers, and Silents—and What They Mean for America's Future*. New York: Atria Books.

Underwood, M. K., and Ehrenreich, S. E. 2017. "The Power and the Pain of Adolescents' Digital Communication: Cyber Victimization and the Perils of Lurking." *American Psychologist* 72(2): 144–158.

Valkenburg, P., Beyens, I., Loes Pouwels, J., van Driel, I., and Keijsers, L. 2021. "Social Media Use and Adolescents' Self-Esteem: Heading for a Person-Specific Media Effects Paradigm." *Journal of Communication* 71(1): 56–78.

Valkenburg, P., Beyens, I., Meier, A., and Vanden Abeele, M. 2022. "Advancing Our Understanding of the Associations between Social Media Use and Well-Being." *Current Opinion in Psychology* 47(5): 1–17.

Valkenburg, P., Meier, A., and Beyens, I. 2022. "Social Media Use and Its Impact on Adolescent Mental Health: An Umbrella Review of the Evidence." *Current Opinion in Psychology* 44: 58–68.

Vandebosch, H., and Van Cleemput, K. 2008. "Defining Cyberbullying: A Qualitative Research into the Perceptions of Youngsters." *Cyberpsychology and Behavior* 11(4): 499–503.

Vandenbosch, Laura, and Eggermont, Steven. 2012. "Understanding Sexual Objectification: A Comprehensive Approach toward Media Exposure and Girls' Internalization of Beauty Ideals, Self-Objectification, and Body Surveillance." *Journal of Communication* 62(5): 869–887.

Van Geel, M., Vedder, P., and Tanilon, J. 2014. "Relationship between Peer Victimization, Cyberbullying, and Suicide in Children and Adolescents: A Meta-analysis." *JAMA Pediatrics* 168(5): 435–442.

Vanner, Catherine. 2019. "Toward a Definition of Transnational Girlhood." *Girlhood Studies* 12(2): 115–132.

Van Ouytsel, J., Walrave, M., Ojeda, M., Rey, R. D., and Ponnet, K. 2020. "Adolescents' Sexy Self-Presentation on Instagram: An Investigation of Their Posting Behavior Using a Prototype Willingness Model Perspective." *International Journal of Environmental Research and Public Health* 17(21): 1–15.

Vares, Tiina, Jackson, Sue, and Gill, Rosalind. 2011. "Preteen Girls Read 'Tween' Popular Culture: Diversity, Complexity, and Contradiction." *International Journal of Media and Cultural Politics* 7(2): 139–154.

Varghese, Neema, and Kumar, Navin. 2022. "Feminism in Advertising: Irony or Revolution? A Critical Review of Femvertising." *Feminist Media Studies* 22(2): 441–459.

Vidal, C., Lhaksampa, T., Miller, L., and Platt, R. 2020. "Social Media Use and Depression in Adolescents: A Scoping Review." *International Review of Psychiatry* 32(3): 235–253.

Viljoen, J. L., O'Neill, M. L., and Sidhu, A. 2005. "Bullying Behaviors in Female and Male Adolescent Offenders: Prevalence, Types and Association with Psychosocial Adjustment." *Aggressive Behavior* 31(6): 521–536.

Vogels, Emily A., and Gelles-Watnick, Risa. 2023. "Teens and Social Media: Key Findings from Pew Research Center Surveys." *Pew Research Center.* April 24. Retrieved July 30, 2023. (https://www.pewresearch.org/short-reads/2023/04/24/teens-and-social-media-key-findings-from-pew-research-center-surveys/).

Vogels, Emily A., Gelles-Watnick, Risa, and Massarat, Navid. 2022. "Teens, Social Media, and Technology." *Pew Research Center.* August 10. Retrieved December 4, 2022. (https://www.pewresearch.org/internet/2022/08/10/teens-social-media-and-technology-2022/).

Vyas, A. N., Nagaraj, N., Genovese, J., Malhotra, G., Dubey, N., Hingorani, R., and Manning, L. 2020. "The Girl Rising 'We Dream, We Rise' Social Media Campaign in India: Reach, Engagement and Impact." *Journal of Creative Communications* 15(1): 106–124.

Waasdorp, T. E., and Bradshaw, C. P. 2015. "The Overlap between Cyberbullying and Traditional Bullying." *Journal of Adolescent Health* 56(5): 483–488.

Wade, Ann, and Beran, Tanya. 2011. "Cyberbullying: The New Era of Bullying." *Canadian Journal of School Psychology* 26(1): 44–61.

Wade, Ashleigh. 2019a. "To Be Girl, Digital, and Black: Black Girls' Digital Media Production As Cultural Discourse." Doctoral dissertation. Rutgers University.

Wade, Ashleigh. 2019b. "When Social Media Yields More Than 'Likes': Black Girls' Digital Kinship Formations." *Women, Gender, and Families of Color* 7(1): 80–97.

Wade, Ashleigh. 2024. *Black Girl Autopoetics: Agency in Everyday Digital Practice.* Durham, NC: Duke University Press.

Waldman, Katy. 2013. "Young Girls Ask 'Am I Pretty or Ugly?' on YouTube." *Slate Magazine.* October 15. Retrieved November 9, 2013. (https://slate.com/human-interest/2013/10/am-i-pretty-or-ugly-youtube-videos-alarming-or-maybe-ok.html).

Walker, Rebecca. 1992. "Becoming the Third Wave." *Ms. Magazine* 2(4): 39.

Walker, Susannah. 2007. *Style and Status: Selling Beauty to African American Women, 1920 1975.* Lexington: University Press of Kentucky.

Warren, Carol, and Karner, Tracy. 2010. *Discovering Qualitative Methods.* New York: Oxford University Press.

Waters, Mark. 2004. *Mean Girls*. New York: Broadway Video. DVD.

Weinstein, E. 2018. "The Social Media See-Saw: Positive and Negative Influences on Adolescents' Affective Well-Being." *New Media & Society* 20(10): 146144481875563.

Weisskirch, R. S. 2011. "No Crossed Wires: Cell Phone Communication in Parent-Adolescent Relationships." *Cyberpsychology, Behavior, and Social Networking* 14(7/8): 447–451.

Weitz, Rose. 2010. "A History of Women's Bodies." In *The Politics of Women's Bodies: Sexuality, Appearance, and Behavior, 3rd ed.*, edited by Rose Weitz, 3–12. New York: Oxford University Press.

Weitz, Rose, and Kwan, Samantha. 2013. *The Politics of Women's Bodies: Sexuality, Appearance, and Behavior*. New York: Oxford University Press.

Wendell, Susan. 1997. "The Rejected Body: Feminist Philosophical Reflections on Disability." *Hypatia* 12(2): 219–223.

Wenner Moyer, Melinda. 2022. "Kids as Young as 8 Are Using Social Media More Than Ever, Study Finds." *New York Times*. March 24. Retrieved July 10, 2022. (https://www.nytimes.com/2022/03/24/well/family/child-social-media-use.html).

West, Candace, and Zimmerman, Don. 1987. "Doing Gender." *Gender and Society* 1(2): 125–151.

Westbrook, L., and Schilt, K. 2009. "Doing Gender, Doing Heteronormativity: Gender 'Normals', Transgender People, and the Social Maintenance of Heterosexuality." *Gender and Society* 23(4): 440–464.

Westbrook, L., and Schilt, K. 2014. "Doing Gender, Determining Gender: Transgender People, Gender Panics, and the Maintenance of the Sex/Gender/Sexuality System." *Gender & Society* 28(1): 32–57.

Willem, C., Araüna, N., and Tortajada, I. 2019. "Chonis and Pijas: Slut-Shaming and Double Standards in Online Performances among Spanish Teens." *Sexualities* 22(4): 532–548.

Willig, Carla. 2013. *Introducing Qualitative Research in Psychology*. New York: McGraw-Hill Education.

Wiseman, Rosalind. 2003. *Queen Bees and Wannabes*. New York: Crown.

Wolak, J., Finkelhor, D., and Mitchell, K. 2008. "Online 'Predators' and Their Victims: Myths, Realities, and Implications for Prevention Treatment." *American Psychologist* 63(2): 111–128.

Wolf, Naomi. 2002. *The Beauty Myth: How Images of Beauty Are Used against Women*. New York: Harper Perennial.

Wood, Adam. 2010. *Barbie in a Mermaid Tale*. El Segundo, CA: Mattel Entertainment. DVD.

Yau, J. C., and Reich, S. M. 2019. "'It's Just a Lot of Work': Adolescents' Self-Presentation Norms and Practices on Facebook and Instagram." *Journal of Research on Adolescence* 29(1): 196–209.

Ybarra, Michele. 2012. "Measuring Cyber-Aggression: The Difference between Harassment and Bullying, and the Influence of Differential Power." Presented at the 120th Annual Convention of the American Psychological Association. Orlando, FL.

Young, Iris Marion. 2005. *On Female Body Experience: "Throwing Like a Girl" and Other Essays (Studies in Feminist Philosophy)*. New York: Oxford University Press.

Zaslow, Emilie. 2009. *Feminism, Inc.: Coming of Age in Girl Power Media Culture*. New York: Macmillan.

Zeisler, Andi. 2016. *We Were Feminists Once: From Riot Grrrl to CoverGirl®, the Buying and Selling of a Political Movement*. New York: PublicAffairs.

Zillich, A. F., and Riesmeyer, C. 2021. "Be Yourself: The Relative Importance of Personal and Social Norms for Adolescents' Self-Presentation on Instagram." *Social Media + Society* 7(3): 1–11.

Index

Katherine A. Phelps is teaching faculty in the Gender and Women's Studies Department at the University of Wisconsin-Madison.

www.ingramcontent.com/pod-product-compliance
Lightning Source LLC
Chambersburg PA
CBHW020349270326
41926CB00007B/355